BLOOD ON THE TRACKS

CLIVE BROOKS
BLOOD
ON THE
TRACKS

Published by
Kingfisher Railway Productions
65A The Avenue, Southampton SO1 2TA

Dedication
To Amanda and Sophie, and to Roger Hardingham for having the
foresight.

Acknowledgements
I would like to thank everyone who has assisted me in this project,
with special reference to Judith James at the Watercress Line, together
with Rosemary Bromley, Roger Hardingham, Pauline Moore, John
Joseph Design, Nick Girdler of BBC Radio Solent and Chris Masters
for character illustrations.

All characters in this book are fictitious. However, the locations
are all real.

© Clive Brooks &
Kingfisher Railway Productions
ISBN 0 946184 59 3
1989

Typeset by
PageMerger
Southampton

Printed and bound by R Booth, Bookbinders Ltd, Mabe, Penryn
Cornwall

Crime of Passion

The sweet, insistent pressure of his mouth on hers tempted her lips to part and she settled deeper into his arms, allowing her body's softness to relax against his strength.

Clickety-clack. Clickety-clack.

The 'Flying Scotsman' continued its relentless swaying motion as it dashed up-country on its east coast route towards Edinburgh. The movement coming smoothly and regularly to the inhabitants of the locked first class compartment, some half way down the speeding train.

The woman suddenly let out her breath in a long sigh and lay back onto the upholstered seat, her frou-frou petticoats, foamingly soft and adored with their pink silk ribbons and lace insertions, riding up enticingly.

With a quick glance over his shoulder to ensure that the door was still locked and that the corridor shutters were securely drawn, he drew her to him. The touch of his hands quickly became more immediate, more demanding, and he ran a finger up the inside of her slender, stockinged leg, then bent to take possession of her sensual mouth once again.

Twenty yards ahead in the mid-morning sunshine, the great locomotive sped on, the line of the boiler unbroken between the chimney and the huge brass casing that enclosed the safety valves just ahead of the cab where the driver and fireman toiled on the footplate. The scene, a picture of calm, unpassioned beauty and power like a full-rigged ship with all her canvas set.

With a high pitched groan like a hot rush of escaping steam, the woman threw her head back, tossing the wide, flat-brimmed hat from her head. It dangled momentarily on the edge of the seat, then slid silently to the floor to land in the soft folds of her flared skirt that cascaded out across the trembling carriage floor. She lifted her arm, a fashionable puffed sleeve riding up as she did so, and shakily loosened her collar.

Voices rose in the corridor outside, then died to a mumble before being swallowed up completely by the rumble of the train as they continued on their way towards their respective compartments.

Inside the shuttered, first class carriage, the temperature rose fast to match that of the pleasant summer weather outside.

Pleasure.

The supremely beautiful locomotive, brainchild of the celebrated engineer Patrick Stirling, forged on ahead, its single pair of eight foot diameter driving wheels thundering along the permanent way. The huge cylinders pumped hard and relentlessly in the sunshine, their graceful twenty-eight inch action clear under the elegant sweeping curve of the footplate.

On past a village where a grey church spire thrust itself up into the clear blue sky, then further on past the gentle farming countryside with its tilled soil and lush grass.

An absolute greyhound.

In the carriage it was over and the woman was overtaken by a light-headed almost overwhelming relief. He smiled and ruffled her 'Princess of Wales' curly fringe, running a satisfied hand through her close-set chestnut brown waves, then down across her voluptuous bodice. She looked up at him through a pair of singularly-bright blue eyes, stripped now of every vestige of virginity.

He smiled again, warmly at first, but then, as she gazed back at him, the fire of erotic passion ebbed and his eyes grew cold and hard below the brows which became knitted together. Silently and disgustedly he looked her over, his soft, flexible mouth drawn now into a hard, uncompromising line.

For the woman it seemed an uncomfortably long period of time, and she became flushed and disturbed by the unexplained and sudden hostility. She instinctively drew back from his strong arms unsure of how to cope with the slow scrutiny that she was being subjected to.

He smiled a third time, but only the merest flicker on this occasion.

The summer sunlight blazed through the half-open carriage window and the sweet fragrance of new-mown grass invaded the compartment to mingle with the strong Sainsbury's lavender water scent that the woman wore. The peaceful black and white cattle that watched the progress of the train serenely with their large, bovine eyes were the only witnesses to the cold, steel blade that rose up and glinted in the light before it was plunged savagely into the female flesh.

She let out her last breath with a half-stifled gasp and her eyes bulged wide as a dark scarlet stain gradually spread out across the bodice of her white dress.

As if in answer, the whole train inexplicably shuddered and vibrated and the woman rolled from the seat to the floor and slipped silently into death.

He left the swan-like figure limp and cold as the celebrated train rushed on...

*   *   *

"Are you alone, madam?" Henry Chesterfield enquired, an excited gleam coming into his delicate blue eyes as a tall, queenly young woman squeezed past him in the narrow corridor of the speeding train.

"Really, sir. You are very presumptious."

"Quite so. But you are very beautiful."

The woman giggled, politely putting her hand up to her generous lips as she did so before turning and walking slowly and sedately on down the corridor, running a hand gently and seductively against the soft aureole of narrow waves and curls that were brushed back in rippling waves over her forehead.

"A poco a poco," said the man under his breath, his dark moustache twitching keenly as she disappeared into a first class compartment. "Little by little."

"Excuse me, sir."

Henry Chesterfield turned around as a tubby ticket inspector pushed past him and made his way down the train. Just then, the basset hound that had been sitting patiently at Chesterfield's feet slipped his collar and romped off after the official.

"Enough, Wilbur B." Henry Chesterfield hurried up the corridor past the first class compartments after the animal. "Sorry," he said, bending down and dragging the stubborn black, white and tan dog away from the railway official. The dog looked up at its master through deep hazel-brown eyes, brimful of intelligence and affection. Its sad face a picture of reposeful dignity. "I do apologise, really I do," Chesterfield continued. "He slipped his collar. Bassetts do that, it's their flabby necks."

Maxwell Shore, Great Northern Railway ticket Inspector.

Flabby was one of many descriptions applied to him over his forty years – along with well-built, tubby, and a dozen or so more that he didn't care to recall. None of them were really accurate. In short, Max was simply fat. Fat with a capital 'F'. His minute, grey piggy-eyes were like tiny solitaires in his red, clean-shaven and taut face. The railway uniform that he wore was clearly struggling to contain the poundage within, and it was easy to imagine the seams of the well-worn trousers and long sleeved waistcoat crying out for mercy. Yes, Maxwell Shore was fat, there was certainly no doubt about that.

Fat and friendly, Henry Chesterfield decided as the fellow leaned over and patted the sad-eyed dog that gazed up at him. Chesterfield smiled and his delicate blue eyes twinkled under the heavy black brows that almost met in the middle. "Don't worry," he said. "He has got a ticket."

"That's as maybe," came the reply. "But it don't mean he can gambol all over this whole train." As he spoke, Max withdrew a grey handkerchief from his trousers and proceeded to remove the dollop of canine slobber that had attached itself to his leg. "What did you call him?" he said.

"Wilbur B. Well, er, actually it's Walhampton Wilbur Blendeques if you really want to know. He's from Major Godfrey Heseltine's new pack. The most successful in the country already, and only formed this year. Still a bit playful I'm afraid." Chesterfield pushed a leather collar with lead attached over the dog's head, flipping his long velvety ears free.

Chess, as he was known to his many friends – a large proportion of which happened to be female – was twenty-five and possessed enviable olive skin and dashing good looks. Confident and outgoing, he had just graduated from the Guildhall School of Music in London where he had spent the last few years playing a mixture of classical guitar and a field of ladies. As the only son of James Chesterfield, the tobacco millionaire, he was well taken care of financially and had been bought an enviable 'bijou residence' in the fashionable Mayfair quarter. Now the music studies were over, he had decided to join the railway's 'grouse traffic', and hoped to get in some good summer sport in Edinburgh while he mapped out his musical career.

Max chuckled, a high tremulous sound that made Chess remember the vibrato technique that he'd been taught (and instantly mastered as usual) at music school.

"What's your name?" he enquired in a friendly tone.

"Max. Maxwell Shore," came the reply.

"Tell me, my good man. Were you involved in those east versus west railway races a couple of summers back?"

"Aye," came the rather proud reply. "We won. Made it to Waverley in seven hours, twenty six and three-quarter minutes if I remember right."

"Molto Presto! A one and a half hour speed up!" remarked Chess. "Most impressive. When's the next one? Today?"

The fat man laughed again. "There's a truce on at present, sir. But 'tis an uneasy one at that. I shouldn't be surprised to see another race in the next four or five years. Now I must get on, sir, if you'll excuse me." He turned and walked a few paces down the swaying railway carriage corridor, pausing at the door of a first class compartment. His podgy hand tugged at the closed sliding door. It held fast.

"Tickets please," he called in a deep baritone. Chess raised his eyebrows at the fellow's surprising vocal range as he recalled the squeaky chuckle earlier.

There was no reply from within the compartment which had the blinds pulled firmly down.

Again Max tried the door, then tapped impatiently on the connecting window.

Still no answer.

"Some people," he said, raising his eyes to the carriage roof in a gesture of mock desperation. "They think we've got all damn day, I reckon."

"Perhaps the inhabitants are otherwise engaged," said Chess with a flash of his perfect, white teeth. "Rather an exciting location, don't you think?"

"No, I do not," said Max. "Really, that is quite a preposterous and disgusting thought."

The musician noticed how the ticket inspector's voice had risen a semitone into a sharp key. He smiled, more mischeviously this time. "Don't be such a prude," he said. "Try again."

The ticket inspector hesitated, hoping that Chess's deductions were erroneous. He cupped his hands round his mouth and pressed them to the window. "Hello?" he hollered, his breath steaming up the pane. "Tickets if you please now." Again Chess recalled his music studies, observing with interest how the six-syllable phrase resembled the notes of a mournful descending minor scale, almost as if the fat man was following some invisible piece of sheet music.

"Only one thing for it," Chess said excitedly, wandering the few steps towards the compartment, keeping Wilbur B. on a short leash. He stooped down and peered through a place where the blind had eased away from the varnished wood frame.

Suddenly his hard, strong body stiffened under the fashionable lounge jacket and tweeds. "Dear God," he gasped spinning round to face Max, his face suddenly exhibiting a deathly white pallor. "She's dead."

"What?"

"There's a woman in there, sprawled on the carriage floor with a dagger in her chest. She's dead," he said again in stunned disbelief.

Max's mouth dropped open and his small, grey eyes widened. Without a word he pushed Chess gently aside and looked through the gap in the blinds to verify the dreadful statement. A second later his head jerked back away, and he turned to Chess, dazed and scared.

"Bloody 'ell!" he said.

"Fortissimo!" Chess hollered, kicking out savagely with his foot and smashing the connecting window. He reached inside the splintered pane and unsecured the door from the inside.

The two men entered the compartment, Chess hooking his inquisitive dog on the door handle as he did so. The appealing hound whined briefly in protest, but on this occasion Chess turned away from the doleful, lozenge-shaped eyes sunk deep into their orbits. The animal's keen nose quivered and his muscles strained under his short, smooth coat as he struggled to get close to the incumbent form on the floor. But it was no use, and he gave up and flumped to the floor at the end of his lead.

"Suicide!" exclaimed Max gravely surveying the body, it's head lolling from side to side with the motion of the train. "Dreadful. I saw her at King's Cross just afore we left at ten this mornin'. She looked happy enough. She was writing a postcard. I had to hurry her along."

Chess stared down at the body. He wanted to look away but a strange fascination made him utterly unable to do so, and he found his attention gripped by the small dagger that was sticking, amid a large scarlet stain, from the woman's chest. He wiggled his black moustache nervously and narrowed his delicate blue eyes. "Straight through the heart," he said softly. "Almost instantaneous death presumably."

The pair stood in silence. Chess eyed the body in front of him, his gaze traversing the generous mouth and then down to the voluptuous curves of the bodice. He drew breath through his teeth. "What a most delectable figure."

Max felt a sudden combination of embarassment and annoyance at Chess's comment. "For God's sake," he barked. "Surely her sexuality is the last thing on your mind."

"Sexuality is never the last thing on my mind," came the reply.

Max shook his head in disbelief and turned his attention back to the body. "Why?" he groaned. "Here on the Scotsman. On my shift. Twenty-eight years the Flying Scotsman's run. Every year she covers enough miles to take her five times round the damn world, not a sniff of trouble. Now this - a suicide in first class."

"Or a murder," said Chess quietly.

"Don't make it any worse than it already is, Mr Chesterfield, for pity's sake," said Max in a pained tone.

"Call me Chess, everybody else does," came the reply. "As for murder, it is a possibility, my friend."

"I don't see how. The door was locked from the inside. If someone killed the poor woman then they must have jumped out of that window," Max said, pointing to the half-open pane. "We haven't made no stops today since Grantham, and she was alright then. I saw her in the corridor." He looked at Chess. "Anyroad, murderer would be dead if he jumped from that there window, that's for sure. We've been on a constant run of over fifty miles an hour."

Chess frowned hard and his thick, black eyebrows drew into a single line. "You're quite right," he said after a few moments. "That is unless our metaphoric fellow scrambled through the window up onto the carriage roof and re-entered the train by another open window."

"He'd be absolutely filthy," said Max in a puzzled voice. "Look here, Mr Chesterf- I mean Chess, this conjecture's all very fine, but that's all it is, conjecture. I'll fetch the guard. He'll stop the train. I'd be grateful if you'd stay on here and –"

"Wait up," interrupted Chess. "With respect, that's a stupid idea. If this is murder, the culprit will surely jump the train the moment it stops. Far better to keep it moving, it's like a prison that way. And anyhow think of the panic that it'll cause. What would you tell the passengers?"

Max stopped at the compartment door, his fat face drawn and fraught with anxiety.

Chess withdrew his Benson's keyless pocket-watch with its three quarter plate movement and eighteen-carat gold, engine-turned case – another present from his millionaire father. "How long before the lunch stop at York?" he enquired peering at the hard, white enamel dial with its sunk seconds.

"'Bout an hour and a quarter. I'd estimate it being around seventy five miles from here. It's eighty two from Grantham."

"Then we haven't got long to solve it, we'd better get started."

"Look Mr Chess, I'd go along with you, really I would if we had some proof that it is murder, but the way it is, it's more than my job's worth not to report it."

Chess's eyes returned to the dagger in the attractive, young body. "Perhaps we do have some proof," he said suddenly. "It's a long shot though. Max, you said you first saw the woman at King's Cross station, just before we pulled out. She was writing a postcard?"

"That's it, but I don't see what relevance that –"

"A long shot, Max, like I said," Chess interrupted. "Which hand was she writing with?"

Max pushed back the cheese-cutter railway cap on his massive head, blew his cheeks out and considered.

A few moments later he let the breath go through his puckered lips like a rush of escaping steam. "Left hand," he said at last.

"Can you be sure?"

"Positive."

"Then it's murder all right," said Chess excitedly. "Look at the angle of that dagger. She couldn't have stabbed herself with that hand, and being a woman, she wouldn't have had sufficient strength with her other one. Besides, she's laying on it." Chess eyed the ticket inspector coldly. "No, Max, this wound must have been caused by someone facing her. This is murder, not suicide."

Max was silent, just staring at the body.

"Look at the clothes, too," Chess added, shooting Max a knowing glance. "They don't get that dishevelled falling off a seat."

"You do seem to be a connoisseur of such matters," Max said distainfully.

Just then Wilbur B. growled and the two men turned to see the dog tugging and shaking its head, a bowler hat locked firmly in its drooping jaws. "Where'd you get that, Wilb?" said Chess striding across the carriage and retrieving it.

"I didn't see it when we came in," said Max.

"It must have been there," replied Chess with a shrug of his broad shoulders. "I suppose we were too pre-occupied with the body, and besides, Wilb's line of vision is a lot lower than ours."

"Perhaps it was on the floor under the seat" Max ventured.

"What the hell, it's a clue wherever it was, and a damn good one. There can't be many men travelling bare-headed on this train," said Chess looking at his pocket watch again. "Come on, we haven't got much time. You start at one end of the corridor section, I'll start at the other and we'll meet back here and decide what to do."

★   ★   ★

"How many?" Chess enquired as Max came hurrying back up the corridor, his massive frame labouring with the effort and his face the colour of an over-ripe tomato.

"One," he said, squeezing the word out between wheezes. "You?"

"The same," replied Chess. "He's in the next carriage with that delectable young creature that I met in the corridor earlier. We'll try him first, come on, allegro, allegro."

"What?"

"Sorry, Max. Silly of me. Talking in musical jargon's got to being a bit of a habit. Quickly, that's all it means."

Henry Chesterfield made off down the train hiding the bowler hat behind his back, his body moving like some hard, flexible metal under his fashionable well-tailored clothes. Wilbur B. pattered along behind, his head carried low so that the skin fell in loose pendulous ridges and folds over the forehead and sides of his hangdog face. More rolls of loose skin on the animal's belly waggled comically from side to side in precisely the same fashion as that of the corpulent ticket inspector who followed the hound.

Chess opened the compartment door boldly. "Good morning," he said in a silvery smooth voice. "Aha, my dear lady. What a pleasure it is to re-new our aquaintance." His eyes flickered approvingly over her beautiful womanly form. "You really are quite the most softest, sweetest and tenderest piece of humanity under heaven, madam. What more could any woman wish to be. Do you not agree, sir?"

The hat-less man at her side bristled and his weasel face coloured up to a deep, angry crimson.

"A word outside," he barked. "In the corridor, sir. Now. If you please." He jumped to his feet as he finished speaking and strode out to join the trio, slamming the door forcefully behind him so that the glass rattled and shook. "What do you mean speaking to my Elizabeth like that, she —"

"Please," intervened Max, holding up his hand for a ceasefire. "It's his way, sir. He didn't mean it."

13

"I would not have said it if I did not mean it, Max," replied Chess with a wicked smile.

The man fairly roared with anger and rounded on Chess. Max stepped between the pair and inadvertently took two heavy body blows. He winced, then heaved the pair apart, his fat frame acting as a barrier. "What the flippin' hell are you playing at, Mr Chess," he said in his ear. "For God's sake treat this dreadful affair with the gravity it deserves."

"Ah, yes!" exclaimed Chess, his face becoming serious. "I almost furgot. The murder!"

"Gracious me. When? Where? Who?" said the hat-less man, the questions shooting from his mouth like bullets from a gun.

"Further down the train," Chess said levelly. "Really, I do apologise for my behaviour, it is most unforgiveable."

"Accepted. You want my help? Excellent. Charles Ginsberg. At your service. Where do we start?" came the excited, staccato reply.

"We start," said Chess in a calm voice, "by asking you a few questions."

"Smashing. Super. Fire away."

"Mr Ginsberg, where is your hat?"

"Hat. Oh yes. Aha, well spotted. Didn't wear it today. Good weather. Get a bit of sun to the old bonce. Make the hair grow, eh?"

Chess smiled briefly, then his handsome face took on a grave expression. He brought his hand out from behind his back and produced the bowler hat that Wilbur B. had found. "This is not yours then?"

"Ugh. Dreadful thing. No. Wouldn't be seen dead in it. Frightful. Far too high. Went out with the ark." He hesitated briefly. "Don't like to say, but I saw a chap earlier. No hat. Might wear a thing like that."

"Thank you, Mr Ginsberg." said Chess. "May I ask what your occupation is?"

"Locksmith."

"Most interesting. We may want to speak to you again. I would be most obliged if you would remain in your compartment until we reach York. And not a word about this to anyone."

"How exciting. Detective I suppose you are. Correct?"

Chess exchanged glances with Max. "Yes," he said at length. "I suppose I am."

"Locksmith. That fits, but what about the hat. How do we know if he's tellin' truth?" asked Max when Mr Ginsberg had returned to his compartment.

"We don't," replied Chess. "Not yet anyway." Again he flipped out his pocket-watch that hung on a rather grand close-curb gold double Albert terminating in a green semi-precious stone fob engraved with the initials H.C.

"One hour before York," he said. "One suspect to see."

*   *   *

"He was on his own," said Max as they made their way to the other end of the corridor. "In a first class smoking compartment. Funny though, he didn't look the first class type. A bit disreputable if you ask me."

"Have you checked his ticket?"

Max nodded. "It's all in order," he said. "But for heaven's sake, if we're going to do this, try to be rather better behaved. Your dog's got the blinkin' edge on you for manners."

On reaching the compartment, it became quite clear that the isolation in which the fellow was travelling was due, in no small part, to his appearance. He was indeed dirty and disreputable to the point of being tramp-like. His frock coat exhibited a considerable propensity of grime down one side, and his light tan trousers were streaked with muddy dust.

"What do you think, Mr Chess?" whispered Max as they peered cautiously through the connecting window. "No hat and dirty with it. Maybe he did climb out of that carriage window back there and over the roof like you said."

"Perhaps," said Chess thoughtfully. "Let's see what his story is." With that they entered the compartment, leaving Wilbur B. hooked by his lead to the door outside, looking every bit as ancient as his fifteenth century ancestors.

"What do you want?" barked the man, slapping his copy of The Times down on his knees and glaring, first at Chess, then at Max, through a pair of singularly vicious-looking dark eyes that resembled raisins pressed into his thin, sallow face. "Can't you see I'm busy?"

"Would I be right in assuming that you're a businessman?" enquired Chess, raising his dark eyebrows for an answer.

It came savage and fast. "It's obvious isn't it?" the fellow blazed. "I wouldn't be reading the financial pages of The Times if I wasn't, would I?"

"I er-suppose not," replied Chess, momentarily at a loss for words.

The angry man capitalized on the oral lull and continued in a biting, sarcastic tone. "What is it? You'll tell me next that you're Sherlock Holmes, and this," he gestured towards a very worried-looking Max, "is Doctor Watson."

"Not exactly," said Chess recovering his nerve. "However, we are looking into a murder."

The musician counted himself through the silence of a two semibreve rests before the businessman spoke up.

"What murder?" said the man slowly and mysteriously, his hands clenching together tightly on his lap.

"On this train," Chess continued looking straight into the fellow's dark raisin-eyes. "I have to inform you that you are one of the prime suspects. What is your name, sir?"

The angry front fell from the fellow. "P-Peterson," he said with a nervous chuckle. "John Peterson, why?"

Chess was silent and sat down on the empty carriage-seat opposite, his face hard and serious. Suddenly he twitched his moustache and simultaneously stabbed his index finger in the direction of Peterson's frock coat. "A few questions about the state of this," he said quietly, "if you don't mind."

Peterson's thin, greasy face coloured up and one or two beads of perspiration appeared on his furrowed brow. "You noticed," he said. "Is it really all that obvious. I tried to clean it off best I could, I–"

"Do you often travel without a hat, Mr Peterson?" Chess interrupted.

"Yes. Well, no. That is to say, well..." He stopped and his eyes appealed to Chess. "Please, this really is all most embarrassing. I can assure you I do not make a habit of parading in this disreputable fashion."

"I don't for one moment expect that you do," Chess said with a slight smile.

"Thank God," Peterson said, breathing a heavy sigh and relaxing his clenched hands somewhat.

Henry Chesterfield's delicate blue eyes became as cold and hard as ice, and he ran his upper lip over his lower one slowly and deliberately from one side to the other, so that his moustache seemed to drift mesmerisingly first to the left, then right, across his dark, handsome face.

Peterson read the signs and stiffened once more, the whites of his knuckles visible as he re-clenched his hands on his lap. "W-Was there anything else, gentlemen?" he said hesitantly.

Chess nodded solemnly and made a clicking sound through his teeth like a metronome. "We have good reason to believe that the dirt that has attached itself to your clothing has emanated from a certain exterior part of this train," he said clearly and positively. "What have you got to say about that?"

"No, no! It isn't that at all, really it isn't. It's just the outcome of an unfortunate accident. I had to get away quickly. I couldn't go back."

"Accident?" said Chess. "Or murder?"

"No, you've got it all wrong."

Peterson was shaking now and a muscle twitched nervously in his gaunt cheek. "It was at King's Cross Station, just outside actually. I tripped, that's all."

"Go on," said Chess gravely, exchanging looks with Max who was still standing silent and poker-faced next to the compartment door, keeping an eye on Wilbur B. The dog had decided to lay down in the corridor outside, his long ears laying out on the dusty floor at right angles to the rest of him.

"I don't know what you think, but I took a hansom to the station this morning and, as I alighted, got my coat caught in the flap door. It fairly bowled me over it did and I found myself lying in the gutter. It was almost nine forty-five. I didn't have the time to return home to change, so I brushed myself down best I could and came on along to the platform."

"I see," said Chess thoughtfully. "Is there anything else that you wish to tell me?"

Peterson shook his head. "No," he said. "Honestly, that's all there is to it."

"If what you say is true, then there must be numerous witnesses to your appearance both back at King's Cross, and also here on this train. Perhaps Mr Shore and I should speak to some of them?"

"No, please," Peterson burst out.

"Surely you want your story verified? Your name cleared?"

"Yes, but... Well. Look, I don't want my unfortunate appearance brought to the fore. Bad for business. I've told you the truth, really I have."

"Everything?"

"Yes, everything," Peterson said.

"There is still the question of your hat."

"What hat?"

"Exactly," Mr Peterson. "What hat? This one perchance?" Chess turned to Max, and the ticket inspector withdrew the bowler hat from behind his back for a second time. "This was found at the scene of the crime."

"No," said Peterson, shaking his head. "Really, it's not mine."

"Then where is your headgear?" enquired Chess. "You just said that you'd told us everything."

"That I have, well, nearly. That is – I mean. There may be some details."

"Recount them, and quickly," said Chess leaning forwards and staring deeply into Peterson's scared eyes.

"It's quite simple," came the worried reply. "Mine fell off when I tripped at the station. It fell into the gutter. A four wheeled cab – a growler – ran over it before I could retrieve it, then it was snatched away by a mendicant." He paused then, unclenching his hands, he gestured towards the bowler hat that Max was turning nonchalantly over and over in his podgy hands. He continued, his face breaking into a weak smile. "Wouldn't be anything like the good condition of that one," he said.

Chess nodded. "There is one other thing," he said snatching the hat from Max and standing up.

Without warning he gripped the brim of the bowler with both hands and shoved it down upon Peterson's head. It dropped on easily, right down over the fellow's eyebrows and made his large ears flap out almost as far as Wilbur B's.

"I told you," said Peterson.

"You did, didn't you," said Chess removing the hat once more. "Don't leave this compartment before we reach York, Mr Peterson, there's a good chap."

"What now?" enquired Max when they had walked a few yards up the corridor.

For the first time since discovering the body, Henry Chesterfield felt worried. He groaned aloud. "Perhaps this is biting off a bit more than I can chew," he sighed. "Maybe they are innocent. Maybe it is suicide."

"And maybe I should call the guard in now," added Max. "It's my job I stand to lose, Mr Chess."

"I do realise that," came the reply. "Look, will you give it one more shot?"

"What sort of shot?"

"Another word with Ginsberg. It won't do any harm, we've still got over half an hour before that twenty-minute lunch stop at York. What d'you say?"

"We'd best be quick about it," said the ticket inspector apprehensively.

"Good man, Max," said Chess, clapping the fat fellow on his back. "Come on, let's beetle back to his compartment."

*   *   *

"Mr Ginsberg, another quick word please?"

The fellow was up out of his seat like a shot and joined the pair in the corridor, closing the door behind him. "Got the blaggard?" he snapped enthusiastically. "Locked up is he? Under guard now?"

"Not yet, Mr Ginsberg, but I am working on it."

Chess smiled inwardly and visualized on a music stave, the brisk semiquaver speech pattern that the fello exhibited. "You said earlier that you were a locksmith," he continued

The weasel-faced man nodded. "Quite right. Thirty years. Family firm. Father a locksmith. Grandfather a locksmith. Me too. Three generations."

Chess held up his hand to silence the relentless blasts of rapid dialogue. "Mr Ginsberg. A woman has been murdered on this train. She was found in a first class compartment. It was locked."

"A woman. Dreadful. Shocking business. Locked in. How can I –" He broke off, the last part of his staccato sentence lost in a mumble. Suddenly realisation dawned and a look of absolute horror cast itself across his features.

"Locked in," Chess said, repeating Ginsberg's words, nodding knowingly as he did so.

"Surely you don't think I murdered her?" the worried man gasped.

Chess simply nodded again, his moustache twitching violently.

"Good Lord no. I won't have it. My reputation," he said, lowering his voice with every passing sentence. "Can't," he continued. "No! Ridiculous suggestion. Preposterous to even think it."

Chess turned and took the bowler hat from Max's hand behind his back.

"Yours I believe," he said.

Charles Ginsberg's face dropped a mile and a look of desperation clouded his features. Before he had chance to speak, Chess plopped the

19

hat on his surprised head. "A perfect fit," he remarked. "Just as I expected."

"Smart man. I like that. I confess."

Chess raised one of his dark, thick eyebrows.

"To owning the hat," Ginsberg added quickly. "Not this other business."

"Don't play games," said Chess ruthlessly. "Your hat was found in the locked compartment that I have already spoken of. The other passenger in there is now laying dead on the floor. You lied earlier when I remarked that you had no hat. Said something about letting the sun get to your head."

"Joke. Didn't want to arouse suspicion. Simple."

"You have done just the opposite," said Chess.

"Not me. Never. Don't know a thing about it. Truly." Ginsberg's words came quick and fast with muted gasps between them. He wrung his hands together momentarily, then shoved them into his pockets, withdrawing a lighter and cigarettes. By now his hands were beginning to shake uncontrollably and his palms were smeared with sweat. He fumbled to light the cigarette, but it fell unused to the carriage floor. Wilbur B. sniffed at it, then devoured it whole, wagging his tail and looking up through sad, drooping eyes at Ginsberg, hoping for another.

"A confession, Ginsberg, or it'll be even worse for you," Barked Chess.

"Dear God. Look. Believe me. I was travelling in the same compartment as a woman. Probably the one you say. I don't know. Never spoke a word. Left my hat on the seat. Showed it was occupied while I went to the bathroom. Came back. Blinds drawn. Door locked. Guessed she wanted privacy. Left her to it. Simple."

Henry Chesterfield's keen young face was expressionless, the only animation coming from the shafts of sunlight that filtered through the rushing trees outside the speeding carriage to fall on his perfect olive skin. "I do not believe a word," he said at length. "Not for one moment."

"It's the truth. Changed compartments. Was going to pick up the hat later."

"Prove it to me." said Chess.

"How?" came the frightened reply. "Impossible. Can't be done."

"Then prove it to a jury."

With that, Henry Chesterfield advanced purposefully on Ginsberg, his muscular body flexing under his clothes, and his jaw square and determined.

At that moment, Ginsberg's face brightened. "Wait," he pleaded, flexing his cerebral muscles. "The guard. He saw me. In the corridor. Coming up the train when I went out to the bathroom. He'll vouch for me. Bound to. Get this over and done. Capital, eh?"

Chess stopped in his tracks and drew back. Max turned to whisper in his ear. "Well, Mr Chess," he said in an undertone. "We'll have to see him sooner or later, may as well get it finished with."

Henry Chesterfield nodded and turned his attention back to the quaking fellow in front of him. "Alright Mr Ginsberg," he said sharply, consulting his gold pocket-watch. "The way I calculate it, you've got about ten minutes to convince us of your innocence, otherwise, when we pull into York, I'm turning you straight over to the police. Understand?"

"Yes. Bear with me. Few moments. This way. Alright?" Charles Ginsberg hurried off down the train that was already beginning to slow down for the approach to the great station a few miles ahead.

"A descant," remarked Chess. "With our friend here's little bleating countermelody added above the main murder theme, this affair is turning into a most complicated composition." The pair followed Ginsberg, with with Wilbur B. trotting at their heels on the end of his lead, oblivious to the whole curious sequence of events.

*   *   *

"Mr Kilburn, hello?" Called Max, peering into the gloomy guard's van. "Are you there?"

"What is it?" came a gruff voice as a face appeared above a pile of parcels at the rear of the van, near the brake compartment.

Chess stared hard at the figure which, he quickly decided, rather resembled Robinson Crusoe.

Under the regulation cheese-cutter cap it was completely fringed with a thick propensity of fiery, red hair. So much so, in fact, that it was impossible to ascertain accurately where the hair finished and the wiry whiskers began.

Max swallowed hard and was about to explain the situation when he noticed that Mr Kilburn's tunic was soaking wet. "What happened to you?" he enquired.

For a few moments the guard was silent, then he spoke up in a deep voice. "Blessed tap in the washroom," he growled. "Got a mind of its own, I reckon."

Chess scrutinised the fellow who was taking care to keep to the shadows. After a few moments, he plucked up courage and broached the subject of the dead woman. "Sir," he said somewhat gingerly. "There's been a murder on the train. I've been investigating it with the help of Mr Shore here, we –."

"You saw me. in the corridor. Remember? Eh?" Peterson burst in. "Two hours back. Halfway down the train. Right?"

The guard narrowed his eyes. "Never set eyes on you before," he said resolutely. "Certain of it."

Peterson was dumbfounded.

"We squashed past each other. You do remember. Must. Utmost importance. Really."

"It's a woman," Chess said sadly, hauling the conversation back to the murder. "A young woman."

"Think man. Now. Jump to it. Emergency," pleaded Peterson.

Chess ignored this second interjection and continued. "She's on the floor of a compartment in first class."

"And you're sayin' this chap stabbed her?"

"Precisely," Chess replied. "There's been some sexual interference too."

Peterson, who was about to plead again, snapped his mouth shut like a sprung trap. He stared curiously at the whiskery guard, then at Chess.

"How?" he said quietly after a time.

Henry Chesterfield turned to face him. "I think I should tell you that what you say could be used as evidence against you, Mr Peterson," he said crisply. "It looks black for you now."

"No. No. You don't understand," Peterson blazed. "How? How did he know she'd been stabbed? No-one told him. And that washroom tap. Alright when I used it. Perfect."

Chess turned his attention back to the guard, just as a shaft of sunlight traversed the van from left to right, illuminating Kilburn's face clearly for the first time. As it did so, it became clear that the man had been weeping. His eyes were obviously red-rimmed, and there was evidence of smears on his positively grimy cheeks.

"Why is your tunic wet?" said Chess. "The truth please."

A forest of trees along the trackside blotted out the cheery sunlight and plunged the van into gloom once more. Through the gloaming, Kilburn replied hesitantly in a scared voice. "I-I washed it. It was dirty, see."

"Bloodstained more like," Peterson retorted. "You did it. Tell them. Blaggard. Murderer."

There was a long, tense silence. Then Kilburn spoke in a low voice.

"My wife," he said, his throat sounding dry and constricted. "She was my wife. She left me. Went on the streets. Wanted more than me wages could give her." He stopped and eyed each of the faces around him before continuing, louder this time. "She made me pay for her services. My own wife! Here, on the train. Pay or nothing she said. I wanted her bad."

Henry Chesterfield's dark, handsome face was grave. His eyes had suddenly become a cold ice-blue. They penetrated deep into the shadowy guard's van. "Mr Kilburn," he said slowly and deliberately. "Did you kill your wife?"

"No," he gasped, his voice rising almost an octave in pitch, causing him to sound like a completely different person. "Not me. Harry. Harry did it. I couldn't stop him. He was too strong. Harry locked her in with this." Kilburn fished a piece of bent wire from his pocket and tossed it onto the floor. "Picked lock he did."

Max and Chess echanged confused glances. "Who is Harry?" said the latter.

"Harry. Harry's inside me. In my brain, waiting, lurking. I talks to him now and again, but he don't like to listen. Harry's with me always."

Max turned away, his brain spinning, a confused mixture of revulsion and perplexity hammering at his skull. He fumbled in his trouser pocket and withdrew his ten-shilling carbolic smoke ball and inhaled deeply, hoping that the stated cure for headache would hold good, as a sharp pain was stabbing relentlessly at both of his temples. This done, he forced himself to centre his attention on the pleasant view through the nearby carriage window. The sun still beat down on the landscape, and now the Flying Scotsman was slowing down and about to enter the great curve of York station, the finest and largest of its kind in the world. Max considered the cast-iron columns and longitudinal wrought iron girders supporting the grand triple-arched roof, trying to block out the matter in hand.

As he watched, the familiar lines of the station came into view, the sunlight flashing and glinting on the large glazed end-screens that still looked as bright and clean as when the station had opened some thirteen years previously. He recalled himself as a younger, slimmer man on that summer Sunday in the June of 1877, standing on the platform witnessing the opening ceremony.

It was the sudden clatter of the guard's van door being pulled back that shook him out of his brown study and hauled his attention back to the dreadful matter in hand. The train was still travelling at almost forty miles per hour.

"Harry's going to jump," screamed Kilburn. "Harry wants to die… Off you go, Harry."

Henry Chesterfield rushed forwards and threw his strong body into a flying rugby tackle but his muscular arms could only clench at the air where Kilburn had been, and he landed in a heap on the van's floor, his head adjacent to the open door.

The station platform rushed past his eyes, and there, at the end of the the long, curving, concrete premonitory lay the guard where he had fallen, his whiskery face smashed. His body bent and twisted.

Chess looked away.

A crowd of well-dressed ladies at the station did likewise.

The queue at the refreshment counter broke up.

The readers at the bookstall tossed down their magazines.

Kilburn died.

Harry died with him.

Diamonds in D Minor

Henry Chesterfield simultaneously pulled up his Venetian blinds and his underwear and gazed out over Hyde Park. Already, under the spreading trees, were smart white-robed nurses with their lovely little charges, preserving an air of studied hauteur as they slowly pushed their perambulators past elderly ladies who drove to and fro in decorous equipages. Chess's eyes traversed the scene from background to foreground, first studying the beautiful women who walked under the shady trees with their attendant swains, and then the horticultural extravaganza next to the park railings – tulips, geraniums and asters, all in luxuriant masses and well-blended shades made Park Lane a very harmony of colour, contrasting against the splendid black carriages that were drawn up, here and there along the thoroughfare.

He yawned lazily and rubbed his delicate blue eyes.

"Chessie?" A young woman's sweet voice drifted into the exquisitely furnished drawing room. Chess smiled. "Ah, apassionata," he said quietly. "Good morning my little plaything."

"Don't call me that, you know how I hate it." A slender and attractive blonde-haired girl wandered into the room and flumped down on the Amersham suite, doing up her bodice as she did so.

Henry Chesterfield's Mayfair residence, purchased for him by his tobacco millionaire father, was marvellous. The drawing room's contents alone represented thousands of pounds. There were Sheraton cabinets with fortunes in bric-a-brac visible through their glass panels, and exquisite miniatures painted on the satinwood frameworks harmonizing with the parquet floors, inlaid tables and bronze statuettes – the latter being quite the very perfection of grace and sex in their so-called 'eurythmic attitudes'. On a more conventional note, there was quality china of every tint that had ever bloomed in a garden or reigned in the sky, all arranged perfectly under the decorative ceiling whose centrepiece was an oval of blue, as soft and uncertain as a gossamer cloud.

The owner of this little palace adjourned to his bedroom and completed his dressing, returning some ten minutes or so later in a finely tailored lounge jacket with matching waistcoat and lighter coloured tweed trousers, just as the post arrived. One solitary letter comprised the morning's correspondence which he opened after settling at the table and pouring two cups of tea from an elegant silver pot.

"Dear Mr Chess," it read. "Many thanks for your kind offer. Yes, I should be happy to accompany you to Southampton and look forward to enjoying your classical guitar recital there. I shall meet you, as suggested, at Waterloo Station tonight at 10.00 p.m. to catch the night express down. See you again soon, Max."

"Am I on your menu today, Chessie?" said the girl, watching as her lover began enthusiastically tucking into a boiled egg.

"Sadly no," came the reply. "I have a musical recital tomorrow evening down south. Practice makes perfect. Now be a dear Catherine, and leave me to my musical studies."

*　　*　　*

Dusk had already fallen on the sprawling city when Henry Chesterfield and his faithful bassett hound, Wilbur B., began their journey in a bow-fronted brougham from Park Lane to Waterloo.

Rattling along Constitution Hill with the seemingly endless wall of Buckingham Palace gardens on the right, the Guildhall trained musician withdrew his guitar from its velvet-lined case and engaged his attention in adjusting the gut strings which had reacted to the change in temperature and dropped in pitch by almost a complete semitone.

By the time the cabbie had reached the end of Bird Cage Walk and left the verdant acres of St James's Park behind, Chess was picking out a soft, delicate tune on the instrument that lent a magical beauty to the lights that twinkled on the dark waters of the Thames as the cab traversed Westminster Bridge. In fact, by the junction of York and Waterloo roads, the cabbie had given to whistling merrily along with the moorish melody, and it was only with reluctance that he pulled up outside the great station to terminate the unexpected musical performance.

Waterloo Station was a strange, oddly arranged terminus where you could easily lose yourself in a Hampton Court maze of platforms. It was a place where fashionable London would calmly exchange smiles and greetings while engines screamed and porters shouted through the throngs of well dressed people, all mixed up in picturesque confusion. However, when Chess arrived, the night had become well-established and the terminus was almost deserted save for a light scattering of weary travellers that lounged here and there on the station seats and against the large supporting pillars.

"Mr Chess!" The familiar deep baritone echoed the length of the long, shadowy platform.

"Con amore, Max! Lovely to see you again. Glad you could come."

"Pleasure!" said the fat man. "I had some leave owing. I'm looking forward to hearing you play." The ticket inspector's taut, rotund face beamed a genuine smile. "Hope we don't get into another caper like that Scotsman affair a while back, though."

Chess was about to re-assure him when his attention was caught by a flurry of activity at the far end of the platform. An attractive woman breezed along, looking somewhat like a cross between Lillie Langtry and Sarah Bernhardt. She wore a heavy brocaded mantle with a luxurious fox fur trim, and possessed an unusual grace and perfect slimness about her that provided her with an almost royal air. A maid, no less attractive, tagged behind her. And further behind still – but catching up fast – came a news-hungry pack of reporters, their pencils and writing pads poised ready to capture any comment and rush it back to Fleet Street.

"Miss Jacquelle, are you performing abroad?"

"Is the romance with Lord Clitheroe off?"

"What's the name of your next play?"

The questions came thick and fast, but the attractive actress brushed them all professionally aside with several deft flicks of a long, slender and wellmanicured hand, before being lost in a cloud of steam as the powerful Adams 4-4-0 locomotive with its formidable quartet of seven-foot one-inch driving wheels rumbled slowly along next to the platform and came to rest with a loud hiss like a dying dragon.

Chess raised an eyebrow at the actress and her maid as they boarded a first class carriage. "Perhaps those beauties will make an interesting diversion," he remarked as he struggled aboard carrying both Wilbur B. and his classical guitar in its hard case. "How about forming a pair of couplets? We could make some very melodious music, don't you think?"

"Look Mr Chess," said Max, "I-I don't think I. I mean... The girls... Look I–"

The two men made their way along the corridor and found an empty compartment. Chess settled back in his seat and eyed the fat man with interest. "So, Max. The girls. You were saying?"

"Well..." Max hesitated, feeling awkward and embarrassed. "It's

27

just that I don't have much success with the fairer sex. Haven't really had any sort of relationship since – well since my Millie divorced me."

Chess smiled mischievously. "I'll soon change that," he said. "All you need is a quick lesson. It's quite straightforward, really it is. You play the woman, I'll play the man..."

*   *   *

Some fifteen minutes later, Chess and Max were at the door of the actress's first class compartment.

"Miss Dierdre Jacquelle, really it is quite the most exquisite pleasure to see you in the flesh so to speak. Allow me to introduce myself. I am Henry Chesterfield and this is my travelling companion, Mr Maxwell Shore. We are both admirers of your well-known talents." He smiled at the double meaning and his moustache twitched eagerly. Miss Jacquelle looked up at his handsome face, darker than ever now in the golden glow of the flickering gaslight.

Chess continued. "We were rather wondering whether we could join you in your journey to Southampton," he said.

"If you wish," came the soft, demure reply. She turned to her maid. "Edith, move next to me so that these gentlemen may occupy the opposite seat."

The train rushed on through the darkened Hampshire countryside, which was relieved only by the tiny lights of villages that loomed up and twinkled here and there before being swallowed by the inky blackness once more as the locomotive hurled itself onwards at a mile a minute.

*   *   *

The impressive portals of the South Western Hotel in Southampton were bathed in an incandescent light when the pair, together with Wilbur B., alighted from the train. Instead of a night sky above their heads, there shot the huge platform roofs that connected the hotel to the adjacent station and blocked out the fine drizzle that had begun to fall, covering the station surroundings in a thin film of damp mist.

In Southampton it had long been clear that the profitability of the railway would depend upon the traffic generated by the docks and vice versa, and consequently the Dock Company had just sold out to the London & South Western Railway. A good move, Chess decided, especially as the Inman Line were showing a healthy interest in the port. He eyed the hustle and bustle – a steamship had evidently just docked, and a connecting train was standing nearby disgorging its passengers. Within a few minutes the quiet late night scene was transformed into one of animation and hurry, and the deserted platforms were thronged with people. A mixture of different accents, both European and American, mingled with the hiss of steam that drifted clear of the locomotive and floated silently across the platforms in large, warm clouds.

Outside the circle of activity, in the darkness, a wide belt of lights in green and white, ever and anon twinkling and changing their colours, took on the appearance of a fairy land as they blinked along the trackside lending a theatrical, vaguely ghostly quality to the scene as the smoke from the resting locomotive drifted across them.

A distant whistle sounded away down the line and another night train came creeping in amidst a great cloud of steam, which was lit up by the furnace fire and the shooting sparks underneath. To Henry Chesterfield it all seemed most romantic. He had been invited to Miss Jacquelle's suite of rooms for a nightcap, and already he could feel the thrill of anticipation course through his whole eager body.

To Max, on the other hand, things were far from ideal. Despite Chess's brief lesson on female flattery, the actress's maid, Edith Todd, had barely responded to him at all throughout the journey and his hopes of any remotely romantic liaison were fading as fast as the steam clouds in the drizzle. However, he gallantly offered to carry the girl's baggage. As Chess breezed past, arm in arm with Miss Jacquelle with a willing porter in tow, Max struggled gamely with suitcases, hatboxes and all manner of secondary items of luggage, puffing and panting fit to burst. His fat face had become the colour of an over-ripe tomato, with enough moisture springing from his brow to fill the boiler of the towering locomotive that he staggered past.

*   *   *

"Tired, Madam?" Chess enquired on reaching the door of Miss-Jacquelle's rather grand suite on the second floor of the South Western Hotel.

"Mmm," came the reply. It was a soft, negative sound and Chess's nerves thrilled with the excitement of it. "You can come in for that nightcap now if you like," she added, looking at him through half-closed lashes, "that is as long as you keep that hound at bay."

Once inside the suite, Chess secured Wilbur B. to a chair leg just inside the door, while Dierdre Jacquelle draped herself enticingly across a large red-velvet sofa that was a feature of the high ceilinged room. Chess sat down beside her. "Where are you bound?" he enquired in a husky voice.

"Broadway, the Luami theatre. I believe we sail in four days time."

Chess nodded and eyed the room with its expensive velvet drape curtains, thick pile carpeting and marbled walls. His gaze came to rest on a table which was well stocked with alcoholic beverages. "Shall we partake in a brandy?" he enquired.

The woman shook her head. "No, I never take it myself. Though you are most welcome."

Chess waved the offer aside and lowered his voice. "You really are a most attractive woman," he said seductively, simultaneously running his hand through the actress's blond, silky hair before planting a light kiss against the locks.

He waited for a reaction. A slight shudder trembled through him as she snuggled closer and gazed at the strong, handsome profile of his face, a lazy smile tugging at the corners of her generous mouth. Chess picked his moment and leaned to kiss her. Her mouth moved in instant response to his, and as his lips tasted hers and he felt a contented glow flow through his veins.

After a few delicious moments, Dierdre Jacquelle pulled gently away and spent the next few minutes carefully removing the sparkling array of gaudy diamond jewellery that hung from her ears, wrists and slender neck. Chess watched in silence as she slipped it all into an ornate wooden box on the nearby table, realising that there must be literally thousands of pounds worth. On completion of this she eyed him seductively, searching into the deep blue depths of his delicate eyes. He felt his heart race, and his thick, black moustache twitched involuntarily over his expectant mouth. He took her lips again. This time the hard contours of his body crushed into hers and the weight of his mouth pushed her head back gently as he kissed with a hungry, pillaging force. She responded to his potent brand of sexuality and relaxed deeper into his arms, not resisting the progress of his hands on her clothing.

Tugging.

Undoing.

Caressing.

Pleasure erupted in Henry Chesterfield in a gold shower as he slid his hand softly beneath her corset to mould his palm to the firm roundness of the underside of her naked breast.

At that precise moment, Wilbur B. let out a deep growl and, as if in answer, the door was opened.

"Gawd, not another one."

The words were flung across the room hard and sarcastically, and Chess had just time to twist his head in their direction and see Edith Todd before the door slammed shut once more and the couple were left alone. Recovering quickly from the shock and embarrassment, both at his compromising position and at the maid's unwarranted display, Chess turned his attention back to the apparently unconcerned and willing woman beneath him, musing that Edith Todd would surely be unemployed on the morrow.

*   *   *

It was approaching eight the next morning when Chess and Max were awakened by Wilbur B's deep, melodious barking. As Chess came to, he became aware of a considerable commotion taking place in the corridor outside. "What d'you make of all that, Mr Chess?" said Max through bleary eyes, "a bevy of beauties queueing up for your affections perhaps?"

Chess said nothing but his face beamed. He pulled on his dressing gown while Max disappeared back into his bed chamber and did likewise, returning with the material stretched like a second skin over his bulbous body.

"A successful liaison last night, Max?" Chess enquired. "How did you fare with that maid? Was there Fuoco?"

"Was there what?"

"Fire, Max. Fire and passion."

Max glared at his friend. "Really, Mr Chess. Whatever do you take me for. I have morals, unlike yourself. I hardly know the girl. We simply talked. It seems that we have very little in common if you really wish to know."

"Time will tell," replied Chess with a smile as he opened the door of the apartment. "As I always say, Poco a poco – little by little."

Suddenly his smile vanished and the scene outside the door fairly took his breath away. The whole corridor was swarming with policemen and the air buzzed with their voices. To Chess, the sight reminded him of the bluebottles in his millionaire father's huge conservatory at his boyhood country home.

"What's going on, my good man?" he barked, grabbing one of the constables as the fellow went hurrying past the open doorway. "Quick now, presto, presto."

"Robbery with murder, sir," came the rapid reply. "Early hours of the morning it seems."

"Who? Where?"

The constable looked cautiously around. "Shouldn't really be sayin', but it's the actress. The famous one. Dierdre Jacquelle. She's stayin' here, y'know, just down the way."

Chess's heart missed a beat. "She's been murdered?" he gasped.

"No sir," came the reply. "Never said that, did I? It's her that's been robbed. All her jewellery. She's famous for it ain't she. Now it's all been nicked. Twenty thousand's worth my sargeant said."

"So who's been murdered?"

"An old lady, sir. Dear old soul by all accounts." He shook his head sadly. "Found at the bottom of the stairs. Strangled to death then pushed down the whole flight."

"It really doesn't bear thinking about," said Max from behind.

"Eighty-five they say she was too," the policeman added. "Dunno what the world's coming to these days. Now look, I must be getting along." The constable shook himself free of Chess's grasp and hurried off around the corner.

Chess closed the door slowly and turned to Max who was standing at his side. "Best go to her," he said quietly. "She's sure to be in need of some genuine consolation. It's the least we can do."

*   *   *

After some fifteen minutes both men had dressed and, locking Wilbur B. into their room, made off in haste towards Dierdre Jacquelle's suite, just up the corridor.

Their reception was totally unexpected:

"You dare to come in here," the actress blazed as Edith opened the door.

Henry Chesterfield was completely taken aback and stared blankly at the dishevelled woman before him. A woman who, just a few hours earlier, had been the very epitome of gentleness and affection. He was

was about to speak when he was prevented from doing so by a rapid fire of speech. "Where are they? Where are my jewels? What have you done with them?"

"Miss Jacquelle, please," said Chess in a cool, level voice. "If you would at least be good enough to invite us inside."

The actress nodded curtly and Edith stepped aside. "Was it not enough that I gave myself to you last night? Was it necessary to steal from me as well?"

"You insult my integrity," replied Chess. "Truly you do. And besides, would I come here now if I were the guilty party?"

"You were in my room last night. You left me asleep. When I awoke my jewels were gone."

"But I assure you, I–"

"Assure me nothing, Mr Chesterfield. Let me assure you that your name will be given to the police if you do not return my sparklers in the next twenty- four hours. You will be their prime suspect, understood?"

"Look, I didn't take them them, I–"

"I said understood?"

Chess exchanged glances with Max, shrugged and nodded. "Alright," he said at length. "But I swear to you that I know nothing of the affair. Let me look around and see if I can find any clues."

"The police have already done that, but as you wish."

"Surely you were insured?"

"The pieces are irreplaceable. Besides, that is none of your business. I must leave now. The police want a word with me. Remember, Mr Chesterfield. Twenty-four hours and then I tell them to arrest you. You will have no defence. It will be an open and shut case."

"We really are in serious trouble again," groaned Max when Jacquelle and her maid had breezed out. "There's no doubt about it, you'd be hard pushed to convince a jury of your innocence in this one. Things do look terribly black."

"Well thank you for those uplifting words of encouragement, Max," said Chess sarcastically. Then his face turned hard and serious. "It looks as if I'm about to play the great detective again," he said snooping around the apartment. "Perhaps it's my vocation after all." He began peering into this and that and scanned the floor minutely before making a careful examination of the side-table on which he had seen Jacquelle place her jewels on the previous night.

Max drew breath through his teeth and scratched his rotund head. "Where do we start?" he said haphazardly.

"How about here," Chess replied. "Look."

He pointed to the large sash windows, and Max noticed a broken pane. He crossed the room and peered out. Below stretched the long station roofs. "It'd have to be a jolly fit fellow to scale those and climb in at this window," he said, "and think of the noise the glass smashing must have made. It would surely have woken Jacquelle. The bedroom's just next door."

"Maybe," said Chess. "But it's a small pane. She could have slept through the sound. The thing I don't understand is why the devil there's no glass in here on the floor."

"Perhaps the fellow didn't come in this way," Max ventured, "but simply used it as an exit."

Chess shook his head. "What's the point of breaking the window at all. If that was the case, he could just have opened it from the inside. No, Max, there must be some glass on the floor, perhaps we've just over-looked it."

"Surely the police have noticed the window," Max said.

"I daresay," replied Chess, getting down on his hands and knees and proceeding to scrutinise the floor for fragments of glass, "but we'd be best keeping well out of their way until I can clear my name." He scrabbled around for a few more moments while Max watched in silence. Suddenly his hand darted into the gloom under a nearby sideboard and he shouted in triumph. "Brillante! You said a fit man, Max, right?"

The fat man nodded.

"Sailors are fit, are they not?"

"Yes I daresay, but–"

"Fit and careless – at least this one was!" Chess drew himself up to his full height, clutching a small photographic card. He tossed it, face up onto the side-table next to a doilly, a table lamp and an empty brandy glass. "What an elementary bungle on the thief's part," he chuckled. "A burglar who leaves his own carte de visit! I think we should pay Mr John Nash of 17 Ogle Road, a visit, don't you?"

"Thank heaven for small mercies," Max replied, breathing a sigh of relief as the two men turned to leave. "You ought to be careful with that dog of yours though," he added as he reached for the door handle. "Look!"

Chess followed the direction of his friend's gaze and raised his eyes in desperation on noticing a puddle on the green lino adjacent to the door. Already someone had trod in the liquid and there was a footprint nearby of a well-worn sole.

"I knew it was a mistake to bring him here last night," Chess said. "Still, it'll have to stay, no time to clear it up now."

*   *   *

Chess had no trouble hailing a hansom outside the hotel, and soon the pair were on their way to Ogle Road. Henry Chesterfield was silent on the journey along Canute Road past the many busy dock gates of the fast emerging main terminus of the the empire, and it wasn't until the Royal Pier came into view that he spoke. "I do apologise for all this," he said. "Really, Max. I seem to have a dreadful knack of getting us into the worst scrapes imaginable. Why don't you just hop on a train home. You're not currently under any suspicion as far as we know."

The fat man smiled. "Mr Chess," he began warmly. "I don't know how to rightly put this, but I haven't really had many friends in my life to speak of. I've seen you twice, and on both occasions I've had the most exciting time of my life. Besides, hang it all, this Nash fellow's likely to be pretty desperate when you confront him with your accusations. I reckon you could use some extra muscle."

A smile lit Henry Chesterfield's face. "Muscle?" he said with a chuckle.

"Well..." Max hesitated. "Bulk anyway," he added at length. The pair exploded in great guwaffs of laughter, just as the cab pulled up in Ogle Road.

After alighting, Chess rapped on the street door, and after a few moments a dark-haired woman with narrow, distrustful eyes opened it.

"Mrs Nash?" Chess enquired.

"What if I am?"

"Is your husband in?"

"Who is it, dear?" came a slow, drawling voice from somewhere deep within the little terraced cottage.

"My name is Henry Chesterfield. I simply wanted a few words," he said loudly, directing the sentence at the voice within.

"Best let 'im inside dear, see what 'e wants like."

Chess and Max were ushered into a small, dark sitting-room with plain painted walls that were only relieved by a selection of rather tatty

35

nautical sketches. Wooden beams shot low overhead, and the whitewash between them was stained a deep yellow from the relentless, feathery touch of tobacco smoke. Most sailors brought home a breath of the ocean in their rolling gait and had clean, clear eyes that twinkled as they issued forth their cheery exclamations. However, John Nash was entirely the opposite. He was sullen and surly with bleary eyes and a breath that smelled, not of the salt of the sea, but of the tobacco of Virginia.

"What d'you gents want?" he enquired between puffs on a clay pipe, his weatherbeaten face expressionless as he sat in a disreputable brown fabric-covered armchair.

"I'd just like to ask you a few questions about the caper up the road the other night," Chess began. "A murder and a robbery with a haul of twenty odd thousand in jewellery."

John Nash was silent. He beckoned Chess and Max sit down, then eyed them severely.

"I trust you ain't accusin' Johnny here," Mrs Nash barked, looking very agitated as she lent on the door frame. "He works for a livin' at sea. Good honest livin' too."

"I fully realise that," said Chess, not taking his eyes off of the man sitting before him. His gaze traversed the strong, supple body and came to rest on a bandage that covered one of the fellow's hands. "Cut yourself?" he enquired. "Glass was it?"

"Aye, that it was," came the reply as Nash puffed once more on his pipe, sending a wispy curl of blue-tinged tobacco smoke up to the ceiling where it nestled between the beams, further perpetuating the ochre colouring of the room. "What's it go to do with you, like, eh?" he added. "My wife asked if you was accusin' me. She never got no answer. Now I'm askin'. Are you, or what?"

"Perhaps," Chess said carefully, his delicate blue eyes narrowing and becoming cold as ice.

"Look, about me hand. I cut it at sea if you must know. Workin' alleyway was like a rockin' 'orse comin' back on the Atlantic. That good enough, f'you?"

"Do you know Dierdre Jacquelle?"

"The actress?"

"The very same."

Nash nodded and withdrew his pipe. "Seen her picture in the journals, like, why?"

"You have never met in person then?"

36

Mrs Nash interrupted before her husband had chance to speak. "Johnny's faithful. If you're tryin' to intimate that-"

"Shut up, Mary," Nash barked suddenly and unexpectedly. "I'll deal with this, whatever it is. Now look," he said getting to his feet and flexing his muscles which stood out clearly under his shirt. "You ain't the police so I don't have to answer to you. Get up off yer asses and bugger off out while you still can."

"Not until you explain the presence of this in Miss Jacquelle's hotel suite," Chess persisted, withdrawing the carte de visit and holding it up for Nash to see.

His wife's mouth fell open. "You was out late last night," she said a look of disbelief clouding her features. "You said you was drinkin'."

"I was," blazed Nash.

"At Dierdre Jacquelle's apartment?" Chess ventured.

"At the Oxford pub actually," retorted the man. He fell silent, then drew a long, deep breath. "Alright he said. For Christ's sake, are you tryin' to break up this 'ome, like? I did meet the bloody woman, but not last night. It was a while ago when I was at sea. I'm a bedroom steward."

Chess raised his eyebrows.

"Nothin' funny about it," blazed Nash. "She was good for a few tips, worked 'ard for 'em I did too. I gave her my card in case she travelled on ship again."

This time Chess smiled knowingly. At this, Nash rolled up his sleeves, placed his foot on a stool and lent over to reach a greasy frying pan that lay on the table. As he did so, several carte de visits fell from his trouser pocket. "If you ain't gone in 'alf a minute, your mothers won't recognise you," he shouted. "Talk to Jacquelle's maid. She's a strange one, make no mistake. Don't come round 'ere 'ome breakin' them that ain't got nothin' to do with it."

"Alright, alright," said Chess, holding up his hand. "We're going."

★   ★   ★

"Well, what do you think of his story, Mr Chess?" Max enquired excitedly when the pair were in the cab rattling back towards the South Western Hotel.

"I don't know," came the thoughtful reply. "He does seem to have rather a flurry of grace notes into his little opus that have served to muddy up the affair. He may be straight about what he said. I suppose we could verify some of his statements with a little research."

Chess considered for a few moments, then he spoke again. "I suppose I believed him," he said. "That was until those other cartes fell out of his pocket when he lifted his leg onto that footstool."

Max looked confused. "I don't follow. What are you getting at?"

"I conjectured that the same thing could easily have happened if it was Nash who climbed in at the window of Jacquelle's hotel suite late last night."

"By jove! You're right," gasped Max. "Well done, Mr Chess, that's blown his story to blazes, truly it has."

"Maybe," Said Chess levelly, "but it hasn't secured us the loot and saved my bacon, and my times running out fast, it's almost lunchtime already."

"What about Edith the maid," said Max. "Do you think she's worth questioning or d'you reckon Nash's comments were just a blind to sling us off the scent?"

Chess shrugged. "Well, Max," he replied with a wry smile. "You know the lady in question somewhat better than I. Why don't you quiz her tactfully on the matter while I take Wilbur B. out for his lunchtime gambol? That is, assuming the maid's still around. I rather thought that she would be unemployed by now."

"Of course I'll speak to her," Max replied, "though I don't hold out much hope of her confiding in me, and anyway, what do you mean about her being unemployed?"

"Ah yes, well, um, when Jacquelle and I were... Well-er-shall we just say, 'involved' last night, Edith burst in and made a most objectionable and unrepeatable comment. If she had been in my employ, I should have had no hesitation in firing her at the earliest opportunity for gross insolence."

By now the cab had completed the journey to the hotel and the pair alighted. Chess paid the cabbie and they walked through the towering doors into the marbled entrance hall beyond. "I'll give it my best shot," said Max as they climbed the wide sweeping staircase to the right. "But as you know, I'm not particularly good with girls."

"As I've said before, practice makes perfect Max," said Chess. "Consider my success rate."

"I'd rather not," came the prudish reply. "Look at the bloody mess that your latest conquest has got you into."

*　　*　　*

The weather, which had been dry all morning, had taken a turn for the worse when Chess emerged from the marbled entrance hall of the hotel behind an eager bassett hound. A light yet persistent drizzle was falling, cloaking everything in sight in its cold, depressing spray. The forest of tall masts and majestic funnels in the nearby docklands were almost totally obscured in the watery mist, and an air of gloom seemed to hang heavy over the busy landscape. The feeling was further perpetuated by Chess's growing concern regarding the bringing about of a solution to the puzzle into which he had inexplicably been thrown. The worried man pulled the all-round cape on his tweed Inverness waterproofs tightly around him and ventured out into the weather, making off in the direction of the small park adjacent to the rear of the hotel. Once there, he let Wilbur B. off the lead and he ran free.

The verdant acreage was deserted save for a lone police constable that trudged, head bowed and cape drawn around him, along the central walkway. "Afternoon, Henry Chesterfield's my name. Nice to meet someone else in this murk. Didn't expect to."

"No sir," came the reply. "P.C. Plumridge at your service. Frightful weather isn't it, just like last night."

Chess nodded in agreement. "On duty then too were you?" he enquired, looking at the young man before him, who could not have been more than twenty-one.

"'S right, late turn for me it was."

The pair walked on, stopping for shelter under a nearby tree where the thick foliage above had kept the ground perfectly dry. "I suppose you were involved in the affair at the hotel then?" Chess enquired nonchalantly.

The constable shook his head. "I saw nothing untoward," he said. "And I'm the only P.C. on this beat. In fact, first thing I heard was when I came back on duty this morning. The station was fairly buzzing with it. Never seen the woman save in magazines." He shook his head again. "No, I was over the Royal Pier way last night sorting out a spot of bother there."

Chess lowered his eyes to the floor. "Shocking business, the murder," he said sadly. His gaze lazily traversed the floor around their feet. About Plumridge's, he noticed that there was a considerable puddle forming.

"Anything troubling you, sir?" said the policeman somewhat uneasily, "It's not my damn socks again is it? Forever slipping right down over my ankles they are, sir. Bloody nuisance, I don't mind admitting."

As he finished speaking, he placed one hand on the trunk of the tree to support himself while he lifted, first one, then the other foot off of the ground to tug his socks up. As he did so, Chess made a sudden start and he centred his attention on the soles of the policeman's shoes. When he spoke, it was with an air of confidence and determination.

"Constable Plumridge, you are a liar," he said.

The policeman stared aghast. "What do you mean?" he replied.

"You were in Dierdre Jacquelle's apartment last night. You cannot deny it, I have proof."

"I can and I will," Plumridge retorted. "In the strongest possible terms."

"Shut up, constable. Your fledgling police force career will come to a very premature end if you do not admit to, and provide a plausible solution, for your nocturnal behaviour."

The policeman looked suddenly white-faced and worried. He eyed Chess with an air of resignation.

"Come on, out with it, molto presto. I haven't got all day."

"I suppose I'd better come clean and tell the truth," Plumridge said at length. "You detective chaps are smart. Everything I aspire to be."

Chess smiled inwardly at the elementary mistake, but played up to it. "Quite so," he said. "It is the soles of your boots that have given your game away, together with this infernal drizzle."

Plumridge frowned.

"It's really quite simple, just a case of putting two and two together." said Chess.

"And making five," the policeman interrupted. "I want to make it clear before I say anything about last night that I'm not responsible for the murder or the robbery, if that's what you're driving at." Plumridge's young face began to look extremely uneasy.

"We shall see about that in due course," continued Chess, rather enjoying his role of detective. "It is, as I have already mentioned, quite clear that you visited Miss Jacquelle's apartment after midnight last night. I was there myself up to that time."

Plumridge's eyes widened, but he said nothing.

Chess continued again. "When I returned this morning to the scene of the crime, my colleague directed my attention to a puddle just inside the door. At the time I confess that we believed it to have been made by my sleuth hound. However, it is now quite clear that is not the case. It was caused by someone soaking wet. Someone who had been out in the drizzle for a long time."

"Today, under this tree, I observe that my clothing has caused no puddle as I have not long been out in this infernal rain. However, around yourself there is a considerable propensity of water. It is unlikely that there were many people out last night in the rain. In fact, I would think that the only souls who would traipse around outside would be people paid to do so – such as police constables. You said yourself that you were the only policeman on duty in the area last night, and if any further proof was needed, next to the aforementioned puddle lies a bootprint, which I am now certain, matches your own."

"Quite formidable," Plumridge replied. "I have to admit you are quite right."

Again, Henry Chesterfield couldn't help feeling rather pleased with himself, and he smiled making his black moustache quiver slightly. "I'm sure that you are well aware that it is utterly against police rules to consume brandy on duty," he went on. "I saw the empty glass on the side-table in Jacquelle's apartment. She doesn't drink alcohol, and I had none. You'd better have a damn good reason for being there or else I'm turning you in. That is, of course, after you've made a full confession to the lady and returned the gems."

"Look, like I've said, it's true that I did go into her room." Plumridge was getting frantic with worry now. "I admit I was there, but I don't know anything about the other ghastly business. I saw Miss Jacquelle coming back into the hotel. I recognised her from the pictures in a recent copy of the Illustrated London News that happened to be laying around at the station. Anyway, it must have been late because the last train had been and gone a long while. I was nearby and plucked up the courage to go and ask her for her autograph. Funny thing was, she suddenly got all flustered when I spoke to her."

At this, Plumridge stopped, and his face coloured up slightly.

"Go on," said Chess. "I am still all ears."

"Well, she… She came over all sorta sexy and invited me up to her room," Plumridge blurted. "Offered me a nightcap in return for me promising to keep quiet that I'd seen her. Didn't want to publicise the fact that she was in town, she said."

Chess nodded, "plausible I suppose," he said, "although those types usually like to court publicity."

"It's the truth, really it is," said Plumridge. "She went up first and told me to follow five minutes later. I did like she asked and she gave me a brandy and a peck on the cheek. I never moved from the doorway, Mr Chesterfield, on my life I never did."

"Constable Plumridge, you look a fit man. What do you do to keep in trim?"

The policeman relaxed slightly at this change of subject. "Ah, climbing, walking and so on. The wife and I took a holiday in Snowdonia this year."

Chess suddenly looked grave. "Most interesting," he said. "Come on Wilbur." The hound romped through the grass towards its master. "We could well meet again soon Constable Plumridge," Chess said in an authoritarian voice as he clipped the dog's lead on and made off towards the hotel. "Do make sure you're available to talk to me if I need you."

*   *   *

"I think I've cracked it, Mr Chess," said Max excitedly as soon as the damp man and his dog had returned to the cozy hotel room. "It's the maid that did it, just like Nash suggested. Has to be."

"Why do you say that?" Chess enquired, settling himself in the easy chair and proceeding to dry Wilbur B. off with a towel.

"I had a long amiable chat with her," he continued, "and everything points to it. She's been skivvying, as she calls it, for Dierdre Jacquelle for over ten years. She's sick of it by all accounts."

"Why doesn't she find another job then?"

"That's exactly what I said, Mr Chess. It turns out that Dierdre Bagstaff – that's her real name apparently – has been promising Edith a share in the proceeds of her dramatic work, but none of the money's been forthcoming. Edith started letting it all pour out to me in a steady stream when I hinted that we thought she may be responsible for the crime. I suppose she was trying to form some sort of cover-up."

"A dreadful one, she's only succeeded in drawing more suspicion to herself," said Chess, "correct, Max?"

"Precisely," said the fat man. "We're getting rather good at this lark aren't we? She went on to say that Jacquelle, or whatever you want to call her, was originally an East End prostitute. She's been bribing Edith to keep her past quiet all these years with the promise of a large nest egg."

"Aha, so that's why Edith gets away with her dreadful behaviour. Go on, Max, this is most interesting, you my have something here, she really does seem to be dropping herself in it. From what you've said so far, she has an excellent motive for stealing her employer's jewels."

"And she had access to the room without arousing any suspicion," Max added triumphantly. "It all adds up, Mr Chess."

"Well, it amazes me that Jacquelle hasn't given her maid the money that she promised her," Chess said. "After all, she's hardly destitute is she?"

"I'm not so sure," replied Max. "From what I can gather, there's not much money around. Edith said that if this Broadway season flops, they'll both be on skid row. She said she's seen Jacquelle's bank statements and for quite some time they've been the colour of ripe tomatoes."

Chess shrugged. "I just don't know," he said. "I can't go accusing anyone else, though you're right, a lot does point to Edith Todd. But there's still the broken window and the other clues."

"Perhaps you're reading too much into this whole business," Max said. "Maybe they mean nothing at all. Perhaps Nash was telling the truth."

"I'd be inclined to agree," Chess replied, "that is if I hadn't met anyone during my walk with Wilbur B. Policemen ARE fit aren't they? And they can go anywhere without arousing suspicions, even at the dead of night can't they?"

Max groaned loudly. "Not more flippin' complications," he said. Chess nodded solemnly and proceeded to explain the events of the previous half hour. By the time he had finished, Max's face had clouded over and a look of complete confusion had spread across his rotund features. He shook his head slowly.

"Blimey, I just don't know what to think now," he said. "What about you, Mr Chess?"

"Likewise," he said, "Looks like we're making a right bloody pig's ear of it again." He fell silent and stared at the floor, his gaze eventually coming to rest on the rug in front of the fireplace. He suddenly registered that it was empty. Immediately he became alert and his delicate blue eyes traversed the apartment. "Wilb's gone," he gasped. "That's all we need, trust me to leave the blasted door open." He jumped to his feet and hurried across the room, peering out of the open door down the long gloomy hallway. At the end, another door was ajar. A door which Chess instantly recognised as belonging to Jacquelle's suite. As he watched, Wilbur B. padded out of it, a picture of dignified nonchalance with a powder puff between his drooping, slobbery jaws.

"A slow largo tempo as usual," Chess grumbled. "Here," he called anxiously under his breath. "Good dog. This way. Come on. Hereboy."

Wilbur B. made no attempt whatsoever to hurry, and simply continued to plod slowly up the corridor, his sad, droopy eyes appealing to his master's better nature. As he approached, Chess grabbed him by the collar and yanked him quickly inside, slamming the door shut.

"Bloody hell!" exclaimed Max, holding his nose. "What's he brought in now? It smells bleedin' awful."

"One of Miss Jacquelle's powder puffs," Chess said with a smile. "He's been in her suite."

"Amazing," Max laughed. "No-one seems to get caught stealing from the damn woman. What's our next move on the main affair, Mr Chess? We've got three suspects, any of which could have carried out the business. But still we've got no solid proof. How long have we got?"

Chess pulled at his grand close-curb gold double Albert and consulted the white enamel dial of his Benson's pocket watch. "About eighteen hours and counting – twelve or so less than that if you discount the night time." He sat down on the sofa. "Well, I don't know what you propose to do, Max, but I have to rehearse for my concert tonight. There a few demanding phrases in some of the works. I really must run through them, and I've also got to put a few finishing touches to an original composition that is still wanting a title."

"It beats me how you can be so calm. Jacquelle has threatened to turn you in to the police, for heaven's sake."

"Quite true," Chess replied in an offhand manner, "and I do confess that this morning I was worried. However, this afternoon I am not. I shall simply visit her before I go to the concert and recount each of our suspect's stories to her. She can make her own decision on what to do from there on in."

"And if she still blames you?"

"Then there's nothing I can do about it. However, perhaps a dose of the old charm and the offer of the best seat in the house may persuade her to relent."

"Unlikely if you ask me," said Max, "especially judging by what we've learned about her today. She seems as hard as nails. Still, you know best I suppose, Mr Chess. I'll leave you to practice in peace."

With that Max strode out of the apartment, every inch of him a picture of worry and concern. Chess withdrew the powder puff from

Wilbur B's mouth, tossed it onto the table, and took up his cherished classical guitar.

* * *

It had just turned five when Max returned to the hotel room to be greeted by a beautiful, haunting and melodious air that Chess was effortlessly producing on his guitar. "Marvellous!" he exclaimed, his voice full of genuine admiration for the flawless playing.

"Nothing particularly special," came the reply. "Simply something constructed on minor scales with a little syncopation on the occasional quaver triplets." He set the instrument down carefully. "Would you care to accompany Wilbur B. and I on our evening constitutional?"

"Certainly," Max replied. "Then I suppose it's time to face Dierdre Jacquelle. Have you thought any more of the affair?"

"Not for a moment," Chess replied with resignation tinging his voice. He clipped on Wilbur's lead and continued. "It does not do to clutter one's mind when one is performing music. The whole brain really must be concentrated upon the job in hand. It is a maxim that was passed on to me by my tutor at the Guildhall School of Music, and one which I live with no matter what."

Once outside the hotel, Henry Chesterfield removed Wilbur B.'s lead and turned towards the nearby park. However, the dog had other ideas and put its keen nose close to the ground, trotting rapidly off along the station platform adjacent to the hotel.

"Oh no," groaned Chess. "Obstinate and uncontrollable – a basset trait if ever there was one. Wilbur. Heel. Come on. Here, boy."

Chess's calls did nothing whatsoever to shake the animal from its chosen course and it continued bounding along towards the far end of the platform, its tail held high, the white tip waving to and fro like a flag, while its long ears dragged along the dusty concrete throwing up little clouds of dust and grime as he sniffed along, nose to the ground.

"Looks like it'll be us getting as much exercise as him tonight," remarked Chess with a look of desperation as he and Max hurried after the errant animal. Chess sprinted along, while Max, labouring with the effort, puffed and panted far behind, his cheeks blown out fit to burst like two large red balloons on each side of his rotund face.

Notwithstanding his athleticism, Chess wasn't in time to prevent Wilbur B. from scrambling down off the far end of the platform and scampering along the trackside. "Here Wilbur. Good dog. Wait!" Chess called. But it was to no avail, and the determined bassett continued relentlessly along the trackside past a line of stationary goods vehicles and onwards until he reached a ramshackle shed set on a grassy bank overlooking the permanent way. Once there, he began scrabbling furiously at the old wooden door, emitting his distinctive deep, melodious bark.

Chess hurried up and tugged at the handle. "What is it, Wilb?" he said. "What's up? Cats?" The door opened with difficulty, emitting two discordant squalks from the oil-starved hinges.

"What the hell's he playing at?" gasped Max, puffing more than a goods locomotive. Chess shrugged and put his head into the dark depths of the shed.

"Euugh!" he exclaimed. "He's been following a scent, in quite the literal sense of the word. This whole place reeks of that Jacquelle perfume that he smelt earlier on that powder puff."

"Perhaps he's onto something," said Max excitedly. "Is there anything in there?"

Chess peered into the darkness a second time, and waited until his eyes became accustomed to the gloom. "My good God!" he cried suddenly, his voice rising to a high and excited squeak. "They're in here! The Jacquelle jewels!" With that he backed out of the shed with a small wooden box. He yanked the lid open and the late evening sunlight fired the glittering mound of diamonds and bright shiny gold within, bathing the riches in a soft pink light.

"Peughh!" cried Max pulling his face away. "That bloody perfume again. It stinks."

Chess nodded and held the box at arm's length. It did indeed reek of the heady concoction. "Lucky for us it does," he said. "Otherwise old Wilb. here would never have sniffed it out."

"He certainly does seem to have his uses," said Max, bending down and patting the sad-eyed dog who was wagging his tail furiously and trying to climb up his leg, convinced that it was all some sort of wonderful game. Max pushed him down and turned back to Chess. "Let's get them back to Jacquelle post-haste so we can get this robbery business over and done with."

Chess considered for a little time. "No, Max," he said "She doesn't want them."

Max was dumbstruck.

He stared incredulously , first at Chess, then at the glittering box. "Doesn't want them?" he exploded. "But they're worth thousands."

"I should say 'doesn't want them at the moment'," Chess said. "I'm certain of it."

Max thrust his podgy hands deep into his trouser pockets and furrowed his sweating brow. "Mr Chess, with respect, what the hell are you going on about? We've got the blasted things back. The case is closed apart from the fact that we can't tell Dierdre Jacquelle who did it."

"We don't need to. She already knows."

"Nash?"

Chess shook his head.

"Edith Todd, the maid?"

"No, Max."

"Constable Plumridge?"

"Wrong again."

"Who the deuce was it then?"

"Dierdre Jacquelle herself," Chess announced. "It's obvious to me now."

Max's mouth fell open and his eyes widened. He didn't speak, he just stared at his friend in stunned disbelief.

"It's quite simple really," Chess continued, smiling at Max's expression, "or perhaps I should say 'elementary', like that skinny detective fellow from over Marylebone way does. Jacquelle was seen by Constable Plumridge coming very late last night. She bribed him to keep quiet about it. I never thought anything much of it when he told me, but now it's obvious. It's clear that she was returning after hiding the gems here."

"But why?" interrupted Max. "What's the point, tell me that."

Chess looked grave. "I'd wager the entire contents of this box that she has a massive insurance policy covering this lot, and that a claim has already been lodged. If you recall, she was quite dismissive about insurance when I enquired whether she was covered for her loss. She would doubtless have recovered the jewels herself when she had been provided with the huge pay out."

"A remarkable scheme," Max said, "and one that would certainly have succeeded had we not somehow stumbled into the affair. But are you absolutely certain of your facts, Mr Chess? We don't want to end up in more trouble for making any unfounded accusations."

"Don't worry Max," Chess replied. "If any further proof was

needed then I could cite the Luami theatre – it doesn't exist. There's no such place on Broadway, I checked. Jacquelle has no dramatic season booked abroad, and her career is on a downward spiral here. You learned that from Edith Todd, her maid. It's obvious that she would have boarded the steamship and disappeared somewhere deep in the United States with the money and the jewels, leaving me to face trial for the theft. She would doubtless have re-surfaced a few years later with another name, probably successfully pulling the stunt several more times. Quite frankly, I wouldn't be at all surprised to find that these jewels are extremely good fakes, and that Jacquelle sold the originals long ago to help support herself in the manner that she had become accustomed."

"Why did she give you twenty-four hours? Why not turn you in straight away?"

"Authenticity, Max. She wanted to give the police time to snoop around and fail to add more creedence to her scheme. They'd never have come up with anything. When I was made known to them a day later, they'd have jumped on me, glad to have a suspect. I wouldn't have stood a chance."

"What about Edith, do you think she was in on it?"

"From what you found out about her dissatisfaction regarding her current situation, it seems most unlikely that she was involved in the scheme at all."

"And the murder?"

"Jacquelle again. Carried out when she returned to her apartment and went up the main staircase to her suite. The poor old lady probably saw and recognised her on the way, and perhaps even approached her as a genuine admirer. To keep her movements secret, I believe that Jacquelle grabbed her by the throat and, in a fit of panic, strangling the frail old lady, leaving her to tumble down the first flight."

"But surely Constable Plumridge would have seen the body when he came up to Jacquelle's apartment a few minutes later."

"Not if he used the lift."

Max fell silent and considered. "I think you're right," he said at length. "But there's just one more thing – the broken window."

"I thought of that one. Remember how I remarked that there was no glass inside?"

Max nodded.

"Well, before I began practising this afternoon, I asked the maintenance staff at the hotel about it, and they said that it happened a while ago when they were painting the frames. They simply haven't had time to fix it yet."

"So that's why there was no glass inside,"

"Exactly," said Chess, "and it looks as if Nash was telling the truth when he told us the story of his carte de visit." Chess flipped out his engine-turned watch. "Gracious," he gasped thrusting it back into his waistcoat pocket. "I must hurry along to the concert hall." He pushed the box of jewellery into Max's hands. "Be a good man and take these to the police station and sketch out the story for them. They can investigate the finer points. Oh, and Max, nip Wilbur B. back to the hotel room, would you? I'll see you at the concert later."

With that, he turned and ran off down the platform at top speed.

* * *

The applause in the concert hall was deafening.

"Thank you," said Henry Chesterfield, adjusting the tuning on his guitar as he spoke. "My last piece tonight is a brand new original composition which was only completed this very afternoon. I've called it Diamonds in D Minor. At least one person here will understand."

49

Death in Devon

"Ow-dee-do, sir? Sherlock Holmes said 'eed be 'elpful," said George Mallock in his broad Devon accent. "Said 'ee's too busy to look into me problem, but that he'd heard that you be gaining a prapper good reppytation as detective. He show me a newspaper clipping about that affair that you be havin' with the actress's jewels a while back. His friend, that doctor fellow, said he daresay it'd make a good yarn for a magazine, that."

Henry Chesterfield closed the large picture window that overlooked Park Lane, in an effort to prevent the clatter of hooves and rattle of carriages from invading his luxurious apartment and intruding on what promised to be a most interesting conversation. He strode across the expensively appointed drawing room and sat down on the sofa, bidding the stocky, well-built West Country man to a nearby chair, and offering him a cigar from an ornate box on the side table.

Two curls of tobacco smoke were soon drifting up to the exquisite ceiling. The conversation was resumed by Chess who was secretly rather surprised at being approached for the first time as a consulting detective, and more than a little chuffed that the recommendation had come from none other than the celebrated Holmes.

"Tell me," Chess said taking a long draw on his cigar. "What exactly is your problem?"

"It be th' 'elp, Mr Chesterfield. A few days back." He shook his head. "Suicide the police be reckonin' 'twas, but I bain't so sure. Dear lill' zaul. She wouldn't have done herself in. No reason to."

"How did it happen?"

"Drownin'. She left my house, Greenlawns Manor down in Torquay, De'bn, last Friday morn' to go visitin' her gawky ol' mother. Friday's be 'er day off, she gaw there every week without fail. Anyway, next thing we knows is she be washed up on Torre Abbey sands with 'orrible lukin' head injuries, been driven against the rocks round the coast the police reckon."

"When was she found?"

"Sunday morning. My Gar, it be terrible." George Mallock stared down at the Wilton carpet. He had no chin to speak of and his head just continued into his collar which was half-obscured by a super-abundance of flesh.

"Where does her mother live?" Chess enquired.

Mallock looked up. "Be a place perched on rocks overlookin' Hollacombe beach," he said sadly.

Chess continued with his relentless questioning. "Is your house within walking distance of the station?" he enquired.

"That-ee-be. Torre be just down St Michael's Road, but on the Friday, my wife took th' 'elp, Judy Kenwyn, to the station in my carriage. She be late leaving for her train, and my wife be goin' t' Newton Abbot, which be that way. She give her lift. Even then they be only in jus' in time, cuz Anne say that as they arrived, she see smoke of train's chimley comin'. Stands out clear against the woods at back of station it do."

"So how far did this Judy Kenwyn travel on the railway?"

"Not much more than stone's throw, Mr Chesterfield. Just down to Torquay station. Next stop on the line it be, only a mile or so, as crow do fly."

Chess frowned. "Surely it's hardly worth taking the train for such a short distance. Why the devil didn't she walk or take a trap?"

"Ah, that be easy. Old Mr Kenwyn, long daid now, twas 'elpful in getting the railway extenshun through from Torre, even talked with Brunel himself they do say. Anyroad, he and his family got gave free passes for the railway. Judy, she had one. She would always use it no matter how short a distance she be travellin'. Used to say it remind 'er of her awl dad."

"I see," said Chess. "Tell me, did she have much luggage?"

"Only a mite," came the reply. "Just a couple bottles of me dair wife's home-made scrumpy cider for her awl mother. We treat our staff well Mr Chesterfield. They t'would 'ave no reason to do suicide. I do everything I can to make 'em 'appy."

Chess nodded and considered. Mallock spoke again. "I want get clain to bottom of it. It be playin' on me mind, makin' me un-cum-ferable. Money be no object. I be a wealthy landowner and I'll pay what-ever charges you be wantin', and more too if you can solve it." His voice was full of enthusiasm. "Will you come down to Deb'nshur?" he pleaded. "You can have your own room at Greenlawns. There be plenty of space."

Chess spoke levelly and slowly. "I have an assistant, a Mr Maxwell Shore. I shall be happy to look into the matter if he is available, and assuming that you will cover his fees too."

51

"Certainly," said Mallock, a smile casting itself across his droopy face. "T'will be no question 'bout it."

Henry Chesterfield got to his feet. "Alright Mr Mallock. Should there be any problems then I shall send a wire. If you hear nothing, then you can expect us tomorrow afternoon. I trust you have no objection to Wilbur B."

The bassett hound that had been lying on Mallock's feet throughout the conversation thumped its tail on the floor at the mention of its name, but elected to remain stretched out.

"That I don't," said the Torquinian, stubbing out his cigar and getting up out of the chair, easing Wilbur B. gently aside as he did so. "It be a pleasant trip down, zummat f'you to enjoy."

"I was under the impression that there was a lot of engineering work going on at the moment - something about a change from broad to standard gauge. It won't hold us up will it?"

George Mallock shook his head. "No, that be all finished up now," he said. "Twas started Thursday last week, open again by the Sunday, all be standard now."

"Excellent, brillante," said Chess seeing his visitor to the door. He placed his hand on the large brass handle, then hesitated. "Oh," he said. "There's just one more thing, Mr Mallock. Did anyone in your household have any sort of quarrel with Judy Kenwyn, the dead girl?"

This time it was Mallock's turn to hesitate. "Naw," he said at length. "She be gude lill' gurl. Everyone git along purty well, far as I know."

*　　*　　*

"I'm not really sure about all this, Mr Chess," said Max, looking worried as he eyed his friend across a first class railway carriage that was speeding through the Devon countryside. "My ticket inspector's job on the Great Northern's not the best in the world, but at least it's secure."

"Secure and boring, Max," Chess retorted. "Becoming a professional consulting detective's infinitely more exciting, and besides, it pays better. Mallock invited me to name my own price."

"Well, I still don't know, I–"

"Look, Max, what would you say if I guaranteed you one and a half times your railway salary – out of my own pocket if we haven't got a case on?"

"I'd say alright I'll do it."

Chess beamed, then leaned forwards and extended his right hand. The fat man shook it. "We have an agreement then, Max?"

"Indeed we do, Mr Chess," came the reply. "Indeed we do. I just hope I'm doing the right thing, that's all."

"No question of it. We've almost no competition. There's only Sherlock Holmes, and until recently, I thought he was lost over some waterfall or other with that Moriarty chap." Chess shrugged. "Whatever, we're definitely onto a gold mine if we can come up with the goods."

*   *   *

As the train gathered speed on leaving Exeter, Max could feel the now-familiar pangs of excitement and anticipation gripping at him. He stood up and peered out of the window at the sprawling patchwork-quilt countryside speeding past.

"Not long before Torre now," remarked Chess. "Presto, presto!"

"You and your musical expressions," laughed Max. "Don't get too excited, there are quite a few halts yet, I'm looking forward to seeing Starcross. Always wanted to."

"What's so interesting about that?"

"The pumping station. Brunel introduced his clever atmospheric railway on this section back in '46. Well ahead of its time, it was."

"What do you mean atmospheric?"

"There were pumping stations three miles apart here that exhausted air from a fifteen-inch diameter pipe between the rails. It caused a piston inside the pipe that was attached to the frame of the leading carriage by an arm which ran in a horizontal slot along the top of the pipe, to be drawn along."

"So why isn't it here now?"

"Lack of the right materials," came Max's studious reply. "Couldn't make a good airtight flap or a durable enough piston. Mind you, it did work for a while. I heard that there was a report of a train reaching seventy under atmospheric pressure. There's still supposed to be some of the bits and pieces of pipe laying around."

"You really do seem quite knowledgeable about all this," said Chess in admiration. "I confess that I hadn't realised your talents."

"Ah, Mr Chess, railways aren't – I mean weren't – just my job, they're my hobby too."

*   *   *

Torre station was busy when Chess and Max arrived with Wilbur B. mid-afternoon. A team of workmen were putting the finishing touches to the alterations that had recently been made to the line. As Chess lifted his stubborn basset from the carriage to the platform, a brawl between two members of the workforce suddenly and unexpectedly broke out.

"If yu'd git t'work on time I wouldn't ha' to reprimand thee."

"I be tired. You make us work like 'orses." A tall, thin man with a distinctive black beard retorted, slogging out at his supervisor with a left that hit home hard on the man's weatherbeaten face.

"Sack f'you if yud don't pack ee in."

Chess, Max and Wilbur B. gave the pair a wide berth and let them get on with their disagreement. The trio made their way towards the exit of the tiny station, at which Max turned and gazed at the steep, wooded slope behind the italianate styled buildings, admiring the rural scene.

Brunel had designed a low-pitched roof that formed a canopy over the entrance, and this was supported beneath by wooden brackets, each with a four-sided pendant knob that produced the effect of a hammer-beam. The whole building, although of horizontal boarding, had the appearance of rusticated stone, aided in no small way by the wooden 'keystones' above the windows.

Max turned and walked on, stopping after a few more yards to examine the footbridge and nodding appreciatively at the fine spiked finials to the roof and the fluted columns at the foot of the stairs with their twisted band and cast iron rosettes. "Beautiful," the fat man remarked.

Chess smiled. "If you say so," he replied with a shrug, "a boring adagio as far as I'm concerned." His uninterested gaze passing quickly over the columns that to him looked like something out of Egypt. His line of sight continued to wander until his interest was caught by a poster pasted on a nearby noticeboard. "Friday 20th," he read out loud. "Last day for broad gauge trains." In smaller letters was a further note. He read again. "Workgangs please note, a goods special will travel the route late at night after closure. Please ensure all rubbish possible is transferred to this." He turned to Max. "Well, they certainly do seem to have had the whole of this gauge change affair well organised," he said handing over his ticket to the inspector. "Seems to all be running pretty smoothly now."

"Apart from the problems back there with the workforce," Max remarked, jerking his rotund head in the direction of the fisticuffs that seemed to have broken up at the other end of the platform. "Never seen a display like that on the Northern," he added, "in all the years I've been working for them."

"Beggin' pardin, but d'you be Mr Chesterfield and Mr Shore?"

Chess spun around to see an attractive, young dark-haired girl leaning against a pillar near the station entrance. "That's quite correct," he said eyeing the girl's fine late-teenage body before meeting her quite catlike emerald green eyes. His black moustache wiggled and his handsome face broke into an easy smile.

The girl spoke again. "I knew 'twas you 'cuz of the dog. Th' maister told me ee'd be comin' along." She bent down and patted Wilbur B's head. The dog looked up appealingly at the girl who giggled. "He be right luvverly," she said. "Well, we'd best be getting on. My name's Mary, Mary Fish. I'm stable-gurl up at Greenlawns. I've got th' fly outside. Mr Mallock reckoned on you be 'avin' some baggage and 'tis hard walk up St Michael's hill."

Soon they were rattling away from the station forecourt, and a few moments later, turned into St Michael's Road. The steep gradient was bordered on either side with high stone walls, their jagged tops fringed with trailing ivy and all manner of other fresh, green vegetation, all gaining a beautiful natural luminosity as the warm afternoon sun shone upon them.

"You two be here 'bout poor lill' Judy Kenwyn," Mary stated suddenly. "I heard the Mallocks talkin' 'bout you. Detective they said you be. Funny though, I thought you'd be a reglar old fuddy-duddy. Never reckoned on you being—"

"Please," interrupted Chess, "Spare my blushes. Likewise, I never thought that I should be greeted by such an attractive young thing as you, appassionata indeed."

Mary giggled again, more mischievously this time.

Max tutted under his breath and averted his gaze. The stone walls on the roadside were relieved here and there by occasional stout, wooden doors that provided access to the stone cottages that could be spied along the route, rising like tiny castles as if to guard the steep track.

"I mus' say, Mr Chesterfield," began Mary, "that I be a mite scared about Judy bein' daid. It makes me worry 'bout meself, 'specially if you think she be murdered."

"I don't think anything of the sort at the moment," Chess replied.

Mary fell silent and drove the horse on a little faster.

On the right, the ground rose above the track, and the tree-line was broken in several places by two or three larger, grander houses that were built, one behind the other in tiers on the steep slope. "That be Green-lawns," Mary said pointing her whip towards a large, white building further on up the road, half-obscured by trees.

Max glanced at it, then craned his neck around in the direction they had come, and there, in the distance lay the sparkling blue waters of Torbay, gradually gaining a prominence on the landscape as the cart climbed higher.

Mary re-opened the conversation once more. "I be mos' obliged if you tell me of what you finds out, Mr Chesterfield. It'll help me rest easier at night. You can alluz find me at th' stables round th' side of house. I've got a little room above them away from everyone else."

"I'll come to you tonight and give you all I can," Chess said with a wicked smile. "Alright?"

The girl shot Max a quick glance, then looked away blushing.

Several seagulls cried overhead, their calls fighting for a prominence over the clattering of the wheels and the clip-clop of the horses hooves as they turned into the cobblestone entrance of Greenlawns Manor.

The inhabitants of the country fly alighted before an imposing and distinctive building, separated from the road by a large, flat lawn from which the house had obviously derived its name. It was built in a com-manding position and, looking across the garden, Chess could see a large part of the bay and even the distant shores of the fishing village of Brixham beyond.

"I'll take Wilbur B. to his quarters and give ee zummat to eat, shall I?" Mary said. "Maister thought he'd be best com-fer-ble over in th' stables alonga me. I've done aside a special place."

"Yes," said Chess. "You carry on."

Mary smiled and took up the dog's lead. Chess and Max watched, squinting, as the pair walked along the patio in front of the gleaming white walls of the sun-drenched house. As they went out of sight around the corner, Chess turned to Max.

"Well," he said. "What do you think?"

"About the girl or the house?" the fat man replied.

"Both."

"I think you should leave the girl alone and concentrate on the case. We're professionals now. You can't go gallivanting with members of client's households."

"You really are a prude sometimes, Max. Anyway, what do you think of the house?"

Max turned again to the building and squinted at it. It had eight windows facing the sea, the ground floor ones opening out onto a patio that ran the length of the property. These were protected overhead by a canopy that curved out from the masonry to create what looked like an effective suntrap, the pillars of which were draped with well-established creeping wisteria that was already blooming in pale purple. "Lovely," Max said at length, gazing at the first floor windows, each of which had been provided with pale green slatted shutters. "A real haven of peace," he added lazily, as he followed the progress of a pair of rooks that circled in the blue heavens before coming to rest gently on the grey slate roof.

"Perhaps," Chess said. "Or maybe a maelstrom of murder!"

*   *   *

The late May night was warm and clear, and it had just turned ten when Chess strode into the darkened stables.

"Wilb," he called. "Here boy." Almost immediately there came the pattering of feet, and a cold, wet nose nuzzled his hand. He bent down and patted the delighted dog. Then, hearing the scrunch of straw behind him, turned round and straightened up to see the silhouette of the stable girl that he had met earlier.

"Thank ee for comin', Mr Chesterfield," she said, lighting a lantern that cast large, flickering shadows over the straw-covered floor. "Do ee 'ave anythin' for me?"

"Plenty," Chess said coyly.

Mary put a hand up to her face to stifle an excited giggle. Chess walked the couple of paces forward and gently pulled it away, taking her mouth and kissing her. She slid her hands around his waist, then slipped them under his lounge jacket.

"Con amore!" exclaimed Chess, responding by pulling the girl down onto the fresh straw. She groaned with pleasure as Chess pushed his warm hand inside her tight riding breeches. Wilbur B. nosed the writhing pair, and then made off uninterestedly into the shadows to lay down.

"You must tell me," Chess said caressing the contours of the girl's fine body, "how did the family get on with Judy?"

"Mmm, Mr Chesterfield, I..."

57

"Tell me or I'll stop," Chess teased.

"I-I don't think Mrs Mallock liked her. I think she be wantin' to sack her."

Chess kissed the girl again, and this time she parted her lips enticingly. After perhaps a minute he pulled away, his heart pounding and a longing ache starting to become established in his loins. "Why'd you say that about Mrs Mallock?" he said, pecking at the soft, creamy flesh of Mary's neck and lazily exploring with his hands.

"Twice," Mary hissed softly, a shudder of pleasure running through her. "I heard Mrs and Mrs Mallock having words about her. But darn, do we have to talk about -"

"Yes," Chess interrupted, whispering softly in her ear, and moving his hands across to Mary's generous chest and one-by-one undoing the buttons on her cotton blouse. "Go on," he continued. "What else do you know?"

"Noan. I be getting tired of this job. Thinkin' of setting up stables mezel'."

The blouse fell open and Chess pulled away the underclothes to reveal the beautiful orbs. He bent down and his mouth tugged gently at one of the pert nipples, his thick moustache tickling the flesh as he did so. Mary threw her head back and closed her eyes.

"How can you afford it?" Chess said suddenly, drawing back and rubbing his index finger gently across the damp, sensitized peak.

"Relative gone an' daid," Mary panted, "left me mort lot of money." Her breath began coming in short gasps. Suddenly she could hold back no more and grabbed Chess with both hands, pulling his strong, hard body down on top of her...

*   *   *

It was almost eleven-thirty when Chess eventually left the stables and the sweet warmth of Mary Fish. "By the way," he enquired as he walked out onto the darkened courtyard. "Do you know where Judy Kenwyn's mother lives?"

"Course I do," came the reply. "I'll write her address for you if you be that keen."

"Thanks," Chess said. "It could be useful, Never know, eh?"

Mary shrugged. "You be the detective, I suppose," she said, hunting in her breeches. She found a scrap of torn paper after a while and

Chess handed her a pencil, watching as she scribbled the address down for him. "It's over at Hollacombe," she said. "It be right on the cliffs looking over th' bay. You can't miss it, it's got blue shutters."

"Thank you, my girl," said Chess, his moustache twitching and his handsome face breaking into a mischievous boyish smile. "You've been most – um – useful!"

Mary giggled. "I haven't learned much about the case yet," she said, "but that azide, I baint scared no more with you here."

★   ★   ★

Next day was Thursday, and Chess and Max sat down to breakfast in the grand Greenlawns Manor dining room with their hosts George and Anne Mallock. The usual pleasantries revolving around the weather, which was something of a heatwave for the time of year, were exchanged before the talk turned to the death of Judy Kenwyn.

"I do believe that George be entirely wastin' your time," said Mrs Mallock. "The police bin an' given their verdict. They said accidental death - suicide in other words. Surely that be enough?"

Mr Mallock glared at his wife. "Don't be so crabbid, woman, I'll be judge of this damn affair," he retorted. The air seemed suddenly charged with a tension that built up steadily in the silence that followed. Chess finished eating a rasher of bacon, then lay down his cutlery and spoke...

"I'll come straight to the point. Did you get on well with Judy, Mrs Mallock?"

The husband and wife exchanged glances.

The tension increased further.

Silence.

"Course she did," George Mallock exploded, the phrase rushing from his lips like escaping steam. Chess narrowed his blue eyes and his moustache twitched.

"Are-Are you sure?" he ventured gently.

Suddenly Mr Mallock exploded. "I didn't bring you here so that you could be callin' my wife a liar over brexis," he blazed, waving his knife menacingly in Chess's direction.

Max, who had been sitting next to his friend throughout the intercourse, groaned inwardly. "We do apologise," he said hastily in a bid to ease the situation. He wiped his brow. "Whew, it's another hot one today, isn't it?" he remarked, nodding at the sun streaming in through the window as he tried desperately to change the subject. As his piggy-eyes glanced around the room, he caught sight of a large earthenware barrel on a wooden stand in the corner. He smiled. "I've heard that most folk round these parts make their own cider," he said enthusiastically. "Is that what that is?"

Anne Mallock returned his smile. "You be right," she said in a pleasant voice. "But 'tis only a small wee drop. If you and Mr Chesterfield would like to come on down under stairs, I'll show ee where I makes it."

Ten minutes later, after Chess had fetched Wilbur B. from the stables ready for his morning walk, the trio, accompanied by an enthusiastic Anne Mallock, ventured down the steep, stone steps into the dark, musty-smelling cellar, an oil lantern lighting the way.

"Good heavens!" Exclaimed Chess surveying the rows and rows of bottles and jars that circumnavigated the room on three levels of wooden shelving. "There must be literally hundreds of gallons of cider here. You must be completely blotto for most of the time."

Anne laughed, a high-pitched sound that echoed around the chamber. "Not all the time," she said, "and in Deb'n, we don't call it cider. Down here it be called scrumpy."

"How apt," said Max, "and abbreviation of scrumptious perhaps?" He cast his eyes around the bottles, noticing that every single one was exactly the same, having three moulded-glass rings just below the neck. "Are these unique?" he asked.

"That they be," came the reply. "We have 'em made special for the Greenlawns brew. George likes tidiness and order, even down here."

Suddenly Wilbur B. let out a couple of strange barks, and the trio looked down to see him rolling on his back waving his short, stubby legs in the air. As they watched he clambered back to his feet and pawed the ground with his back legs like a bull preparing to charge, before giving out two more excited barks and rushing forwards to clamp his jaws firmly around a bottle that had rolled out across the stone floor and come unstoppered.

The onlookers roared with laughter. "Old Wilb. seems to like your scrumpy," Chess remarked. "How about us trying some?"

"Sorry," said Anne. "Here, you best be 'avin' a bottle each, avore you be daid of thirst."

The detective pair sampled the brew and were soon in agreement over its considerable strength and pleasant, unique taste.

* * *

Still feeling somewhat inebriated, Chess, Max and Wilbur B. boarded a country fly that rattled off down St Michael's Road towards the Torre Abbey sands. Chess felt that he should examine the spot where Judy Kenwyn's body had been washed up...

"Nothing," Max said, walking along the smooth, wet sand. "I reckon the sea would have washed any clues away by now anyway. The tide comes up almost to the road by the look of the seaweed line."

Chess nodded in agreement and gazed along the shoreline before turning and surveying the land behind.

"A penny for your thoughts, Mr Chess," said Max.

"I don't think that Judy had her date with destiny here," came the thoughtful reply. "Mr Mallock said she was found with head injuries, probably caused by rocks. There's none along this stretch of beach, but look!" He pointed to the headland just visible through the morning mist on the right of the seascape. "Round there the coast is much more jagged. Let's hunt there."

The coastline that Henry Chesterfield spoke of turned out to be that which had become known as Hollacombe Beach. It was approached through several acres of well-manicured gardens, and as the intrepid trio walked through them they were met by a dense fog that hung in the morning air and drifted in silent, wispy wreaths in off the glassy sea. Cormorants were their only companions as they made their way across the gardens and down through a cold, dark and dripping tunnel that led under the railway line onto a beach with fine red sand.

Chess surveyed the bay. The distant Torquay coastline to the left was partially obscured by the fog making it appear to be hovering, a tiny, ghostly island, in the grey air. The tide was out and shiny, seaweed-covered rocks jutted up here and there along the shoreline, half-hidden by the clinging atmosphere. Behind rose tall ochre-coloured cliffs, at the foot of which, hundreds of sea-worn rocks lay, smooth and hard like monoliths to some unknown God.

"What a flippin' eerie place," Max remarked in an undertone, feeling somehow afraid to raise his voice to its normal level. "The perfect spot for a suicide."

"Or a murder," Chess added, his face hard and serious.

The isolation that the pair felt was only relieved by an old man and woman, she carrying a stick and wearing a tartan wrap, he in shorts and shirt, carrying two large butterfly-type nets in one hand and a black bucket in the other. Chess and Max watched the distant figures as they worked their way silently and purposefully through the rockpools.

"Biologists or shrimp catchers?" said Chess, nodding in their direction.

Max peered through the murk. "I'd favour the latter," he said without much hesitation. "Shall we take a gander round there ourselves?"

"Lead the way," said Chess, letting Wilbur B. off of his lead. The dog gambolled happily down the gentle slope of the beach while the two men followed some distance behind.

Suddenly Max gave a start. The absolute tranquillity was broken by the sound of a steam whistle, and the pair turned around to see a locomotive, drawing two carriages, puff past along the very edge of the cliff above the beach before being lost again in the fog bank, the smoke from its chimney serving to add to the thickness of the atmosphere.

Silence reigned again and Chess felt a warm, slobbery sensation on his hand and looked down to see Wilbur B., his tail wagging enthusiastically, a bottle clamped in his drooping jaws.

"Blimey!" exclaimed Max. "Look. It's got three rings on it, and its full too. It's one of the Greenlawns bottles. Where'd he find it?"

Chess peered down at the wet sand. The dog's tracks were clearly visible on it and the pair lost no time in following them for twenty yards or so to a rockpool near the water's edge. Max sifted carefully through the clear waters but there was nothing else to be found. Chess, who had extracted the bottle from his pet's jaws, scrutinised it carefully. The three distinctive rings were clearly visible and it was indeed still completely full of what Anne Mallock had called scrumpy.

"Well, Mr Chess. D'you make anything of it?" Max enquired, straightening himself up and wiping his wet hands with a handkerchief that he withdrew from his pocket.

For a moment Chess said nothing, then all of a sudden his delicate blue eyes gleamed with excitement. "A vital clue!" he cried. "I remember now. George Mallock told me that Judy took two bottles of home-made scrumpy with her on the fatal day that she visited her mother. I'll wager that this is one of them."

The fog was gradually lifting as the morning became established, and Max cast his eyes along the clifftops at the far end of the bay that were, for the first time, becoming visible. "That's Judy's mother's place," he said, stabbing one of his fat sausage-like fingers towards a small single-storey building that was perched precariously on the cliff-edge and that offered a commanding view of the bay. Chess nodded, noticing the distinctive blue shutters that his stable-girl lover had mentioned.

"Apparently the old dear's going a bit doo-lally," he said. "You don't think that she could have played any part in this whole affair do you, Max?" Chess said. "After all, if someone fell from that balcony they'd stand absolutely no chance on the rocks down here."

Max nodded his rotund head in agreement. "And with these tides, a body could easily be washed up round at Torre Abbey sands," he said, re-enforcing Chess's thoughts. "Maybe you've got something there, Mr Chess," he went on. "But surely it's a bit of a long shot isn't it? A mother murdering her own daughter."

"Long shots can sometimes be the best to go for," came the reply. "I think we'd better pay old Mrs Kenwyn a visit doppio movimento, if to do nothing more than eliminate her from our enquiries."

"Doppio what?"

"Sorry, I mean at the double basically."

"How about now then?" Max said. "There's nothing much else for us here, we'd—"

Something caught his attention at the edge of his vision and he broke off in mid-sentence, turning to see the old shrimp-collecting couple waving frantically in his direction. "Over here," the man shouted. "Please, it's a body!"

Chess and Max exchanged incredulous glances and then hurried off towards the far end of the beach in the direction of the distant figures, with Wilbur B. romping along at their side considering the whole activity as quite jolly fun.

The body in question was lolling in the gentle surf, obscured from the rest of the beach by an outcrop of rock that had thrust itself up out of the sand. "Dead God!" Chess gasped, bending down to examine the mortal remains, his moustache twitching nineteen-to-the-dozen.

The old woman began wailing like a siren and her husband tried unsuccessfully to console her, his own composure visibly shaken by the ghastly find. Chess took no notice of either of them, instead proceeding to rifle the fellow's pockets looking for some form of identification. There was none, but what he did locate made the whole grisly episode even more obscure. Each and every pocket in the man's trousers and jacket were crammed to overflowing with soggy banknotes. "There's thousands here," Chess gasped, shaking his head in amazement. "Literally thousands."

"Any marks on the body that you can see?" said Max staring open-mouthed at Chess's incredible discovery. His partner shook his head again.

"Nothing," he said. "He's drowned, that's for sure."

"Maybe he was a man overboard from one of those American steamers. They carry a lot of rich people."

"No," came the staccato reply. "Passengers on those don't dress in ragged old clothes like this."

"Suicide?"

"Could be," replied Chess. "We can certainly rule out money problems as the motive, that's for sure."

Max agreed and, for the first time, dared to peer closely at the fellow. As he did so, a smile of recognition lit his fat, frowning features. "The labourer!" he exclaimed. "The one we saw fighting with his superior at Torre Station. Remember?"

Chess transferred his full attention back to the body once again and recalled the tall, thin man with the distinctive black beard. "By heaven, I reckon you're right Max," he said. "It IS him."

"I wonder if it's got anything to do with the other affair," Max said.

Chess shrugged. "God knows," he said haphazardly. "I don't."

*　　*　　*

After calling at Torquay police station to report the finding of the body, Chess and Max boarded a train with Wilbur B., bound for Torre, a mile or so up the track, taking the trip that Judy Kenwyn had made, albeit in reverse, on the day of her disappearance in an effort to shed further light upon what could have befallen her.

"Well Mr Chess," said Max after they had settled down in the compartment. "Any ideas?"

"Maybe I have," came the thoughtful reply. "They might not come to much though, and I'd rather not speculate and create a fuss just yet, at least not until I'm quite sure of my facts."

Max raised his eyebrows. "Well, I can't see anything amiss at all," he said patting Wilbur B., who sat panting by his side. "What have you got up your sleeve, Mr Chess. Come on spill the beans, we are in this together."

Chess was serious. "It's only a theory, and I'm keeping it to myself for a while. But there are other things too."

"What?"

"Well for a start, we should consider what could have happened to Judy on this very train on the fateful day."

"Not much, that's for sure," said Max. "There must have been people everywhere. Not only are the tail-end days of the week busy on most railways, but added to that, there was the gauge change gangs. I'll tell you for nothing, Mr Chess, these carriages wouldn't have been deserted like they are now."

Chess glanced around the railway compartment. There was only one other inhabitant of the carriage; an old lady travelling at the far end with a wicker basket full of flowers, and wearing a quaint straw hat. "Point taken," he said, turning his attention back to his companion. "So let's think," he said in a low voice. "When was she most alone on her journey from Greenlawns Manor to her mother's at Hollacombe?"

"Easy," came the reply. "When she was in Mrs Mallock's horse-drawn carriage. You told me that she'd given Judy a lift that day when you outlined the case."

"And?" Chess prompted, "so? Presto, presto."

"Well," Max went on, "maybe Judy never did catch that train. We're only going on Anne Mallock's say-so that she did. I wondered about it when it became clear during that breakfast that she was unhappy about us poking our noses into the affair, so to speak. It's as if she's got something to hide. She could even have killed Judy herself for all we know."

"How?" said Chess, shielding his eyes from the hot midday sun that was blazing through the carriage window.

"Dunno," said Max with a shrug. He wiped his sweating brow with the back of his hand. "Phew!" he exclaimed, "it's getting damn warm in here. Maybe I'll think better after a drop of this stuff." With that he withdrew from his pocket the bottle of unopened scrumpy that Wilbur B. had located on Hollacombe beach earlier. He unstoppered it and took a brief swig.

Immediately he wished he hadn't.

"Uurrgh!" he gurgled, leaping to his feet and wrenching open the pull-down window. Chess watched in amazement as he spat the liquid out, shuddered and screwed up his taught face.

"What's up?" Chess enquired. "I thought you were thirsty. Not too strong for you is it?"

"Very funny, I don't think," came the reply. "Blimey, Anne Mallock must have been having an off-day when she made that. It tastes absolutely bloody foul. Here, you try."

Chess shook his head and waved the bottle aside. "No thanks," he said. "I'll take your word for it."

*　*　*

The next day was Friday, and once again Torquay was blessed with clear blue skies. The weather made Henry Chesterfield, for the first time in his life, have some faith in the predictions contained within the current copy of his Almanac. The book had correctly promised a heatwave in the last two weeks of May. He threw back the curtains in his Greenlawns bedroom, yawned, then washed and dressed with the sunshine pitching warm on his strong, muscular body, the extremities of which had already darkened to something approaching the colour of teak.

Ten minutes later he was knocking at the door of Max's room. A weak and feeble voice drifted through the woodwork. "Come in," it said.

"Good heavens old fellow, you look dreadful!" exclaimed Chess as he entered the room and closed the door behind him. "What the deuce is up with you?"

Max heaved his corpulent body, with even more difficulty than usual, into a sitting position in the bed. He looked pale and drawn and his piggy eyes were red-rimmed and exhibited large bags beneath them. "That scrumpy," he said half-heartedly. "Has to be. I've been as sick as a dog all night. Couldn't sleep at all and my belly feels like it's been kicked by a flippin' horse or something. It's poisoned, that stuff I drank. Has to be."

Chess looked grave. "It's lucky you only took a small sip," he said, a look of genuine affection coming into his blue eyes which dimmed slightly, "otherwise-"

"Wait 'til I tell that bloody Anne Mallock, I'll soon-"

Chess held up his hand for silence. "Please Max," he appealed, "I beg of you to keep quiet about all this, if it was poison, then it's the first piece of hard evidence we've had, and anyway, we've got no proof that she was responsible for the contamination."

"She makes the infernal mixture," said Max, still simmering close to the boil. "How many bottles did Judy Kenwyn take to her mother's? Do you know?"

"Yes," said Chess calmly, "she took two."

Max punched the air with a clenched fist. "Well that's the whole affair solved then," he said excitedly, suddenly forgetting all about the

66

way he felt. "Last Friday, the day she disappeared, it was a scorcher over the whole of this half of the country, I'll wager poor Judy downed one of the bottles of the poisoned stuff on the way. She's bound to have been thirsty."

"Good point, Max. You really could have something there," Chess said thoughtfully.

"I've had all bloody night to think about, haven't I?"

Chess smiled. "I suppose you have," he said. "Perhaps in the - circumstances your lucky escape was lucky for us too. I've always thought that Anne Mallock must be hiding something, and after all, it's only her word that she did actually convey Judy to the station. There's nothing to say that she didn't encourage her to drink one of the bottles of deliberately poisoned scrumpy on the way to the station then divert, perhaps to Corbyn Head, or even Hollacombe, and in some desolate spot, dump her body, together with the remaining bottle, over the cliffs."

"Brilliant," said Max. "Or 'brillante' as you always say. But there's just one thing puzzling me. All night I've been trying to come up with a motive. A reason why she'd do something like that. I can't think of one blessed reason on that score."

"No matter, Max," Chess replied excitedly, "I haven't, it's jealousy, that's what it is. Anne Mallock was jealous. My little stable-girl told me that she'd overheard the Mallocks having words about Judy. By all accounts, Anne wanted to sack her but George was dead against it. I reckon he was having some sort of affair with Judy."

"And Anne found out?"

"Precisely," said Chess looking grave, "but hang on, we can't rule out the possibility that she did get on that train just yet. I vote we take a walk down to Torre Station and sniff around again to double-check for any other clues before we make any unfounded accusations. What say you, Max? Are you up to it?"

"I reckon I am, Mr Chess. Just give me fifteen minutes and I'll be right with you."

*   *   *

"I be damn glad it be all over and done, that's all!" exclaimed a well-dressed man to the stationmaster at Torre, as Chess and Max arrived. "Why Brunel had to plump for a different gauge railway in the first place beats me, and to cap it all, d'you know what's gone an' 'appened?"

The stationmaster shook his head and stood aside to let the pair onto the platform. "No idea," he said haphazardly.

"One of them navvies," the other man went on. "Washed up on Hollacombe beach 'ee be. No one be too sorry to see him daid though," he added. "Always moaning like billy-o 'bout pay rates, and a damn unreliable beggar to boot. D'you know, ee'd come in late and expect me not t' dock 'is pay. Twas only yezzerday mornin' we 'ad set to 'bout it."

Chess and Max made no comment and continued along the platform until they were safely out of earshot of the two men. Max was the first to speak; "Doesn't look like our latest suicide victim was a very popular fellow, that's if it turns out it was suicide, I s'pose he could just as easily have been drowned by someone."

"For what?" Chess countered.

"Money?"

Chess tutted. "Largo, Max. Largo. You are a bit slow sometimes. You're forgetting. The chap's pockets were crammed full of the stuff. No, suicide's favourite on that one, but let's not get sidetracked, it's nothing to do with us, and besides, we've got more than enough on our plates trying to make some sense of this Kenwyn affair."

"Quite right," said Max. "So what's the plan here, Mr Chess?" His gaze traversing the busy station as he spoke.

Chess pointed to the opposite platform. "I'd have liked to snoop around behind those buildings over there on the far side," he said quietly. "They back directly onto those steep woodlands. If I was planning to murder someone here then I reckon I'd do it in the vicinity of those."

"Let's take a gander then," said Max eagerly, making towards the footbridge. Chess grabbed at his sleeve and pulled him back.

"Not now Max," he said in a whisper. "Too many people around. I don't want us to be noticed, let's leave it, there are bound to be plenty of other opportunities."

Max shrugged. "You're the boss," he said with a smile, "so what now?"

"Old Mrs Kenwyn at Hollacombe," came the reply. "I can't personally imagine her being much help but we really ought to have a word with the silly old stick. Besides, it won't do for us to be mooching around Greenlawns too much looking idle. Mallock's going to be stumping up good money for our services, we ought to at least be seen to be doing something."

*　　*　　*

Mrs Kenwyn's cliff-top residence lost a good deal of its appeal when viewed up close. From the beach the distant whitewashed walls seemed to fairly sparkle in the sun, and combined with the pleasant blue shutters and matching paintwork, the building had something of a Mediterranean appearance. However, now, as Chess and Max alighted from the country fly, it looked an altogether different place. The paintwork was peeling and the whitewash wasn't really white at all. A seagull squalking on the roof caught Max's attention and he looked up to see that a dozen or so slates were missing. "Fancy letting a place like this go so much," he remarked. "What sort of woman can Mrs Kenwyn be?"

"A damn crazy one by all accounts," Chess replied in an undertone. "Mary Fish told me that apparently she hasn't been told of her daughter's death for fear of it tipping her completely over the edge, so to speak. As I've already said, she could have even been responsible for the dreadful deed herself."

"I've been thinking about that," Max replied. "An old woman like her?" He laughed. "Really it's quite improbable to say the least. How would she do such a thing anyway?"

Chess considered for a little time, then his eyes narrowed. "She could have pushed her off that balcony round the other side of the house," he said at length, "just like we suggested before." With that he strode purposefully through the overgrown garden with Max close behind. He rung the bell and after a delay of what must have been at least a minute, it opened with a creak and a wizened, white-haired old woman peeped round the peeling framework. Her leathery face screwed up into something resembling an animal-like snarl and a pair of singularly bright watery-grey eyes glared at the men on the doorstep.

"What?" she snapped.

"Uh, Mrs Kenwyn?" Chess enquired in a pleasant tone. The woman jerked her ancient head violently to the affirmative.

"We... We wondered if we could have a few words with you about your daughter. We're from Greenlawns Manor where she worked – I mean works."

This time the reply was softer and more pleasant. "Do she be in trouble, the blimmer? Headstrong and hopeless she be. You come 'ee inside an' tell old ma Kenwyn 'bout it."

The rooms that the trio passed through were all decorated in the early Victorian style, with furnishings that were faded and tatty. Added to that there was a considerable propensity of wildlife around. Cobwebs festooned most corners and large spiders scuttled here and there. A hen created a frightful fuss when Max almost trod on the brooding bird by accident, then, once in the lounge, Chess had to protect himself from an over-fed cormorant that, having made several circumnavigations of the room, perched on the back of a filthy red-velvet armchair and pecked at his neck before excreting and then flying off through the large French windows that opened onto the balcony overlooking the bay.

Mrs Kenwyn made no attempt to clear the mess up and as Chess looked, he saw more of the same and came to the conclusion that the whole place was full of filth. "How do ee like my li'll darlin' pets?" Mrs Kenwyn said, her face losing its scowl.

"Well, we – uh – yes, very nice," Chess said, completely at a loss for words. "They're very – sort of – different,"

"They be all I do 'ave now. I can't get out of th' house far. Too many o' they hills. Look 'ee at me tiny boats in th' bath."

Max, who was behind the woman, made a gesture to indicate that he was convinced that she was mad.

Chess, who was facing her, tried to ignore his friend but his face nevertheless cracked in to a half-smile. "I can't see a bath or any boats," he said.

Suddenly and unexpectedly, the woman screamed in anger and grabbed Chess, spinning him round to face the French windows and propelling him forwards with a hard shove. "Prapper idyit you be. There, use them eyes. That's what they be for."

Chess was utterly taken aback, both at the outburst and at the strength that the old woman evidently possessed. He looked dumbly out across the sparkling waters of the bay, studded with all manner of small craft and understood. "Of course, of course," he said. "How very silly of me. I do apologise. Look Max. Boats in the bath!"

Without a word, Max joined his friend at the opened French windows and looked out. "Did Judy visit you last Friday?" Chess enquired nonchalantly.

"She comes and goes," came the woman's vague reply. "What days

I don't know. I don't have clocks nor none of them newspapers. Judy comes now and again. But she be a bad'un."

"How do you mean?" Chess said gently.

A far away look came into the old woman's grey eyes and for a fleeting moment the harsh protective exterior layer of her personality melted away. "We argue," she said in a quiet voice. "She alluz be wantin' to put me in nursing awm." As she continued again, her voice began to rise, both in pitch and volume. "We beller at each other vit t'burst. I want none of it. I won't be goin'. Lived in this place for fifty years a' more. Begger'd if I be movin' now."

Mrs Kenwyn's eyes were blazing and the singular animal snarl had returned to her wrinkled face. She turned to a chest of drawers and hurled the top one open. "I soon makes her hush 'er mouth!" She was shouting now in a crackly high pitched tone. "I shuts her up with this."

Both Chess and Max simultaneously felt the icy stab of fear in their stomachs as the old woman snatched a gun from the drawer and began waving it around in their direction.

"I-Is it loaded?" Max ventured.

"You're gabey, an' stupid too," came the vicious reply. "Course it be loaded. It alluz be. I be livin' 'ere in this housen on me own. I needs per-teck-shun for me pets." Mrs Kenwyn advanced on the two men, forcing them back across the room and out onto the balcony.

"Jesus Christ," Chess hissed under his breath, as he looked in horror at the rocks, a hundred feet or so below.

"I-It's at times like this that I wish I was still a ticket inspector," gasped Max. "For heaven's sake do something, Mr Chess before it's too late."

"Is Judy, your daughter, alright?" Chess blurted. "She didn't go over here did she?" He swallowed hard. "Over this balcony, I mean, you didn't –" He broke off as the woman came forward again, gun in hand.

It seemed hopeless and Max found himself looking for a spot on the beach below that was free of rocks; somewhere where his fat body would stand the most chance of survival.

Mrs Kenwyn spat out her obscure reply; "Judy, she be able t'swim. I taught her." She cackled loudly and cocked the revolver.

Max closed his eyes.

There was a loud retort as the gun blazed its fire. He waited for the searing pain.

It never came and he opened his eyes that immediately stung with the rivulets of salty, cold sweat that ran into them from his fat face.

Old Mrs Kenwyn was scrabbling around on the floor at his feet.

"She's fallen over that bit of torn carpet," Chess cried joyously. "Come on Max. Run for it before she gets up."

Max didn't need a second telling and threw his corpulent body forwards, tearing through the house as fast as his legs would carry him, reaching the garden, gasping and wheezing, a good few yards ahead of Chess, just as another shot rang out.

*　　*　　*

It took the rest of the day for the pair to get over their narrow escape, and come the evening, they were sitting in Henry Chesterfield's bedroom at Greenlawns Manor in something of a quandary.

"What the devil are we going to do, Mr Chess? Do we tell George Mallock how Judy was killed and risk letting him take the law into his own hands? Or do we go to the police and let them handle it?"

Chess ran a hand over his troubled face and then placed a thoughtful finger to his lips. When he eventually spoke it was in a tired, drawn voice.

"It's not that clear cut is it?" he said. "We still can't really be certain that the crazy old bat did do in her daughter. There's conflicting evidence. Take the poisoned cider and Mrs Mallock for a start."

"Well, I vote we get ourselves out of the confines of this room and think," said Max peering out of the window at the fine Greenlawns gardens that stretched for several acres around the house. They looked inviting in the gathering dusk of a fine evening. Although the sun was beginning to fade in the west, firing the distant Torbay shoreline with gold, there was still plenty of light.

"Alright," Chess agreed. "Let's get some fresh air."

As the pair wandered down the steps that led to the lawn, they chanced upon a member of Mallock's staff. "Good evening," Chess said with a smile. "You must be the gardener."

"That be right, sir," came the reply. "John Carter."

He was a big-boned, lumbering man with a weatherbeaten face that was both animated and friendly, if rather grubby. "Just packing up for the night," he added. "Them flower borders be regler 'ard work this part of season. Weeds alluz comin' up ev'ry five minutes."

"Indeed?" Chess said. "Tell me, John, in confidence. Have you any of your own thoughts on the Judy Kenwyn affair?"

Carter thrust his soil-stained large hands into the pockets of his green overalls, then blew his cheeks out and considered. "Don't rightly know what to think," he said after perhaps half a minute's silence. "I'm not one of them detective's like you be."

"Quite, but even so, you may be able to shed some light on the case," said Chess enthusiastically. "Do you know anything about the affair that Mr Mallock was supposed to be having with the dead girl?"

The gardener shook his head vigorously so that his wispy grey hair fell across his eyes. He brushed it back patiently over his balding forehead. "You be barkin' up the wrong tree there sir," he said. "I bain't heard nothin' 'bout maister carryin' on with pawl li'll Judy, God rest her soul. 'Tis Mary, the 'osses girl that he be 'avin' courtin' wiv. She be real sassy baggage."

"How do you know all this?" Max enquired, trying to conceal the surprise that he felt from his voice. "Surely it's not something that's common knowledge?"

"That it bain't sir, but remember I be up and about at odd times 'specially this time of year. I bin workin 'late into night in yonder greenhouse, plantin' out and so forth. Maister Mallock gave me oil lamp to work by, he be wantin' garden alluz lukin' neat and tidy. He be like that, everything 'ave t'be in its place."

Chess nodded. "Yes," he said, "I've heard that. Go on."

"Well, I puts me tools away in a little cubby-hole near the stables, and many a time I've heard things in there."

"What things?" Chess asked, pushing for more information.

"Noises. Y'know. Groanin' 'n' suchlike." The gardener blushed. "Y'know," he repeated sheepishly. "Maister was, y'know...with Mary."

Max nodded. "Have you heard anything lately?" he enquired.

The gardener frowned. "Funny thing that," he said. "After Judy's death, it all gone away, but this last week, just after you cummed, shore 'nuff, I heard some goin's on again one night."

This time it was Henry Chesterfield's turn to blush. However, John Carter continued, blissfully unaware of the detective's embarrassment. "There even be a rumour that the maister be overheard sayin' t' Mary that he was going t' divorce 'is wife fer 'er. But I couldn't be attachin' much t' that caper. It cummed vrum a strapper, y'know, a subcontract painter who was here whitewashin' walls a while back. Couldn't be believin' a word 'ee be sayin' usually."

"Well thank you Mr Carter, you've been most helpful," said Chess.

"'Appy to oblige," came the reply. "I liked the lass, Judy. Have a nice stroll."

"What do you think of that?" Max said excitedly when the gardener was out of earshot.

Chess groaned. "More problems," he said. "It's all getting so damn complicated. This affair is shifting around like sand in the wind. I really don't know what to do next."

"I do," came Max's reply. "You said you wanted another look at Torre Station when it was less busy. Now'll be by far the best time."

Chess brightened at this. "Good idea, Max," he said. "Let's beetle on down there then. I'll nip over to the greenhouse and borrow that oil lamp that Carter mentioned, it'll soon be dark and we want to make sure we don't miss any clues. I'll have it back here within an hour or so. Nobody'll know it was even moved."

★　★　★

Torre Station was indeed deserted, just as Max had supposed, and the only moving object that the pair were greeted with when they stepped out onto the shadowy platform was a thin, wispy fog that had drifted up the curve of track from the lower reaches of Torquay, and now hung over the silent station buildings, shimmering in the pale moonlight like some Arctic ice field. The flickering golden splotches of weak illumination from the gaslamps along the tiny terminus did little to penetrate the gathering murk, and Chess found himself glad of the oil lamp that he had brought with him. "Perfect," he exclaimed. "Not a soul in sight."

Max grunted in agreement, then, instinctively lowering his voice. "Where do we begin?" he enquired.

"In the place I wanted to look before," came Chess's reply. "Behind those buildings on the far platform. Come on Max, before someone turns up." With that he made his way towards the footbridge. Max followed, a feeling of excitement gripping at his insides once more as he did so.

Once on the other side of the terminus, Chess hurried round the rear of the buildings to the spot where the wooded slopes bordered the station premises. For a couple of minutes he scrabbled around enthusiastically, the oil lamp illuminating his features and casting huge, menacing shadows on the fog shroud behind.

"Damn and blast!" he exclaimed at last. "Nothing."

Max shrugged. "Hardly surprising really," he said. "It's been almost a week since Judy disappeared, and what with the gauge change, there's been hundreds of pairs of feet trampling all over this station, they'd surely have–"

"Feet!" Chess cried. "Max, that's it, footprints."

"What are you on about?"

"Here! Look! Leading along the back here!"

Max peered along the beam of the lamp that Chess was carefully directing. "Hardly footprints," he said. "Just places where the long grass has been flattened." He was about to dismiss Chess's discovery, when he noticed the fence. "Blimey, there's a hole there," he remarked, pointing to an area where the chain link had been cut away.

"This could be something," Chess said, his heart pumping hard with excitement. "This could be what we've been looking for. Come on, let's investigate." The two men squeezed through the fence and Chess shone the lamp up the steep, grassy slope that led to the woods beyond. A trail of flattened grass was still clearly visible. "Someone's been along here that's for sure," Chess said. "The flattened grass leads to that clump of trees." Chess hurried on ahead, while Max, his massive bulk labouring with the effort of the incline, struggled on as best he could, wheezing and puffing like a steam engine half a dozen yards behind. "Anything of note?" he managed to call out between breaths.

"Not sure," came Chess's reply. "Looks like there's a bit of greasy old pipe here. I can't see anything else though."

Max arrived gasping for air. Chess smiled. "A perfect greyhound," he said sarcastically.

The fat man ignored the comment and peered at a foot-long length of broken iron pipe. A smile of recognition swept across his sweating face. "Fifteen inch diameter, I'll bet," he said.

Chess frowned. "So what?" he said.

Max tutted impatiently. "You know what this is, don't you?"

His companion shook his head.

"Oh, flippin' 'eck Mr Chess, you do have a blinkin' short memory. I told you about Brunel's atmospheric railway on the trip down here from London the other day. Remember the pipe that was set between the rails? Well, this is a chunk of it."

"Really?" said Chess in a bored voice as Max picked up the artefact. "I should mind your hands," he added. "It seems jolly greasy." He turned the lamp towards his friend and let it play on his hands. What he saw made him give a terrible start and for a moment words wouldn't come. When he did finally manage to speak, the words came tumbling out in a gushing torrent; "Max-it's-blood," he blurted. "Covered in blood. The pipe. And on your hands. The murder weapon. We've found it."

Max looked down. "Ugh!" he exclaimed, dropping the pipe as if it had suddenly become red hot, and looking at the stains on his hands. Chess shone the lamp on the floor and the pair stared down at the chunk of heavy pipe. It was then that Chess noticed a piece of paper poking out of one of the jagged ends. He stooped and gingerly picked it up. It was a half-sheet, torn down one edge, and upon it was written a short, simple sentence.

"10am tomorrow," Chess read out loud before folding the note and slipping it into his coat pocket.

"Any significance?" Max enquired.

Chess replied with a wry smile. "I want time to gather my thoughts, Max," he said. "I'm afraid you'll have to wait until my little theatrical tomorrow at Greenlawns for the answer to that one. However, suffice to say that my nets have closed in at last."

* * *

Henry Chesterfield eyed the sea of expectant faces before him as he stood, with Max at his side, in front of the large marble fireplace in the Greenlawns drawing room. "First off, I'd like to thank you all for assembling here at such short notice," he said, "I can now reveal that Judy Kenwyn was murdered." His moustache twitched rather nervously as he scrutinised each face in turn for a reaction to his statement. Mrs and Mrs Mallock were seated on the large settee, both stony-faced and silent, while Mary Fish, the stable girl and John Carter, the gardener, stood behind exchanging glances.

Max swallowed hard and prayed that his friend was not about to make an absolute buffoon of himself. For a few moments the room was silent, then Chess spoke again, his voice strong and proprietorial. "Old Mrs Kenwyn threatened us with a gun when we went to visit her. In fact," he continued, "She almost sent the both of us over her balcony to crash to our deaths on the rocks below, just as she maintained, in her mixed-up mind, that her daughter had met her doom."

Looks of relief swept over the faces of all those present as they suddenly realised that they were no longer under suspicion. The heavy atmosphere was somewhat relieved by their mumbled exchanges.

Chess held his hand up for silence. "A plausible solution to the puzzle, I am sure you will agree," he said.

The sentence was met with predictably enthusiastic nods.

Chess continued. "The body was, as you all know, washed up on the Torre Abbey sands, and by all accounts it did have head injuries that could easily have been inflicted by rocks. Added to that, Max and I learned that Judy and her mother didn't get on at all well."

"It be an open and shut case," said George Mallock. "I think that be what you be callin' it, bain't it?"

Chess nodded. "The term is indeed correct sir, but there are other complications that have clouded the issue and made me realise that this conclusion was in fact, erroneous." Without waiting for a verbal response from those present, he turned to look at Anne Mallock. "Such as the cider that you poisoned," he added sternly.

George's mouth fell open and his wife's eyes widened. "I-I can explain that," she began.

"So can I," Chess retorted. "The three-ringed bottles were exclusive to Greenlawns. You said so yourself. Your husband told me that the girl travelled to her mother's with two of them. I remember last Friday as being an extremely hot day, and so Max and I conjectured that Judy could easily have drunk from one of the poisoned bottles on her way to the station with you. Initially I believed that you tried to poison her because you thought that she was having an affair with your husband. It was quite clear to both of us that there was some tension there, especially after you flew off the handle when I hinted at it during our first breakfast here."

"I didn't kill Judy," Anne Mallock protested, her face growing pale and scared, "It was–"

"An accident," Chess interrupted, finishing the sentence for her. "I know, I came to that conclusion too. Judy persuaded you to do it didn't she?"

"Yes," said Anne. "That be it. She be wantin' to get rid of her awl mother. Get the money for her awm, afore it fell down 'round her ears. I was just doin' the li'll gurl a favour. She didn't drink none of the scrumpy, Mr Chesterfield. She knew it be poisoned."

Chess nodded gravely. "Spot on," he said. "Though it's clear to me that you did have a motive and opportunity, and it's only your word that I have to go on that you didn't carry out the murder."

"Mr Chesterfield," said George Mallock. "You can't expeck me t' stummick all this. 'Ow could Anne 'ere 'ave killed Judy? An' what d' you be meanin', opportunity?"

"One question at a time, please," Chess replied levelly. "First off, if Judy didn't know that the scrumpy had been poisoned, and had indeed taken some during the journey to the station, your wife could quite easily have covered the body with a shawl and diverted to Corbyn Head and thrown both Judy's body, and the bottles, over the cliff to make it look like suicide. I'm sure that answers your questions. However, as I've intimated, I do believe your wife's explanation." He turned to the gardener. "Incidentally, Mr Carter, I would refrain from lending your weedkiller to anyone in future."

George Mallock breathed a heavy sigh. "So we'd all be agreed that it be suicide after all then, and them police was right. Thank th' Lord we've got th' affair out in the open."

"It's not over yet, Mr Mallock," said Chess. "And you've really hit upon the key to the case. The affair that must be brought out into the open is none other than the one that you were having with Mary Fish, your stable girl."

Anne Mallock pulled away from her husband and stared at him in disgust. George was having none of it and jumped up from the settee and advanced angrily on Henry Chesterfield. "I be payin' you t' investigate this case, not t' pry int' my private affairs," he blazed.

"In this case they are one in the same," Chess replied.

"Keep t' the case of Judy's death," Mallock snarled. "leave my affair out o' it."

"So you admit it be true?" Anne said, with tears forming in her eyes.

George Mallock was trapped and suddenly at a loss for words.

"Sit down and listen," Chess said in a commanding voice. Mallock cooled and did as he was bid, while Mary Fish burned with embarrassment.

All eyes returned to Chess as he withdrew two pieces of crumpled paper from his coat pocket. He held them both up, one in each hand, rather like a magician preparing to astound his audience with a clever trick. Slowly and carefully he brought each piece closer together until at last they touched. "Notice," he said, "how these two sections were torn from the same sheet."

"What do 'ee think all this be t' do with anythin'?" said George, still angry.

"Everything," was Chess's reply. "On one piece is written the address of old Mrs Kenwyn. On the other is a short message which reads '10am tomorrow'. Both exhibit the same characteristic sloping handwriting."

Chess's face was grave and his moustache twitched involuntarily as he surveyed the faces before him. A heavy, expectant silence pervaded the room once more. The young detective took a deep breath and continued. "The address was written by..." He paused, for a moment unsure of whether to go on. Then he turned to face the stable girl. "Mary Fish," he continued suddenly. She took the scrap of paper from her pocket and wrote upon it when I asked her about old Mrs Kenwyn's whereabouts. It is therefore clear that she was the owner of the other half too, which we found in a bloodstained pipe at Torre Station.

"Surely y-you bain't suggestin' I be Judy's killer?" Mary stammered.

"I am afraid I am my dear," said Chess. "I am fully aware that you do not have the strength to wield a piece of fifteen-inch diameter pipe and bludgeon poor Judy yourself. Instead you paid someone else to. The message '10am tomorrow', is evidence enough of that. It was precisely the time that Judy was due to arrive at the station. The tomorrow in question was, of course, last Friday."

Henry Chesterfield shifted his gaze to George Mallock and his delicate, blue eyes narrowed. "You are as much to blame as anyone else," he said.

Again the room fell into silence. Max couldn't believe that Chess was about to accuse their employer of murder, and suddenly wished that he could disappear into a hole in the ground.

Chess continued, but not in the same vein as anyone was expecting; "You are indirectly responsible for the outcome," he said. "After promising Mary your hand in marriage and a share of Greenlawns estate, you suddenly dropped her and began carrying on with Judy in front of her. Her jealousy boiled over and she was driven to arrange for Judy's death in the hope that your affections would return to her. Isn't that so, Mary?"

"Yes," the girl shrieked. "I did. He said 'ee luvved me. I reckon'd on him tellin' truth, the firkin' beggar, he-"

"Enough," bellowed Chess in a commanding voice. Mary's outburst faded to a quiet sobbing.

79

"For God's sake," said Anne Mallock. "I can't be takin' much more of this, just tell us who Mary be hirin' t' kill Judy. You tell 'ee it bain't George, say bain't, please."

"Don't worry, it's not," Chess said. "The deed was carried out by a labourer who was working on the gauge changeover gang down at Torre Station. The fellow has since met his doom. His was a suicide. Consumed with guilt about what he'd done, he simply walked into the sea at Hollacombe and drowned himself."

"Aye," said Carter. "That fits. He be washed up wasn't he? His pockets wuz all stuffed wiv money."

"That's right," said Chess. "Mary Fish's pay-off for a job well done."

George Mallock shook his head. "Don't 'ee be jumpin' to a few conclusions again Mr Chesterfield," he said. "Where'd Mary be gettin' all that money from?"

"At first I thought that you provided it," came the reply. "But as the case unfolded it became evident that that was out of the question. It just didn't fit with the facts. Then I remembered that Mary had told me how she had been left money by a deceased relative. She even told me she was planning to leave Greenlawns and set up her own stables."

"Don't be believin' a word of all this," said Mary savagely. "'Tis but a set-up. Darn vurriner be tryin' t' make 'imsel' look purty gude. 'Ee be lyin'. 'Ee's failed t' solve it and now 'ee be tryin' t' set me up."

"Hush 'ee up," said George. "You've already gone an' admitted yure guilt once."

Chess raised an eyebrow. "Thank you," he said. "Frankly, if more proof was needed then consider this. Mary came on very strong with me when we first arrived, culminating, I have to admit, in a lovemaking session in your stables."

"So that be what I 'eard," said Carter.

Chess nodded. "At first I believed that she was genuinely fond of me, but as time wore on and I began picking up the threads of the case, it became clear that she only wanted the liaison to hide the fact that she was responsible for the death of Judy. She figured that my attraction for her would prevent me considering her as a suspect. I must confess that it did work for a time. However, her keenness to be informed of all the developments as they occurred soon made me suspicious."

All eyes turned towards Mary, whose young face had gone an embarrassed crimson. George Mallock was the first to look away. "Alright,

Mr Chesterfield, it be lookin' like you bin an' done a good job after all. It's bin a mite painful fer uz awl, but per'aps I should alluz expected that. But there be zummat else. We knows who done it, we knows why, but we dunno know how th' murder wuz done. Do 'ee know 'bout that? After all, pawl awl Judy was found in th' sea, not at th' station."

"It's actually quite simple," Chess began. "Your wife dropped Judy off at the station and the girl hurried in. It was ten o'clock and the labourer, having read Mary's note, was waiting. He approached her and doubtless spun her some yarn or other that lured her over the footbridge to the shadowy far side of the station, then dragged her behind the sheds when the train came in and obscured the view from the opposite platform. With all the noise and commotion going on, no-one would have noticed. As you know, that side of the station borders on woodland, and once behind the sheds, he picked up a piece of Brunel's old atmospheric railway pipe and smashed it into her skull, killing her almost instantaneously and inflicting the wounds that the police took to be caused by the rocks on the beach. It was easy to make a hole in the perimeter fence and drag the body through the long grass into the woods, before getting on with his work on the tracks. However, he made a grave error by tossing down the note with the murder weapon. Had he not done so, then it is quite likely that the case would never have been solved."

"But th' beach?" said Mr Mallock. "She be found on th' beach."

"I was coming to that. The body lay hidden until late that night, when, undercover of darkness, the labourer hauled the corpse onto a goods train that was carrying discarded old sleepers and suchlike from the gauge change."

Max smiled. "Ah yes," he said knowingly. "The sign on the wall saying that there would be no more trains that day, and another posted underneath telling navvies to throw all their rubbish into the goods special that would be through late that night to clear things up. I remember you commenting on it now."

"Exactly," Chess went on. "It's clear that the labourer clambered into the wagon with the body and kept his head down until the train reached Hollacombe. There is a point where the railway runs right along the cliff edge, high above the beach. I noticed it when we visited the place the other day. At this place, the labourer simply hauled the body out of the wagon into the waters below, throwing the luggage, which amounted to a couple of bottles of scrumpy, over afterwards. In truth, it was a perfectly executed job. But even though it made him a rich man, he simply couldn't live with what he'd done."

As Henry Chesterfield finished speaking there was a sharp rap on the door. He flipped out his Benson's pocket watch. "Ah, eleven a.m.!" he exclaimed. "The police may not be particularly good at solving crimes in these parts, but they are at least punctual. I called them earlier." He strode over to the door and admitted two burly constables.

"Goodbye, Mary," he said. "It was – shall we say – interesting knowing you."

The Bishop's Castle Case

The dense, yellow fog that had settled over Mayfair and left its oily droplets on the windows of Henry Chesterfield's grand Park Lane residence, served to further perpetuate the young detective's rather morose mood.

While Max peered through the grimy panes, screwing up his piggy eyes to catch a glimpse of the great expanse of Hyde Park through the silent swirls, Chess lounged around, his face almost as long as the settee that he flung himself down upon. He slouched, classical guitar in hand, and proceeded to play some haunting, dreary air that harmonised perfectly with his feelings.

"What the deuce are we doing wrong, Max?" he barked suddenly, throwing the exquisite guitar aside in mid-phrase. "We haven't had a case for months, ever since that affair in Devon."

Max shrugged and wandered across the large drawing room, finally settling himself in a seat opposite his friend. "I don't know, Mr Chess, I really don't," said the fat fellow sadly. "But what I do know is that it's unfair you giving me free board and lodgings here in your lovely house, just in the hope of a case coming up. I feel that I'm sponging on your good nature."

"Nonsense!" exclaimed Chess, waving his friend's words aside with a flurry of his hand. "A preposterous thought. As I've already said, with you here, we can act immediately something comes along. It's much more sensible than me having to struggle to contact you up-country."

Max nodded. "Yes," he said, "but the truth is, nothing's coming along is it."

"Heaven knows why," Chess retorted. "We've had some good publicity from our first few cases and I've mailed calling cards to all the key people, including that weasel-faced fellow, Lestrade, at Scotland Yard that Sherlock Holmes often works in connection with. But nothing. This new career of ours is going at a dreadful largo tempo, not the molto presto I'd hoped for at all."

Max smiled at the musical dialogue that had a habit of creeping into his friend's speech. "Perhaps we'll have to content ourselves with poco a poco," he replied smugly. "Like you're so fond of saying Mr Chess, little by little." The fat man leaned forward and picked up a copy of the

Illustrated London News from a nearby side-table. "I'll wager that Holmes is busy with loads of blinkin' cases. In this game, it seems that it's not so much what you know, as who you know."

"Maybe," came the reply. "Though I still hold that good exposure to the public is the key to success. Perhaps we need a chronicler to dramatize our cases and get them into the pages of a popular magazine like that Watson chap does for Holmes. Holmes'd never have become the so-called great detective that he is without the help of those short stories."

Max buried his head deeper into the large magazine. "Don't even think about it Mr Chess," he said firmly. "I'm no author."

The room fell silent once more and Max turned his full attention to his reading. After a couple of minutes he spoke in a voice full of enthusiasm. "You know, I reckon if work doesn't come to us, then we should go to it."

"What?" came the reply.

Max smiled. "This should be right up your street," he said, laying the journal down on his lap and stabbing with one of his podgy fingers at a news story on James Payn's 'Our Notebook' page just inside the cover. "A musical mystery!" he exclaimed. "Listen. A concert given by the Cambrian Male Voice Choir at Bishop's Castle had to be cancelled last week due to the strange disappearance of their lead tenor, a Mr Owen Tregaron who was last seen with the rest of the choir when they arrived at Craven Arms, the terminus of the 10 mile Bishop's Castle Railway near the Welsh border. The police were informed, and a worried Mrs Tregaron commented that she was certain that her husband would never have intentionally missed a concert. 'He loves singing like all Welsh people' she said. A police spokesman commented that foul play has not been ruled out, but requested that we print this account in the hope that anyone with knowledge of Mr Tregaron's whereabouts will get in touch, as they admit that, to date, they have drawn a complete blank."

Max shifted his gaze towards a thoughtful-looking Henry Chester-field. "Well?" he said. "What do you think?"

"Brillante, Max" came the reply as the young detective's face lit up. "The more I think about it, the better it sounds. It really would be a good publicity exercise on our part if we handle it correctly and are successful in locating this Tregaron fellow, but I'm not sure how we can best become involved."

"Simple," said Max. "Let's offer our services to Mrs Tregaron gratis, that'll give us some good publicity for a start. It's hardly a very good business plan, and we could end up out of pocket, but I reckon it could be worth it."

Chess shrugged. "Well," he said. "We've got nothing else on, so I suppose we could give it a shot. I'll send a wire to the magazine and get them to ask Mrs Tregaron to meet us at Craven Arms tomorrow. That should get the publicity ball rolling."

"Excellent," replied Max, "and don't forget to offer to keep them in touch with the affair, perhaps's they'll agree to do another story if we can solve this."

*   *   *

Originally no more than a junction with an old posting inn called Craven Arms, the similarly named railway halt had, over the years, gradually grown in importance, being successively the junction for the Central Wales line to Swansea and the Great Western Line to Much Wenlock, before eventually serving the Bishop's Castle Railway. Consequently, when Chess, Max and Wilbur B. stepped down from their train they found the terminus bustling with activity.

"How the hell do we find Mrs Tregaron in this crowd?" said Max peering at the sea of faces that were hurrying past.

"We don't," came Chess's reply. "We wait for her to find us. I told her we'd have Wilbur B. with us, there's no one else here with a black and white bassett, is there?"

The trio stood patiently in the middle of the platform as the crowd thinned around them, with Henry Chesterfield smiling pleasantly at every young woman who happened to glance in his direction. At first, Max conjectured that this was in case one of them was Mrs Tregaron, but when his friend began entering into conversation with a particularly sweet young thing it became evident that he was up to his old tricks again.

Max tutted under his breath and turned discreetly away. A few moments later he felt a tap on his shoulder. "I don't want to hear about her, I just wish you'd..." He said turning round.

He broke off embarrassed in mid-sentence as he realised that it wasn't Chess about to recount the beginnings of another of his romantic liaisons, but a most attractive woman. She smiled.

"Mr Chesterfield?" she said.

Max blushed, "Uh, no, not me. Him, excuse me, Mr Chess. I believe this is Mrs Tregaron."

Chess broke off his conversation with the girl and came smartly across to the pair, extending his right hand in greeting. "Mrs Tregaron, it is indeed a pleasure to make your aquaintance."

"Sir, do call me Margery. Mrs Tregaron is much too formal." She took Chess's hand delicately. The detective's moustache twitched, and Max groaned, wishing that the central figure in their investigation wasn't young, shapely and female.

"A London accent if I am not very much mistaken, Margery?"

"That is quite correct. I moved to Welshpool, just over the border six years ago when I married Owen. Before that I resided in Chelsea."

Chess was about to comment when his attention was caught by a rather large and conspicuously positioned 'wanted' poster on the station wall which gave details of a fellow called Morley, an escaped convict thought to be at large in the area. "Good heavens," he said with a shudder on reading the text printed beneath a picture of a large, savage, bear-like man. "Listen to this, Max; 'We strongly recommend that you keep your doors and windows securely fastened and do not venture out in the hours of darkness.'"

"Flippin' 'eck, what's the fellow done?" Max enquired, a squeak of fear creeping into his voice.

"Killed his wife and two daughters with his bare hands," said Margery. "The police say he's deadly and mustn't be approached."

"And he's thought to be in these parts?" Max asked rather gingerly.

Margery nodded. "Yes," she said. "He's been seen along the railway line. Everyone travelling on the Bishop's Castle Railway fears for their safety, but most have come to terms with it, after all, life has to go on."

"You really are jolly brave, Margery," Chess remarked, eager to slip any compliments that he could into the conversation. "You must be completely shattered by your husband's disappearance, let alone all this."

Margery Tregaron's reply was completely unexpected, and both Chess and Max were taken completely by surprise. "No," she said. "Not at all. I loathe and detest Owen if you must know. Having him permanently out of my life is nothing but a bonus to me. I've been separated from him for a year now anyway. He's a wicked man, Mr Chesterfield, I don't mind telling you. He persuaded me to have children and I produced two daughters for him. They ask about their daddy, but he never visits them, and to cap it all, now he's disappeared I don't get any maintenance money from him. So you see, though I hate him, I want him found, not because I miss him, but because I miss his money."

By this time, the engine was making ready to leave from the north bay of the station, and so the quartet were forced to hurry across the platform and temporarily suspend conversation.

Max's attention was drawn by the 'Bishop's Castle', a smart little 2-4-0 locomotive painted in black and lined in red and white, domeless with a large manhole cover in the middle of the boiler. The fat man would have liked to linger longer, but just then the engine gave out a loud, uncouth cry and the guard signalled that the train, which consisted of two simple carriages, was ready to move off.

Soon the group were rattling at a modest speed along what could rightly be described as a fairy glen; one of the prettiest lines in all of England, where you could reach out from the carriage windows and, in appropriate seasons, pick hazelnuts, wild roses and honeysuckle.

"What a bloody beautiful little country railway," Max remarked. "I've travelled a fair few routes in my time as a ticket inspector on the Great Northern, but I've seen nothing to compare with this."

Even Henry Chesterfield, who was not normally given to showing much interest in railway matters, nodded in appreciative agreement before resuming conversation with Margery who was seated opposite him. "You said that your husband wanted children and now he's disappeared without so much of a word, correct?"

Margery nodded. "Exactly," she replied.

Chess considered. "Well," he said after a little time, "he's either a blaggard or – " he hesitated. "Or he's dead," he added quietly.

Margery shrugged.

Max, who had been listening to the conversation half-heartedly while gazing out of the carriage window, raised his eyebrow and felt he should attempt to bring the talk around to lighter matters. Just then they ran through a little halt known as Stretford Bridge. "Don't the trains stop here?" he piped up as they passed the short, earthen platform to which the only access looked to be through fields.

Margery shook her head, "only occasionally," she replied. "If someone puts their hand out for the train."

"I can see how people around here must be worried about that Morley fellow," Chess said. "He could easily strike in any one of these isolated spots."

The conversation dissolved at this and the three faces stared introspectively out through the carriage window. The stretch of line down which they were travelling ran along the valley of the River Onny which was one of the most picturesque on the whole railway, with hedges and undergrowth gently brushing the panes. "It really doesn't seem possible that any crime could be committed in such a beautiful place," said Chess, "but if there has been, you can rely on us to find out about it, madam."

Margery looked rather worried at this. "Mr Chesterfield," she said after a slight pause. "Really, you are most kind, but I have to confess that I am financially embarrassed at present." The woman lowered her eyes, and her dark eyelashes flickered on her silky-smooth cheeks that had coloured up somewhat. "I am hardly in a position to afford your fee," she went on quietly, "however modest it may be. I think, really, it may be for the best if you just go on back to London."

Chess waved her words aside with a dramatic flick of his hand. "A preposterous thought, madam," he said. "I will have nothing of it. We are at your service entirely free of charge, We will do everything in our power to alleviate your plight, you may count upon it."

"I don't know how I shall ever be able to repay you, Mr Chesterfield," she replied sheepishly, with something of a cheeky glint coming into her attractive brown eyes.

Chess smiled discreetly. "Ah, appassionata! I'm sure we'll be able to think of something," he said.

Once the comings and goings of passengers alighting and departing from Horderley station, which consisted of a modest single-storey brick building, had subsided and the train was making its steady progress once more along the widening and gently ascending valley, Max found himself changing the subject a second time in the hope that his companion's eyes would stop trying to undress their client.

"Could you give us a description of Owen?" he enquired.

"Certainly, that's easy. He's really quite distinctive; brown hair, quite long for today's fashions and broad and tall, the same sort of size as that Morley I suppose. Oh yes, I almost forgot, Owen has a rather distinctive tattoo - it's on his left arm, just above the wrist. Two musical notes - on account of his love of singing, just like you see in books, with little curly tails on."

The sound of the train changed suddenly as it negotiated a bridge over the river and Max glanced out of the window to see the impressive heights of the Longmynd Range rising on the right.

"His clothing," said Chess. "Do you have any idea of what he was wearing when he disappeared?"

"Yes," came the reply. "I saw him get off the train at Craven Arms with the choir. He was wearing a tweed lounge jacket and light tan trousers. Quite nice he looked to be honest."

The train continued to make its way, first through Plowden the largest station on the line and a rather forbidding looking two-storey building, then Eaton with its little brick station curiously constructed on the opposite side of the line as the platform, before making the ascent to Lyndham Heath. Here, Max was quite surprised to witness the locomotive running round in a loop and coupling to the rear of the carriages for the final leg of the journey to Bishop's Castle itself.

During this temporary stop Chess resumed questioning of Margery Tregaron. "Tell me," he began. "What is the situation with the local police at the present time?"

"As far as I know they've given up the ghost. A constable told me that they believe Owen to have left the area. Mind you, they have apparently arranged for small stories to be inserted into some of the national newspapers to help find him."

Chess smiled. "Yes," he said. "It's one of those that brought us here. I wonder, Margery, do you suspect foul play at all?"

"No, not really. Owen's a big, strong man. I think he can take ample care of himself, don't you?"

"Oh yes, quite," said Chess, "but it does seem strange that he simply vanished without arranging to see the children that so wanted and must dearly love."

The train moved off once more and Margery looked thoughtfully out of the window at the deserted countryside. "I thought that too once," she said with a far away look on her face.

"Do you live alone now, save for the children?" Chess enquired, his moustache twitching somewhat.

Margery shook her head. "Oh no, I have a lov- I mean a man-friend. A gentleman by the name of Ivan. Ivan Stockley, another big bear of a man. He looks after me. The trouble is, he's out of work at present. He was a miner, and a good one too, but the coal dust affects him when he's down the pit, some sort of allergy that's prevented him working. He strong though, at all other times."

Chess nodded and Max noticed that he looked rather deflated, having no doubt hoped that Margery Tregaron could have become his next conquest. It was a couple of minutes before he spoke again. "I don't suppose there's anyone you suspect of uh- harming your husband is there?" he began rather awkwardly. "Maybe even Ivan. After all, surely they didn't get on too well," he added quickly.

Margery eyed Chess severely. "True enough, they didn't get on too well, obviously," she said carefully, "but Ivan's not stupid, Mr Chesterfield. He wants to spend his life next to me, not next to four grey prison walls. No, you mark my words, if anyone at all has resorted to foul play then it's that lunatic Morley that's on the loose. He's striking fear into the whole community."

*   *   *

The weather was being kind for late October and Chess and Max found their room at the Castle Hotel in the town adequately warm, without having to resort to lighting the fire. Wilbur B., however, seemed unaware of this and had taken up his normal position in front of the hearth.

"You know, Mr Chess, that must be the damn stupidest dog I've ever come across," Max remarked.

"He's been responsible for solving more than one case though," Chess replied with a smile, leaning forwards and patting the slumbering hound on his shiny black flank. "Well," he continued, "hardly the place where the elite come to eat is it? but I suppose it'll have to do. If our investigations are successful then hopefully we shouldn't be stuck here for too long."

He settled back in the austere cotton-covered easy chair and eyed Max, whose bulk lay sprawled on the nearby bed, his shoes removed and a toe poking through one of his socks. "What do you make of this affair with the escaped convict," he said. "Do you think he could have killed Owen?"

"I'm bloody well sure he could," Max replied. "From what we've heard about him he could also probably kill a herd of wild buffalos single-handed. But I think that Margery's lover, Ivan Stockley, must also rate as a suspect. It wouldn't be the first time that blind jealousy has been responsible for murder."

Chess nodded solemnly. "Quite true, Max. If I was carrying on with a married woman then I'd certainly want the husband out of the way, wouldn't you?"

"I wouldn't be carrying on with a married woman in the first place," came the stern reply, "and neither should you be if you want my opinion, not unless you want to cross swords with Ivan Stockley."

"As prudish and unadventurous as ever, Max," Chess said with a rather overdone yawn.

"Alright, Mr Chess, you know best. So what's our plan of action?"

"Well I vote we give this affair a week of our time, and if we haven't found out anything by then, we admit defeat and come to the same conclusion as the police, that he's done a bunk."

Max nodded. "Agreed," he said. "So where do we start?"

"The local pub," Chess replied. "The nucleus of local gossip. come on."

*   *   *

The moment Chess and Max entered the busy. low-ceilinged pub with Wilbur B., the chatter within, which, up to that point had been animated and friendly, suddenly dissolved like ice in hot water and the two men were met with frosty looks by the locals who were evidently distrustful of unfamiliar faces due, no doubt, to the prevailing problems surrounding the community.

Chess took a deep breath, strode up to the bar and ordered two pints of ale, "and a drop for the dog, too," he added with a smile. "In a saucer please."

Still the pub was silent.

The drinks duly arrived and Chess bent down and placed the saucer of ale on the floor. Wilbur B. plunged his long tongue – and his ears – into the golden liquid and for the next thirty seconds all that could be heard in the room was a most ungracious slurping noise.

A few of the locals exchanged surprised glances. Chess smiled again. "Every since he tasted scrumpy down in the West Country a while back he's been quite partial to a tipple," he remarked to the assemblage.

A few suppressed chuckles ran round the room.

Suddenly and unexpectedly, Wilbur B. began pawing the ground like a bull preparing to charge, gave out two rather high-pitched barks and rolled over onto his back, kicking his short, stubby legs in the air.

This time the public house exploded with laughter.

"Looks like 'us foreigners' have been accepted," said Max through the hub-bub.

Chess nodded. "I'm going to come clean about why we're here," he said. "They'll find out soon enough anyway, may as well get it from the horse's mouth so to speak." he turned to the barman. "Sir," he began. "I am Henry Chesterfield, and together with my friend, Max, we are investigating the disappearance of Owen Tregaron."

"That damn episode," the barman grumbled back. "It's turned my plans upside down, I can tell you."

Chess frowned. "How do you mean?"

"I had the big barn behind the pub all laid-out ready for the Bishop's Castle choir concert, all staging and God knows what else made out of straw bales and so forth, extra ale ordered and then the darn thing goes and gets cancelled."

"Owen Tregaron must have been some fine singer for the choir not to be able to manage without him," said Max.

"That he was," came the barman's reply. "I've seen him many a time, a great tenor, the leading light – sung all the solos."

"So was it cancelled, or just postponed?" Chess enquired, hitching Wilb's lead onto a brass hook supplied for the purpose on the front of the polished mahogany bar.

The barman shrugged. "Still don't rightly know. We're all a bit annoyed about it to tell the truth. The manager of the choir said it'll go ahead just as soon as Owen Tregaron turns up, but heaven knows when that'll be. The thing that's riling the town is that they've all shelled out for tickets - nigh on five hundred by all accounts, at three bob each, and no one's had their money back. 'rescheduling it soon, 'Shouldn't be too long now,' is all we've been getting lately."

"Well, we will certainly do our utmost to locate Owen so that the show can go ahead," Chess said. "You can count on it."

"Show?" said the barman. "Shows you mean, there have been concerts cancelled at Eaton, Lyndham heath, Plowden and Horderley too. Owen's going to be a mite unpopular with folks 'round here when he does show up I'm reckonin'"

"I saw him, mister,"

The voice came from the detective's right and he turned to see a chap leaning against the bar. Chess raised his eyebrows and struck up a responsive pose. "Oh yes?" he said. "What can you tell me?"

"I saw him over Plowden way. I'm an engine driver and in the distance this morning, near the station, as I came on down the line same as always, he ran out of the woods and came towards the train. Then suddenly he changed his mind and headed off back in the direction of new Farm, Mr and Mrs Blake's place, with great lumbering strides." The engine driver paused, supped his ale, then continued. "Quite a stout chap he was, must have a lovely deep voice being that size, no wonder the choir couldn't do without him, eh?"

"Are you absolutely sure that it was Owen?" Max enquired.

"Course I am, I've heard the police description half a dozen times and he fits it exactly. He was wearing a tweed jacket and light tan trousers, just like they said he'd be."

"This really is most interesting, sir," said Chess. "Tell me, have the police been told of this sighting yet?"

The engine driver shook his head. "Like I said, it was only this morning I saw him. I came straight off shift and over here."

"Well this is excellent. We do seem to have rather a head start on the official force for a change." Chess dug into his pocket and withdrew some coins. "Barman," he said. "If you would be so kind as to pour this helpful gentleman a drink."

While the ale was being pulled Chess turned around and leant his back on the bar. His delicate blue eyes surveyed the sea of faces that were fixed on him. "Anyone got anything else to tell me?" he enquired in a loud voice.

"I saw him over Horderley way," came one reply.

"Chap answering his description was on the road to Eaton," said another.

"Swore I caught sight of him on Lyndham heath," piped up a third.

Chess smiled. With the thought of free drinks there suddenly seemed to be a rush of conflicting information. The affluent young detective took a sovereign from his pocket and brushed aside the informative comments with a throwaway gesture of his hand before tossing the coin onto the bar. "Buy them drinks, barman," he said. "To shut them up more than anything else. They must think that I'm as green as grass."

The smiling barman took the orders, then, as he began pulling the ales, he turned his attention back to Chess. "I don't know if it'll help much," he said, "but it might be worth you having a word with the choir manager. If he's planning to reschedule these shows then he must be keeping abreast of developments where Owen is concerned." He turned around and, from between two half-empty bottles of spirits on the shelf behind the bar, he removed a small, white visiting card. "Here, take this," he said. Chess did as he was bid, and peered at it.

"A barber?" he exclaimed in a somewhat surprised voice. "But I thought –"

"No, these chaps only do this singing lark in their spare time."

"And so what's this, chap –" Chess consulted the card again. "Um – Stanley Soper – like?"

The barman hesitated. "Well, he's a bit - uh, shall we say. Well. He. He does the high bits in the choir."

The nearby customers in the public house roared with laughter. Chess nodded. "I do believe I get the picture," he said. "Well, thank you my good man. I will certainly contact him. However, I rather feel that my investigation should commence over in the woods near Plowden, where our engine-driver friend chanced upon our missing man. There's no time like the present. Good night."

* * *

The night had become well-established by the time Chess and Max, together with Wilbur B., had reached the Plowden woods that were silent and eerie in the pale blue moonlight. Max shuddered, not so much from the cold of the conditions, but from a strange, hard-to-explain, feeling of being in the presence of something inexplicably awful. He cast his eyes apprehensively around the dark, deserted landscape and across to the huge towering outline of the heights of the Long Mynd, feeling suddenly insecure and insignificant amidst the awesome natural surroundings.

It was Chess's nearby voice that made him snap out of his introspective thoughts. "This really is an excellent hiding place," he said. "Based here, Owen would have the nearby River Onny for water and New Farm for stealing food."

"And that superb vantage point over the whole area," Max added jerking his rotund head in the direction of the misty mountain range. "So where do we start?"

Henry Chesterfield scratched his head. "I'm not sure," he said at last. "It seemed straightforward when that chap in the pub said he'd seen Owen. I assumed that we could simply come out here, find a few clues and wrap the whole thing up. I must confess that I didn't realise that there was such a large expanse of land here to search."

He sighed and began wandering further into the deep woods, the crunchy autumn leaves crackling under his feet. He gestured to them in annoyance. "I didn't bank on these either," he added. "The slightest wind and they blow all over the place. Even if there were any clues on this forest floor, we'd already be hard pressed to find them. Still, we must try."

Max followed his friend, while Wilbur B. padded along behind, head to the ground and ears flapping through the leaves.

Suddenly Chess stiffened and stopped. Max's heart began beating faster and a combination of worry and excitement spread through his massive frame. "W-What?" he enquired quietly of his friend. "W-What is it?"

"Shh, pianissimo. I thought I heard something."

Max strained his ears for any sound. For a moment there was nothing save for the gentle rustling of leaves in the light breeze. Then suddenly he heard a familiar sound and breathed easily once more. "It's an owl, Mr Chess," he said. "For pity's sake don't do that to me."

But still Chess didn't move. He stood stock still. So still, in fact, that his perfect form could almost have been mistaken for some classical statue in the steely moonlight. "That's not what I heard," he said in a tense, quiet undertone. "Listen again, Max."

The fat man held his breath and his frightened piggy-eyes darted nervously around the tall trees that suddenly seemed to him to be looming menacingly close overhead. All sorts of terrible nightmarish thoughts began to race through his brain as he thought of Morley, and when a wood pigeon fluttered down from a branch almost directly over his head, he broke out in a cold sweat. However, it was as the bird made off that he heard, for the first time, the sounds that Chess had alluded to...

Distant voices.

Shrieks.

The crackling of a forest fire.

"There," said Chess. "Look, Max, way over there, d'you see the red glow?"

Max nodded. His throat had become dry and he had trouble replying. When words did eventually come they were squeaky and fraught with fear. "N-Nothing to do with our case, M-Mr Chess. Best leave it for now, eh? See what tomorrow brings. No sign of Owen here."

"Tut tut, Max," came the reply. "Pull yourself together. We must investigate, it's our job, remember?"

It was evident that Henry Chesterfield's resolve was strong and unshakable, so Max surrendered with a groan and crept along behind his friend who was moving in a half-crouch from tree to tree in the general direction of the flickering light, holding Wilbur B. on a short leash.

Max's brain was racing as they approached. With every passing step the voices were growing louder and wilder. At that precise moment, a most terrible thought struck him and he was almost poleaxed as realisation struck like a hammer blow. He grabbed out at Chess's coat tails and hauled him back.

"What is it?"

"The time" Max hissed is a scared voice. "What is it?"

Chess flipped out his Benson's pocket watch and peered closely at the enamel dial. "Just coming up to midnight," he said. "Why?"

"You know what day it is don't you?"

"Tuesday, what of it?"

"Tuesday the 31st of October," Max provided the extra information. "Halloween," he added. "And almost midnight. I'll wager that we're about to witness something terrible - it's the witching hour."

Another few yards and the pair found themselves on the edge of a forest clearing. Rhododendrons provided ground cover and enclosed a small area that had become the stage for some diabolical ritual. Some half-dozen or so people had stripped stark naked, and, as the pair watched from the undergrowth, they could be seen dancing and chanting around a blazing fire, the flames flickering on their flesh and giving it a warm, golden hue. Max looked across at Chess whose eyes had widened so much that they looked as if they could physically pop out of their sockets.

Whilst the shadows were too deep to make out individual features with any certainty, the bodies themselves left nothing whatsoever to the imagination. The women, all of which were attractively endowed, were making an absolute show of themselves and then men were responding, their eager, gyrating bodies in various stages of sexual excitement.

Max turned away in utter disgust but Chess continued to stare, intrigued and excited himself as a black-cloaked man with a long hook-nose and sunken cheeks raised a dagger above a poor, helpless goat that lay struggling, tied and bleating, on the ground nearby.

Max looked in the opposite direction at the deserted forest, refusing to permit himself another peep at the scene. It was as he did so that he saw a large man break cover from a nearby rhododendron bush and dart away through the woods.

"Mr Chess. Over there," Max gasped excitedly. "Through the trees, look."

With some considerable difficulty, his lecherous friend managed to tear his eyes away from the demonic scene in front of him and re-focus his attention on the figure. However, by the time he had done so, the fellow had almost entirely faded into the darkness. At that moment, Wilbur B. decided to give tongue, and, slipping his lead, rushed off in hot pursuit of the phantom figure. Without a second thought, Chess made off after him with Max, puffing and blowing with the effort, bringing up the rear. "I think it was Owen," he managed between wheezes. "Had a tweed jacket on."

"Big chap too," Chess called back. "About the right build. Come on Max, allegro, look sharp."

The chase continued enthusiastically for about two hundred yards, after which Chess caught up with Wilbur B. who had become disinterested. The pair slowed to a walk and when Max caught up with them, they stopped altogether. "Damn and blast," Chess grumbled. "We've lost him."

"Well, at least we know he's still around these parts."

Chess nodded. "You're quite right I suppose," he said. "It's just that it's so annoying, we nearly had him. We'll come back tomorrow when it's light."

The pair, together with Wilbur B., made their way cautiously out of the depths of the Plowden woodlands, taking care to avoid the ghoulish gathering that they had witnessed earlier. It was as they were within sight of the country road that they came upon a small pond lit by the ethereal light of the moon. "This light really can play tricks on the eyes," remarked Max, gesturing towards the mirror-smooth waters. "They look almost white."

Chess, who was closer to the pond, followed the direction of Max's gaze and made a violent start. "It doesn't just look white," he said, bending down beside the water. "It jolly well is white."

Max, too, went to the edge and ran his hand through the liquid. "Milk!" he exclaimed, screwing up his face, "and phew, doesn't it reek? What the hell's it doing here?"

The moon disappeared behind a cloud and threw the scene into darkness. Chess shrugged. "Only thing I can imagine is that it's goat's milk. Something to do with that sacrifice affair we saw back there perhaps?"

Again Chess scrutinised the pond, peering at the strange, cloudy waters. As he did so, the moon broke through the clouds and afforded him a better, brighter view. What he saw made him recoil in horror, for there, like thin veins running through the white, were dark crimson threads. Threads that could only be one thing – blood.

*　　*　　*

Next morning, which dawned depressing and grey, saw the intrepid investigators alighting from a train at Plowden station. Their moods were much brighter than the weather, however, as Chess was convinced that they were on the verge of locating Owen. Whether or not it was a co-incidence could not be certain, but both men considered it a good omen when they walked past the domeless 2-4-0 locomotive, and noticed the nameplate:

"Progress," Max called out. "That fits us."

Chess smiled and nodded. "Let's hope so," he replied.

Max started prattling on about the engine … "safety valve over the firebox Mr Chess, and see that large brass cover, just like Stirling's earlier Great Northern type."

Chess hurriedly dragged Max towards the station exit ignoring the information that came gushing from the enthusiastic fat man… "used to be the number one engine on the Somerset and Dorset that, Mr Chess. See the large manhole cover in the place where the dome usually is? There's not many around like that, and the tender, it's–"

"The case," Chess interrupted, changing the subject, "could be nearing completion. We know Owen's round here. Let's make for New Farm."

Max nodded. He took another longing look back at the locomotive that was just pulling out of the station, then followed his friend.

From the rather dilapidated look of the buildings and the over-grown nature of the farmyard, it was clear that the inhabitants of the rather inappropriately named New Farm were not having particularly outstanding success with their lands. Chess knocked on the farmhouse door and waited patiently for perhaps a minute before it was eventually opened by a middle aged, weatherbeaten and unshaven individual.

As the door swung open, the pair noticed a woman bundling a young man away into the back room. Neither had time to get a good look at the fellow and all that registered was that the person was tall and dressed in black.

"So what d'you be wantin' round 'ere?" said Mr Blake guardedly, addressing his gruff words to Chess.

"We are looking for a missing person, seen recently in your area, a man named Owen Tregaron."

The farmer's wife joined them at the door. "No," she said nervously. "Not round here. Ain't seen hide nor hair of 'im."

Chess detected apprehension and fear in the voice, so much so that it was almost tangible. Immediately he began to sense some involvement and continued with his line of questioning.

"But surely," he pressed on, "you both being out in the fields all the hours God sends you must have laid eyes on him."

Max noticed a rather nasty look coming into Mr Blake's grey eyes, and, thinking that there was a very real possibility that he may have a gun close to hand, decided to tactfully change the subject and play the pleasant fellow. He had no wish to be at the end of another gun barrel like the one wielded by old Ma Kenwyn in Torquay on their last case. "Lived in the area long?" he interjected pleasantly and with a smile.

This seemed to have the desired effect and the farming pair relaxed their guard.

"Aye," said Mr Blake. "Twenty-six years. Got married up at the wee church in Bishop's Castle."

His wife nodded. "July 1867," she said.

"And you look to have a fine son," Max continued amiably, guessing that it was the person that he had spotted briefly when the door was first opened.

Suddenly all the tension returned and immediately Max realised that he'd somehow put his foot right in it, fair and square. Chess, who seemed to delight in aggravating potentially explosive situations, was next to speak.

"A fine lad, is he?" he said.

The silence was deafening.

"Well?" he continued. "Have I said something wrong?"

The farmer and his wife exchanged stoney-faced looks. Mrs Blake eventually breathed a heavy sigh. "Christian isn't a well boy," she said at length. "He can't speak, well, he can but only in grunts. We understand him, but he don't take easy to no strangers."

Chess nodded sympathetically. "Well," he said. "We really are both most terribly sorry to hear that. We will bother you no further. However, I'd rather like to look around your farmyard and outbuildings to see if I can find any clues appertaining to this Owen fellow."

"We told you, there ain't nothin' round here," said Mr Blake.

Chess was adamant. "Probably not but we'll take a peep all the same," he replied, shooting a look at Mrs Blake who suddenly appeared desperately worried but had no choice but to agree to the harmless request.

Wilbur B. led the way, straining on his leash towards the large barn at the far corner of the farmyard. Once inside and safely out of earshot of the farmhouse, Chess began speaking excitedly. "They're hiding something," he said, voicing the obvious.

"Or someone," Max retorted. "I reckon they're harbouring Owen."

"You could be right, Max," said Chess peering into the dark depths of the barn and tossing heaps of straw aside in a vain effort to locate some sort of clue. "But why?" he added. "What's the point of hiding him, he –" Henry Chesterfield stopped, dropped to his knees and scrabbled on the floor...

"What is it?" Max enquired, hurrying across the shadowy barn with Wilbur B. The dog wagged his tail excitedly so that his whole long, sausage-shaped body moved from side to side in sympathy. His wet, slobbery jaws nosed around a wooden chest that his master had found. As he watched through doleful, drooping eyes, Chess opened it.

"Merciful heavens!" Max gasped, peering at the assortment of daggers, black robes and strange cards with odd-looking symbols on them that were inside.

"Black magic again," Chess said, his voice grave. He snapped the lid shut quickly, half-afraid that some demon from the darker side would rise up out of it and consume them in its power.

Max put two and two together. "Christian Blake," he said slowly and deliberately.

Chess nodded. "Did you recognise him as one of the worshippers from last night?" he enquired, somewhat apprehensively.

Max considered for some little time, then suddenly it twigged. "Of course," he said. "Tall, dressed in black, one of those daggers from that chest in his hand. The one who was about to kill that goat."

"Old hook nose?"

"Exactly," Max nodded. "Christian Blake. We're getting into some deep and dangerous waters now, Mr Chess."

Henry Chesterfield shuddered slightly, and for a moment, his courageous nature took second place to his immediate feelings. "Let's get out of this place it gives me the creeps," he said. "We'll head back to the station and check out the Blakes as soon as we can. Haven't much to go on, save that they were married in July 1867 at Bishop's Castle. We'll start with that."

*   *   *

Plowden station was deserted when the trio returned to it and settled on a wooden bench on the platform to await the arrival of the train back to Bishop's Castle. It came steaming in after about ten minutes. No-one alighted from the two carriages save for the guard, who began shifting a quartet of milk churns stamped with the legend 'Edgton Farm' from a wooden stage, across to the carriage.

At that moment, Wilbur B. gave a well-practised shrug of his head and slipped his collar to bound up the platform towards the railwayman, the deserted station echoing with his deep, barking. The guard turned and looked apprehensively at the animal that came bounding towards him.

"Don't worry," Chess called out, getting up from the bench and following the errant hound along the platform. "He's quite harmless."

The guard looked unconvinced. He shook his head. Pushing his cheese-cutter railway cap back as he did so and scratched his balding head.

"Sorry," said Chess pushing Wilb's collar back on. "His bark's worse than his bite, really it is. Look, do you want a hand with those churns?"

The guards face cracked into a smile. "That's mighty kind of you, sir," he said. "To tell the truth, they do seem a mite heavy today, or perhaps it's just that I'm getting too old for all this lark."

"Max, take Wilb. would you?" Chess called. The fat man hurried up the platform and did as he was bid. Chess gripped the handles of the first churn, manhandled it down from its little wooden stage and out across the platform. His face took on a bright crimson colour and his chest heaved fit to burst. "They weigh a damn ton!" he gasped, offering the container up to the guard who had climbed into the carriage and was leaning out ready to take it. As he was about to lift it inside, Wilbur B. began barking excitedly and his keen nose quivered around the churn. It was as Chess stepped forward that disaster struck: Instead of the churn passing into the guard's hands, Chess tripped over the dog's lead which had somehow caught between his legs and both the churn and Chess tumbled onto the platform. Max groaned as the lid clattered off and

101

dropped down onto the track. But his look of concern turned to one of utter horror when, instead of gallons of creamy, white milk pouring all over the platform, a severed head rolled out across the concrete and came to rest next to where Chess lie. The detective sprang from the floor like it had been a trampoline and stood gaping, open-mouthed at the death-head with it's blood-red eyes, short, black hair and cold, grey skin which was already showing signs of decomposition.

"Dear God!" cried the guard climbing from the carriage, shaking and quivering like corn in the breeze as he peered gingerly at the terrible sight. Mercifully, there was very little blood and, steeling himself, Chess hauled the churn back upright and replaced the head inside where, chancing a brief peep, he saw the mangled remains of a torso. He turned hastily away.

"Anyone on board?" he said weakly, nodding towards the train.

The guard shook his head. "No," he replied. "Empty thank heaven."

Henry Chesterfield's face was like rock as he walked slowly across the platform to where the other three churns remained.

"You don't think -" began Max.

He broke off as Chess lifted the lid of the first churn. The stench almost took him off his feet and he scrabbled in his pocket for a handkerchief which he clapped to his nose before peering gingerly inside.

The container was stuffed with more rapidly-decomposing human remains, but what struck upon his soul with the force of a galvanic battery was the appearance of a tattoo - a tattoo on a severed wrist that depicted two musical notes.

*   *   *

"I must inform Margery Tregaron of her husband's fate," Henry Chesterfield said as he sat with Max in the hotel room at Bishop's Castle. "We're investigating the affair, and frankly it's our duty. I'd rather she didn't hear it from the official force."

"Have you formed any theories about who may be to blame for such a grisly murder?" Max enquired.

"Morley," Chess replied without any hesitation. "Who else but a psychopath would do such and absolutely foul thing to a fellow human being?"

Max raised an eyebrow. "Devil worshippers?" he ventured. "I don't think we should entirely rule out Christian Blake being involved. After all, it's happened close to where he lives."

A pain throbbed with dull persistence at Henry Chesterfield's temples and for the first time in the case he looked tired and drawn. When he spoke it was in a weary tone. "It's becoming deep and tangled again as usual. Nothing seems to be adding up. Take the stench of the remains and the decomposition of the flesh for instance."

"I don't follow, Mr Chess," said Max, his brow deeply furrowed. "What are you getting at?"

"Owen Tregaron has clearly been dead for a good few days. The thing is, Edgton Farm could only have put those churns out last night, otherwise the milk would have gone off. And we saw Owen last night with our own eyes running through the undergrowth."

Max nodded solemnly, "and the engine driver saw him recently too," he added. "You don't think it could have been his ghost do you?"

Chess shrugged. "With all this black magic business, I don't know what to think Max, I just don't know at all."

Henry Chesterfield rose from his chair. "I'm going over the border to Welshpool to get the dreadful business of telling Margery over and done with. It'll be one less thing on my mind. If you'd like to make yourself useful while I'm gone, you could check out the church register and see if Mr and Mrs Blake were married when they said they were."

"Of course I shall, Mr Chess, but what's the point?"

"First off, we can find out if Christian is really their son and if he was Christened there. There's something not quite right about those folks up at New Farm, and we've got to get to the bottom of it."

*   *   *

"Please, Mr Chesterfield, I don't want to discuss it in front of the children. Come upstairs."

Chess followed Margery Tregaron up the steep wooden flight, gazing enthusiastically at the precious flashes of bare ankle as the attractive woman climbed ahead of him. On reaching the top, she showed Chess into a bedroom and the pair perched on the edge of the bed. Suddenly Margery burst into floods of unexpected tears. "How c-can I tell the children what's happened to their daddy?" she wailed. "It's awful. I know I don't care for him but even so."

Chess was silent and his delicate blue eyes dimmed. When, after a few minutes, Margery's grief had not showed any signs of abating, he moved closer and slipped his arm gently around her waist for comfort. She turned towards him and he withdrew a handkerchief from his pocket and softly dabbed away the worst of the salty tears from her eyes.

"I-I'm s-sorry," she sniffed. "It's just come as – as a dreadful shock. To go in that way, it's so..." Her voice trailed off and she threw her arms around the young detective and brought her face close to his. Chess's moustache twitched and he slowly brought his lips to touch hers. Seconds later, the pair were locked in a warm and passionate embrace. "Make me forget," Margery said, sweetly as the couple fell back onto the soft mattress.

"Con amore, my love," Chess said sweetly, and without needing a second telling struggled enthusiastically with the buttons on Margery's blouse, beads of perspiration springing from his brow as he slid his hands over the warm, creamy-white flesh beneath.

It was as his other hand fumbled with the two layers of soft petticoat that the sound of footsteps on the wooden stairs invaded the room and a moment later, the door was flung back.

Chess half-turned and was met with a roar of anger. A huge clenched fist slammed with uncanny accuracy in to his left eye socket, sending him clean off the bed and onto the floor.

"Ivan," cried Margery. "No, I can explain. He–"

"Shut your mouth, woman," blazed the big man, lunging forwards again towards Chess who had managed to struggle, somewhat dazed, to his feet, only to be met with a powerful right-hander that hit home fair-and-square on his lip.

The detective tried gamely to retaliate but it was as one-sided as David and Goliath and he found himself forced to cling on to the big man and content himself with springing ineffectual rabbit-punches.

Still Ivan Stockley came on, slamming a couple of painful kidney punches while Chess held on, his dazed head flopping onto Stockley's muscular shoulder where he got a mouthful of irritating loose hairs down his throat that made him retch.

"I'll take you apart in little pieces, just like Tregaron, if you don't get out of here now, mister," he bellowed, thrusting Chess towards the door. "Now beat it, fella."

For a second time, Henry Chesterfield needed no second telling and fled, hoping the Stockley wouldn't be too hard on Margery, but feeling, in his heart-of-hearts, that there was a very real chance of him never seeing her alive again.

*   *   *

"Stockley's our man, Max," Chess exclaimed as he burst into the hotel room at Bishop's Castle. "He—"

"Flippin' 'eck, Mr Chess. What the hell's happened to you?" the fat man interrupted, staring open-mouthed at his friend's wounds, which were already turning a most alarming purple.

"What? oh, these?" Chess replied, touching his puffed-up eyes gently but still wincing with the pain. "That's just it," he continued. "Ivan Stockley, he's like a raging bull. He threatened he'd take me apart in little pieces - 'just like Tregaron' he said. It was either a dreadfully inappropriate coincidence that he used that figure of speech, or a really bad slip on his part and I favour the latter."

Max frowned. "How do you mean?" he said.

"Well, it's as good as admitting he murdered Owen. News wouldn't have reached Welshpool about our grisly find yet."

The fat man sat down heavily in a nearby chair and considered. "Point taken and understood," he said at last, "but perhaps he's been to Bishop's Castle and found out. We can't seriously point the finger of accusation at him on such a flimsy piece of evidence. Did you learn anything about where he's been recently?"

Henry Chesterfield nodded. "He's been to a barber's shop, that's for sure," he said. "When we were fighting, my head came into contact with his shoulder and I got a mouthful of hairs and a whiff of hairdressing."

Max eyes lit up. "Well that's an excellent start, Mr Chess," he said excitedly. "There's only one barber's shop in the whole of Bishop's Castle, and that's Soper's Salon. The barman gave you the fellow's card and particulars, remember?"

Chess fumbled in his pocket and drew out the crumpled card. "Ah yes," he recalled. "The effeminate amateur choir manager. I could do with a haircut. Alright Max, I'll wander down there and quiz him. If it turns out that Stockley hasn't been near the place then it's going to look very black for him indeed."

Henry Chesterfield smiled, a dangerous, vindictive smile that Max had never witnessed before. "I'd love to pin the blame on Stockley after what he did to me."

105

Max breathed a heavy sigh and eyed his friend severely. "Hardly surprising after what I'll wager you were doing to his girlfriend," he said, shaking his head. "You never learn, Mr Chess."

The detective managed another smile through his bruised and swollen lips as he turned to leave.

"Wait up," Max called. "I've got news too you know."

"Ah, the church? The Blakes?"

"Exactly," replied the fat man. "I checked the records just as you asked, and it seems that they did indeed get married when and where they said."

"Looks like we've drawn another of our famous blanks, then," Chess replied.

"Not quite," said Max. "There's something that you ought to know regarding Mrs Blake's maiden name..." Max hesitated.

"Well," Chess said, "go on."

"It's Morley."

Chess gave a start. "Morley," he repeated. "The same as the escaped convict?"

Max nodded. "Probably her brother. We were right about the Blakes harbouring someone, but it's Morley, not Owen, that's a cert. This cracks the case wide open. Owen was supposed to have been spotted several times in the vicinity of New Farm at Plowden. Now we know that Morley's definitely been in the area it doesn't take much stretch of the imagination to guess who's responsible for the murder."

Chess nodded enthusiastically and his moustache twitched. "You're right, this really does re-inforce the case against the fellow," he said.

"Damn right it does," his friend retorted, "especially with the black magic crowd making ritual sacrifices and heaven knows what in the self same area. Mixing that up with Morley make a very powerful and sinister brew to say the least. It's either Morley, Christian Blake, or both that are responsible, that's crystal clear now, isn't it Mr Chess?"

"I think so," came the replied, "but even so, I'm going to check out Ivan Stockley with Soper to make sure."

"Caution, Mr Chess," warned Max. "Don't turn this Stockley thing into some sort of personal feud and go blowing our chances of bringing this case home. We're on the verge of completing it."

"Don't worry," came the reply as Henry Chesterfield closed the door. "I'm not that stupid."

"Huh!" Max muttered under his breath.

*   *   *

"Just a trim," said Henry Chesterfield sitting down in the barber's chair, looking askance as Stanley Soper breezed effeminately around, placing a white shawl over him, which he tucked in a round his collar while exhibiting a high, rather excited giggle.

The detective was sullen as he surveyed the small bespectacled man before him. The latter had dark eyes that darted this way and that behind horn-rimmed glasses which were perched rather precariously on his singularly narrow nose. His skin, which was clean shaven, had the delicate appearance of a woman's, and the mousy brown hair that topped the soft face was perfectly coiffured and sprayed with a particularly sweet-smelling lotion that could almost have been a french perfume. When the man spoke, it was in a lisping voice in the upper register.

"I must say, sir," he said running his hands through Chess's thick black hair, and peering at the reflection of both of them in the mirror on the wall, "that your locks are in the most exquisitely beautiful condition. Just a trim you say, sir?"

"And a shave while I'm here, it'll save me time later."

"Dearie me. Love to oblige you, sir, but it's no go I'm afraid."

"What do you mean 'no go'?" Chess replied, already tiring of the simpering fellow.

"Trouble with my tools," came the reply. "Problem with the razor. It needs sharpening."

Chess shrugged. "Alright, just the trim then."

"Lovely sir. Can do. No problem. Haven't seen you around this area before," Soper said, giggling again and placing one of his long, thin hands to his mouth to stifle the sound. "Oops, sorry. But I'd have remembered a handsome face like yours."

Henry Chesterfield tutted loudly and began to feel considerably uncomfortable. He changed the subject and attempted to find out if Ivan Stockley had been a customer that day. "How's business, Mr Soper?" he said coldly.

"Slack, dearie, slack," replied the barber, snipping expertly away at Chess's hair. "You're the only man I've had all day. If it goes on like this, I shall move away. I can't imagine why I'm not getting the trade."

Chess smiled, but avoided stating the obvious.

Snip.

Snip.

The scissors flew in deft flicks around Chess's head. "Perhaps the reason you haven't been doing business has something to do with the choir affair. Maybe people blame you for Owen's disappearance."

"You know about the concerts, do you. Dearie me, news does travel fast around here, even to outsiders these days."

"Only to outsiders who make it their business to know," Chess countered. "I am a detective."

He eyed Soper in the mirror and noticed the fellow's delicate skin grow a shade paler. The smooth flurries with the scissors suddenly seemed to grow more jagged and agitated.

"Ouch, steady on," cried Chess, clapping a hand to his ear. "You're cutting me to ribbons. I'll end up in pieces like Owen if you're not careful."

Again he fixed his gaze, via the mirror, on Stanley Soper, who was now visibly shaken. "Are you all right?" he enquired. "What's the matter?"

For a few moments, the barber was silent. When he did speak it was in a weak, hesitant and effeminate voice tinged with terror. "I-It's Morley," he blurted. "The escaped convict. The one who the whole village is talking about. When you mentioned Owen, I-I remembered how scared I am for myself, sir."

"For God's sake pull yourself together Man," Chess barked, "before you have my ear off."

"It's alright for you, sir. You don't have to go home in a trap each night to Edgton. By the time I'm as far as Lydbury North, I'm petrified. And to make matters worse, you're right, folk round here do blame me for the cancelled concerts. I can tell by their looks, their eyes, they–"

"Enough," commanded Chess. "I am going to help you out, though heaven knows why. I am an accomplished guitarist, and my colleague, Max, is a quite excellent tenor. We shall fill-in for Owen and enable you to stage the Bishop's Castle concert. You'll have to make your own arrangements for the others."

Stanley Soper's reply came as something of a surprise. "I'd rather you didn't," he said. "I mean to say, well, after all–"

"It will be a benefit with the proceeds going to his widow. You have no objections do you? I insist."

Stanley Soper eyed his customer, then shook his head slowly and apprehensively.

*   *   *

The barn behind the Bishop's Castle public house was almost bursting at the seams when, several nights later, the choir, together with Henry Chesterfield and Max, assembled in front of an enthusiastic audience to give their much-belated performance. Newspaper reporters milled about with the locals, scribbling furiously on their pads in the hope of cobbling together follow-up stories to their earlier pieces on Owen Tregaron's disappearance.

Throughout the evening, Henry Chesterfield's virtuoso guitar playing thrilled the assemblage and a rather nervous-looking Max displayed his vocal talents to admirable effect, perhaps not entirely up the standard of the man he replaced, but nevertheless, considerably more than adequate. All in all it had been a most successful evening. A large sum had been raised for Margery's benefit and the concern that Morley may strike members of the audience on their way to the barn was unfounded, due in no small part to the presence of a pair of burly uniformed police constables who stood guard at the door.

As the thunderous applause following the final number died away, Henry Chesterfield stood up to speak.

"I am sure that you will all join me in offering sincere condolences to Mrs Margery Tregaron for the tragic loss of her husband," he said. "Perhaps the proceeds of this benefit concert will at least help to relieve the hardship that she must now endure. However, it is really entirely due to one man, a Mr Stanley Soper, that this concert is taking place today–"

Chess was halted be a further barrage of genuine applause, during which time the effeminate barber bowed his head in embarrassment.

Chess's smile subsided at roughly the same rate as the applause, and when the latter had dwindled to silence, he was stoney-faced and grave. "I was about to say that it is entirely due to Mr Stanley Soper that this concert is taking place here today–" he paused... "because he murdered Owen Tregaron."

A shock wave reverberated around the barn.

Chess continued. "Had he not done so, this event would have been over and done with a week or so ago, as scheduled."

Gasps and mumbles emanated from the incredulous crowd.

Again Henry Chesterfield went on, turning towards the poleaxed barber. "If our boys in blue at the door would care to step forward and apprehend the Bishop's castle murderer, then I will be pleased to fill-in the quite singular circumstances surrounding the case."

Max stood open-mouthed at the utterly unexpected turn of events. When he came to his senses, he couldn't help allowing a slight smile to tug at the corners of his mouth as he watched the reporters poised with their pens and realised what an absolutely brilliant publicity extravaganza his friend had engineered.

"Spill the beans, Mr Chesterfield," called one hack. "We're ready and waiting."

Chess waited patiently until Stanley Soper had been led away by the policemen and then launched into his monologue, his clear strong voice holding the audience in rapt attention:

"Stanley Soper looked set to become a wealthy man for the first time in his life up to a few minutes ago," he began. "I confess that, even as a detective, I find it absolutely incredible how far man can be driven by greed. Our murderer was dead against me re-staging this concert, as it would diminish the financial return from his ghastly scheme. He was holding on to the takings from the shows scheduled, not only for Bishop's Castle, but also for Lyndham Heath, Eaton, Plowden and Horderley too. The rogue accidentally let it slip that he was planning to leave the area – doubtless with all the money, and it is there that we have the clear motive for murder – killing Owen Trega-ron ensured that the concerts would be halted, and he was banking on your own good natures to allow him to retain all your ticket monies while he waited for Owen return to the stage – an event that he knew would never happen. Suspicion of any foul play was lifted from him by the fact that the escaped convict, Morley, was at large in the area, and could therefore be blamed for the murder. In fact, I'll wager that it was this that encouraged him to embark on the dreadful business in the first place."

"How did he do it?" piped up one reporter.

Chess exchanged glances with Max and hesitated for a moment. "I can give you those details if you wish," he said, "but be warned, the episode is of a rather macabre nature and I must advise anyone with a nervous disposition to leave now."

He waited.

No one moved.

He shrugged, drew a deep breath and continued. "Stanley Soper killed Owen Tregaron by slitting his throat with a razor from behind, directly after cutting his hair. This fact is re-inforced by my own observations. Margery mentioned that her husband's hair was rather long. However, when I saw Owen's head in death, the hair was cropped short. It was significant."

"Excellent, Mr Chesterfield," a reporter remarked. "But tell us. How come the body was found at Plowden station?"

"I was coming to that," Chess replied solemnly. "Soper conveyed the body in his trap through the darkness to the woods near Plowden. He told me that he travels home after dark this time of year and usually goes via Lydbury North to his home at Edgton. A slight diversion was all that was needed to take him deep into the woods. Woods that he maintained he was petrified of going near for fear of coming face-to-face with Morley. Once there, he stripped the body and hid the clothes nearby before proceeding to cut it up with a combination of his razor and a woodsaw - when I asked for a shave at his salon the other day, he told me that his razor was blunt. Anyway, following this, he dumped the mangled remains into a nearby woodland pool. A pool that we chanced upon during our investigations, but was, by then, empty."

A woman near the back of the hall retched and was helped outside. Chess waited, unsure of whether to continue. However, eyeing the sea of expectant faces before him, he realised that he had no choice and spoke again in a matter-of-fact voice devoid of any emotion or feeling.

"The body decomposed somewhat over the next few days before Soper returned one night in his trap to complete the abomination, having stolen the Edgton farm milk churns which were awaiting collection at Plowden station, and brought them to the pool. Once there, he dragged the water of all the mortal remains, poured the unwanted milk into the pool then filled the churns with the body parts. All was going well until he checked to see if the clothes were still hidden nearby and found them missing. Paradoxically, their removal actually assisted in Soper's plan as it turned out they were found by Morley who used them to replace his conspicuous prison suit. At one point, the convict even considered boarding a train. The engine driver saw him and mistakenly conjectured that it was Owen. I made the same mistake and it was not until I recalled that Margery had told me that Owen was about the same size as Morley that I twigged. If Morley is captured and questioned, then he will no doubt verify my complete story, and incidentally, should one of the constables on duty here like to speak privately with me afterwards, I can reveal the whereabouts of this fellow and clear up another case. But to conclude, Stanley Soper conveyed the milk churns back to the station and placed them exactly where he'd found them earlier, convinced that no-one would suspect him of any involvement in the dreadful business. He should have caught a train there and then and got clean away, taking the concert money with him, it would have made my investigations considerably more difficult and perhaps he may have even pulled the whole thing off. As it was, the affair turned out to be..." Henry Chesterfield paused, "to coin a famous phrase, elementary!"

The reporters finished writing, photographic bulbs flashed and the crowd began chattering excitedly.

"It'll be front page in tomorrow's edition," said one scribe.

"Likewise," said another, rushing to the door.

Chess allowed himself a slight smile, and his moustache twitched.

"I do believe, Mr Chess," said Max, "that we could at last be on our way to success!"

The Mid-Hants Affair

"A Mr Chesterfield and a Mr Shore to see you," said Mrs Hudson, poking her head around the door of the old room of 221b Baker Street.

"Ah, capital," said Sherlock Holmes. "Show them up."

Chess and Max clattered up the stairs and into the room. "It is indeed a pleasure to meet you, Mr Holmes. We came directly we received your letter. You know my colleague, Max?"

"Quite so," came the reply. The great man's inscrutable grey eyes bored, first into Chess, then Max. "Is there anything wrong?" the latter ventured, somewhat gingerly.

Sherlock Holmes considered for a little time and placed his long, spindly fingers in the familiar thoughtful pyramid in front of his ascetic face. "From your point of view, or mine?" came the reply.

"Well, er, ours," said Max, peering at himself.

"Pray forgive me, it is a habit of mine. I notice from your appearance that 'Strides' in Mayfair has finally closed down, and secondly that you were late in leaving for our meeting here. There are several elementary other giveaways, but I shall not bore you with them."

"Jolly simple, all this deduction lark," said Chess haughtily. "You've been in Mayfair on a case lately and seen the chemist in question, and you knew we left late because we were slightly late getting here, 'elementary' I believe you call it."

A brief smile flickered across Sherlock Holmes's gaunt features. "You have much to learn, Mr Chesterfield. I rather feel that your deductions have taken you entirely up the wrong avenue. You are somewhat like Watson. You see, but do not observe. Your accomplice normally wears hair oil, that much is clear from the soiled condition of the inside of the hat that he is holding. However, on this occasion, I notice that the hair is quite dry. As he looks meticulous in all other matters of his toilet, I conjectured that he'd run out of the substance. Knowing where you reside, it is fair to assume that you use the local store, which I know to be 'Strides'. It was therefore a rather straightforward assumption that it had closed down. To reinforce my deductions, I simply drew a connection with the product sale that the aforementioned establishment advertised recently in the newspapers."

"The fact that you were late leaving for Baker Street is evident from your own coiffure, Mr Chesterfield, which, if I may say so, is not in preferred condition, having been rather windblown, due, no doubt to the fact that you have travelled here in an open hansom. Had you been blessed with more time then you would, I do not doubt, in these rather blustery and cold conditions, surely have waited and hailed a covered-in, bow-fronted vehicle instead of jumping in the first public conveyance that came along."

"Excellent," cried Max.

"Elementary," retorted Holmes. "But to business." He gestured Chess to an old wicker chair, and Max to a softer one nearby. "You got the gist of my letter?"

"Yes, Mr Holmes. Something about Elizabeth Clarke, my lady friend."

"Precisely," said Holmes, taking shag from the Persian slipper on the fireplace and preparing his clay pipe. "You are in dangerous waters there, my dear fellow. She is promised to another."

"Promised to another?" Chess repeated incredulously. "Oh, come, come, Mr Holmes. I have known her for several months. She would have said. That's a preposterous notion, and if it's all you brought us here for, then we'll take our leave, guessing about things like that, it's—"

Sherlock Holmes eyed Chess severely and held up his hand for silence. It was difficult to refuse and of Holmes's requests because they were always so exceedingly definite and put forward with such an air of mastery. Consequently, Chess instinctively clammed up, while Holmes took the tongs and lit his pipe with a glowing ember from the flickering fire. Seconds later the familiar blue tobacco swirls that many associated with the celebrated detective, were drifting lazily up to the ceiling.

"Mr Chesterfield," he said slowly and deliberately, eyeing the young detective. "I never guess, it is a shocking habit, entirely destructive to the logical faculty. Is that not so, Watson?"

The doctor nodded and sat himself down on a chair near the bow window. "Quite right," he said as he did so.

Chess shrugged. "Alright," he said with a heavy sigh. "I'm listening. What dangerous waters am I supposed to be floundering in?"

"Elizabeth Clarke is the fiancee of Nathaniel Klinko."

"Klinko?" Chess repeated the curious name. "Never heard of the fellow."

"I do not doubt it for one moment," Holmes replied. "You do not yet possess the experience or ability to move in the same circles as I. Klinko is the head of the most sinister and powerful gang in the whole of England. More dangerous and more ruthless than even the evil web that Moriarty has spun through the criminal world. My current task is to stamp them out before they gain a foothold."

"But surely it's a job for the police?" said Max.

"Psaw!" exploded Holmes. "The police nothing. Lestrade and his blinkered cronies from the Yard would not even believe the existence of such an organisation. No Mr Chesterfield, at this moment I stand alone against their might. I am the only person alive outside the society who knows their plans."

Chess rose to leave. "Well," he said. "Thank you for the warning. I take it that you are suggesting that I do not see Elizabeth any more."

Holmes smiled. "My dear fellow," he said. "Nothing could be further from my mind. On the contrary. I was rather hoping that you would continue with your relationship. Let it blossom and grow. Nurture it."

Chess frowned. "What is all this, Mr Holmes?" he said dropping back into the wicker chair again and leaning forward. "First you tell me that I'm in danger if I carry on seeing a certain young lady, then, in almost the same breath you intimate that I ought to marry her."

"I would never suggest such a drastic step," Holmes said seriously. "I apologise, I rather thought that you would have caught on by now. Mr Chesterfield, I would like you and your partner to work with Doctor Watson and I on this Klinko case."

Chess and Max exchanged surprised glances. "It would indeed be an honour," Chess said after a few moments, "however, I should like to know the facts before I agree," he added.

"Excellent," Holmes replied. "A man quite after my own heart. I will relate them, but must caution you that what you are about to hear is, as you will soon realise, of a very secret nature, and, as such, must not be divulged to anyone outside these four walls."

Chess and Max nodded solemnly and waited for the great detective to begin.

"Klinko's gang have been approached by the Boers who are desperate to prevent British troops from being transported over there to swell the ranks opposing them. Klinko's task is to sabotage all troop movements possible. You will, I'm sure, recall the recent sinking in the channel of the troopship Australasia."

"A tragic accident," Max said shaking his head sadly. "I read the account in the papers."

"It was far from being an accident," Holmes continued. "She did not strike a half-submerged object in the water at all. She was dynamited from underwater. It was calculated and cold-blooded murder by Klinko's gang. The Navy still do not know who was responsible. I do."

"A loss of eight hundred souls," Chess added. "Frightful."

Holmes nodded. "And that is, to coin a phrase, only the tip of the iceberg. Remember the recent gas explosion at the Aldershot barracks in the mess hall?"

Chess nodded. "Klinko again?" he ventured.

"Precisely," replied Holmes. "A clever operation blamed on the new-fangled gas appliances in use there."

"I read that two hundred of our crack infantry lost their lives there," sighed Max shaking his head.

Holmes was grave. "Now you realise the depths to which these people will go," he said, "and the dangerous waters that I mentioned you were getting into, Mr Chesterfield. These men must be stopped. Their interference could cost us the war, not so much through the direct loss of troops, but through the widespread erosion of military morale."

Chess nodded in agreement. "I do understand," he said, "but fail to see how we can do much to assist."

"Tut man!" barked Holmes. "With respect, you really are a dull fellow. Think! Your contact with Elizabeth Clarke! With a little ingenuity you should be able to infiltrate the gang and work undercover."

Chess blistered at Holmes's cutting remarks, and cursed himself for letting the celebrated detective gain the upper hand so much. He had hoped that he could control any situation that may arise out of the dialogue, and had planned to present himself as formidable competition for the great man. Now, his pride bruised and feeling embarrassed and small, he sat in meek silence.

Max scratched his rotund head. "All very fine for Mr Chess," he said, "but how the devil can I help? I hardly think I'm built to go galli-vantin' after some gang of rogues."

"I entirely understand your point of view, and sympathise with your physical condition. However, Mr Shore, your talent lies, if I may say so without offending your colleague, in a more professional and technical area. You are well-versed in railway matters, are you not?"

"Well, yes, but–"

"There are no buts about it, Mr Shore. Klinko and his men are centering their activities around the rail network. The troop trains are their new targets. My investigations have led me to believe that they are planning to strike on the Mid-Hants Railway which, as you have probably seen in the newspapers, is currently carrying large troop convoys from Aldershot to the South Coast. Your technical background will be of the utmost importance in bringing the case to a satisfactory conclusion." He paused, then surveyed the two men before him. "Well?" he continued. "Are you game?"

Henry Chesterfield considered for a little time. "Certainly," he said at length, glancing at Max, who nodded his head in agreement. The fat man looked outwardly confident, but inside, he was wondering what the devil he was letting himself in for.

"Capital!" replied Holmes. "Watson and I have some pressing allied business to carry out here in London, revolving around some young watercress selling aquaintances of ours that we first met in connection with *The Friesland Case. I'd like you to attempt to infiltrate the gang in Hampshire, Mr Chesterfield."

"Mr Shore, I understand that there is currently a position available on the Mid-Hants Railway at Alresford. I would like you to take that. It is a security post which requires the use of a dog. The animal that you call Wilbur B. will, I am sure, make a suitable, if perhaps rather slow candidate."

Chess nodded. "He has proved himself in the past, Mr Holmes," he said, "and I'm sure he will again. But what I don't understand is what the devil the watercress sellers in London have got to do with the affair that you've outlined, aside from the fact that the Mid-Hants is known for carrying watercress, I can see no connection."

"Suffice it to say that I have my reasons," Sherlock Holmes replied. "They will become clear in due course. Now, my dear fellows," he continued, rising from his chair, striding across the sitting room and opening the door. "There is work to be done. Should you become aware of anything suspicious, or learn of any specifics regarding Klinko's diabolical plans, then send a wire and Watson and I will come down directly. And remember, gentlemen, I am relying on you both. It is a matter of the utmost importance."

* *The Friesland Case – chronicled in "Sherlock Holmes Revisited", by Clive Brooks.*

             ★   ★   ★

"What experience have you had in security work, Mr Shore?" The railway official facing Max across the interview table at Alresford station enquired.

"Nothing specifically," the fat man replied. "However, I have had considerable crime fighting experience recently working with Henry Chesterfield."

"The Mayfair detective?" the railwayman enquired.

"The very same," Max replied.

"Then your credibility is no longer in doubt. I read about your celebrated success on the Bishop's Castle Railway. It made front page news in several of the dailies."

Max blushed slightly.

"You've got the job," said the official, his serious face cracking into a genuine smile. "But tell me, why do you want to work here on the Mid-Hants Railway? After all, you must be inundated with crime-solving requests."

Max thought quickly, aware that he must not give the game away. "Um, well, actually I wanted to rediscover my roots," he said rather unconvincingly. "I was on the Great Northern as a ticket inspector and was missing the old iron road."

Luckily, the official seemed pleased with the explanation. "Excellent," he replied. "Well then, Mr Shore. You start tonight at eight."

Max stared across the table in surprise. "Tonight?" he repeated somewhat incredulously.

"That's right. Twelve hour shifts. There's no problem is there?"

Max shook his head. "Uh, of course not," he said, rising to leave. "Tonight at eight then, and thank you."

*　　*　　*

A biting, icy wind whipped through Alresford station, blowing the light drizzle that was just visible in the dim splotches of illumination from the gas lamps on the platform, in stinging needles against Max's face. He positioned himself on the glistening concrete beneath one of the lights and peered at his pocket-watch.

"Eleven thirty, is that all?" he groaned out loud, shifting his gaze to a rather sorrowful-looking Wilbur B, who waited, wet, bedraggled, and a mite confused, at the end of his lead. Max yawned for what must have been the fiftieth time since he came on duty, and began to question why he had allowed himself to be drawn into the scheme. After all, what was he supposed to be doing? Holmes had given no indication of what was likely to happen. "Just take the job," he'd said.

Max was shaken out of his introspective musings by the sound of a locomotive approaching. He glanced lazily up the line and watched as it came into view under the road bridge. Wilbur B. sat at his side, ears back and a look of mild alarm casting itself across his comical features.

Once the train had stopped, Max hooked the hound onto the four-foot railings that separated the platform from the yard behind and clambered into the guard's van to have a few words with the railwayman to check he was having no bother.

"Evenin', how's everything going? Any problems? I'm new here, I–". Suddenly the whole guard's van was whirling around and Max fell to the floor, a sharp pain stabbing at the back of his head...

"Woof, woof," Wilbur B's deep, agitated barking shook Max back awake and he opened his eyes to find himself sprawled on the station platform. He heaved his massive bulk up into a sitting position and, with the rain dripping off of his hair and running in rivers down his face, he surveyed the station which was utterly deserted, save for Wilbur B., who continued to bark from his position near the railings.

Max put a hand up and felt the back of his head that was throbbing with pain. The fact that it was wet was nothing out of the ordinary in the inclement conditions, and it wasn't until he brought his hand back into his line of vision that he realised that the dampness wasn't caused by the rain – but blood.

He scrambled wearily to his feet, staggered over to a lamp and flipped out his pocket-watch for the second time that night. "Alright, Wilb., it's alright," he called across to the worried hound as his eyes focussed on the dial. "Flippin' 'eck!" he gasped. "Three forty-five! I've been out cold for four and a quarter hours."

The fat man unhooked Wilbur B., and the pair made for the shelter of the little station, with Max wondering what he should do – report the attack to the railway authorities, or send a wire to Holmes? After giving the matter due consideration, he decided to do neither, but instead, use his initiative to carry out his own investigation the following night. After all, he thought, there was really very little to report anyway, save that he had been knocked out by someone in a guard's van for no apparent reason.

*   *   *

119

"No, Chessie, I won't care what you do for a living," the brown-eyed girl who was draped enticingly across a luxurious settee in his Park Lane home purred. "You're rich," she said, placing a hand to her face to stifle a giggle. "That's all that matters to me."

Henry Chesterfield strode purposefully across the room and pushed the girl's long, slender legs roughly aside before sitting heavily down beside her to begin his charade. "You wouldn't care then, Elizabeth, if I told you I was a criminal?"

The girl hesitated for a moment. "No," she said firmly.

"Well, consider it told," Chess replied in a harsh tone. "Tough, ruthless and professional. A hired killer, and I'm looking for another job in the old game to pay off some gambling debts, and pay for your sparklers, my little angel," he added, slapping the girl playfully on the side of her face, but with enough force to ensure she felt it. "Your Chessie needs some time to think, Elizabeth, so put those pretty shoes on and beat it."

The girl got up, looking rather startled, to say the least, obviously having never seen this facet of her gentleman friend's character before.

"Are you really a rogue?" she asked quite directly.

Chess groaned to himself. He really liked the girl, and had been seeing her regularly for several months now. This deception was tugging at his heartstrings, and already he was beginning to deeply regret agreeing to assist Sherlock Holmes in his case. He sighed quietly and cultivated an expression of anger. "Are you calling me a liar?" he barked.

Elizabeth shook her head dumbly and pulled on her shoes.

"I don't suppose a kid like you can help me out," Chess continued. "But if you hear of anything going, you be sure you make it known that old Chessie is available, right?"

Before she had time to reply, he grabbed her round the waist and pulled her to him, kissing her roughly on her generous lips before throwing her aside and gesturing towards the door.

When she'd gone, Henry Chesterfield poured himself a stiff whisky and sat down in the easy chair that faced the window overlooking Hyde park. He watched the ebb and flow of peaceful pedestrians parading lazily through the verdant acres. It was when one particularly stout gentleman came into view that his thoughts drifted to Max, and he wondered how his partner was getting on with his side of the affair. Confessing to himself that he was missing his fat friend's companionship in the case already.

*   *   *

Two day's later a telegram arrived at Chess's Mayfair home which he opened over breakfast:

JOB FOR YOU — STOP

BE READY AT TEN — STOP

WE WILL COME FOR YOU — STOP

Henry Chesterfield tossed it down on the table and finished extinguishing his third egg before flipping out his Benson's pocket watch and checking the time. It was approaching ten, and, a few minutes later, having just removed his napkin and withdrawn from the table, there came a sharp rap on the door. He answered it to be met with a short, stocky man with a black beard and dark, sallow skin.

"Come with me," he growled, before turning abruptly on his heels. Chess shrugged and did as he was bid, hoping that he wasn't letting himself in for anything too dangerous, while feeling deep down inside rather depressed that Sherlock Holmes seemed to have been right about Elizabeth being involved with the underworld.

Once out on Park Lane, the fellow walked briskly across to the edge of the thoroughfare to where a rather disreputable Brougham stood.

"In there," barked the small man as he climbed up onto the box and took up the reins in his grubby hands. Again Chess did exactly as he was asked without a word, and climbed aboard, closing the door behind him. Directly he had done so, he knew something was wrong. The interior was in almost total darkness, and he realised that the carriage windows had been painted black. Before his eyes had a chance to become accustomed to the gloom, a blindfold was clapped across them and he became aware of a stench of bad breath a few inches from his face. It smelt like the bottom of a birdcage.

"Right, matey. That'll keep your pryin' peepers out of action."

It was a voice that resembled coarse sandpaper, and Chess couldn't help shuddering slightly at the very sound of it. However, he took a deep breath and tried to make his reply sound hard and bold;

"Where are you taking me?" he said.

"Har har! Wouldn't you like to know," the voice scraped back. "We ain't stupid, mister. 'Til we know if you're sound, we ain't gonna be tellin' you nothin', 'cept that you're gonna meet Mr Klinko."

Chess nodded. "I see," he said, trying to ascertain the direction in which they were travelling. As far as he could make out they were currently rattling south down Park Lane, a fact that was confirmed a few minutes later when they drew up at a junction.

Piccadilly, Chess said to himself. Has to be. He concentrated hard as the Brougham took a right turn onto the main thoroughfare. The sounds of passing hooves and the clatter of carriages invaded his conveyance, but these gradually subsided and Chess realised that they must be heading out of the sprawling metropolis, probably through Knightsbridge and Kensington. However, after that, he found it impossible to ascertain their position with any certainty, and the concentration, plus the movement of the carriage, caused him to fall into a fitful, restless sleep in the airless, smelly cab.

It seemed like an age had passed when, suddenly and unexpectedly, the Brougham came to an abrupt halt, throwing Chess forwards and shaking him awake.

The door was thrown open.

"Bring 'im this way," said a voice that Chess recalled as being the driver's. "And keep the blindfold on 'im," he added.

Henry Chesterfield allowed himself to be led roughly along. Alert and awake now, he strained his senses for any indications of his position. However, without the benefit of sight, it was a thankless task, and all he could be sure of was that he was in a countryside location.

An unexpected stroke of rather painful luck gave him his most comprehensive clue to date. He was being led along what he had taken to be a gravel track, when his companion missed his footing and, cursing his misfortune with a fierce ejaculation of foul-mouthed blasphemy, momentarily let go of Chess, who toppled to the floor, striking his head painfully against something hard and metallic. As he struggled back to his feet, he felt the edge of a block of wood and smiled to himself. It hadn't been a gravel track that he'd been led along, but the side of a railway line, doubtless a stretch of the Mid-Hants if Holmes's deductions were accurate.

"Sit him there, on the floor," a gruff voice bellowed, and Henry Chesterfield was thrust down onto what he took to be floorboards. He sat back against a wall, waiting patiently while someone removed the blindfold from his eyes. After a few seconds, when they had become accustomed to the conditions, he realised that he was in a large, wooden shed, sparsely furnished with what looked like discarded railway items. He looked up at the faces that were staring down at him. There were three of them. One was the black-bearded driver who he had met earlier. Another, with decaying teeth and unkempt mousy hair, he took to be his companion in the Brougham, but it was the third man that made his blood run cold. His expression was entirely blank, and he stood, feet wide apart, just staring down. Chess found himself inexplicably locked in the stare of the menacing fellow, utterly unable to wrench his eyes from the remarkable head.

It was entirely bald, without so much as a single hair on either the scalp or face. Added to that, it exhibited a freshly-scrubbed pink colour. But what was all the more remarkable were the eyes which, sunk deep into recessed sockets, seemed to blaze with a remarkable, almost luminous, ethereal green hue. Distinctly cat-like and highlighted by the fact that there were no eyebrows or lashes whatsoever.

Still the fellow was silent, and flicked up one of his hands to thoughtfully finger a diabolical scar that ran from the outer extremity of his left eye socket, down to the corner of his mouth.

"Good-day," Chess said apprehensively after a time, getting slowly to his feet and extending his right hand towards the frightening individual in greeting. "I'm Chesterfield," he said.

Still the man facing him made no movement whatsoever. Then suddenly, with a lightningly fast flick, he shot his hand from his scar and grabbed Chess's outstretched fingers with a bone-crushing force. Without a word, he squeezed harder and harder until Chess was wincing with the pain of it.

"And I am Klinko," the egg-head said, suddenly letting go and leaving the young detective's hand bruised and throbbing. "Nathaniel Klinko," he went on in a voice as deep and mysterious as the ocean. "Am I to understand that you seek employment?"

Chess nodded, marshalled his senses and recultivated his tough image. "Could be," he said. "What's goin' down?"

"Something major," came the reply. "Clint, take his money, his watch, his identification and any thing else you can find on 'im."

The man with bad teeth stepped forward, grinning disgustingly, and began rifling through Chess's pockets. The detective pushed the unsavoury character roughly aside. "Now wait a minute," he barked. "I ain't made no decisions yet. I've come here of my own free will, put up with bein' blindfolded for bleedin' ages, but I ain't havin' me belongin's taken, least not 'til you tell me what your game is. If you can't do that, I'm gettin' out, right?"

A slight smile tugged at the corners of Klinko's mouth, making his scar tighten. "Perfect," he said. "I like someone who speaks his mind against all odds. Alright, my dear little Elizabeth said she's heard you were good. Very good. I ain't asked how she come to know, but I will. Tell me, Chesterfield. What d'you know about railways?"

Chess shrugged nonchalantly. "A little," he said, secretly thinking how accurate Holmes's initial briefing was turning out to be. He decided to see how much Klinko was willing to reveal about the caper; "you talkin' about robbin', or a big bang?"

Klinko's green eyes bored deeply into Chess. "That," he said, "will become clear soon enough."

"What's the game worth?"

"A few hundred to you, mebbe a thou. if you do the job right."

"And what is the job?"

"To do exactly as I say. Nothin' more, and' nothin' less. This little palace 'ere's our 'eadquarters, an' I don't want no one snoopin' round pokin' their noses into our bizzness. You can prove yerself with the job of look-out. Kids stuff. You keep your beady eyes glued to them windows, an' if anyone comes this way that don't give this sign" - Klinko broke off and lifted his open hand into the air, folding his second finger flat against the palm - "then you blow their bloody 'eads off, no questions asked." He handed Chess a rifle. "We've got bizzness to attend to down the line. You start now, right?"

Chess nodded. "Where are we?" he enquired.

Klinko looked severe. "There ain't no reason for you to be knowin' that," he said. "Jus' do your job." He turned to his partner. "Clint, take 'is belongin's now."

"Why?" Chess protested.

Klinko eyed him with what Chess took to be distrust. "Security," he said. "If you gets your 'ead blown off, we don't want the law drawin' no connections or makin' no traces. Jus' do your job," he repeated. "There'll be some company along soon, my girl, Lizzie. Look after 'er well or else." Chess felt the stab of cold steel as a pistol was thrust into his neck and cocked.

The terrible trio went to the door, and Klinko called back. "No funny business," he growled, slamming it behind him so hard that the whole wooden shed shook.

After they'd been gone a few minutes, Chess picked up the rifle and walked across to the window. Although dusk was falling, he could still distinguish the outline of the trees and the railway line that snaked by. Placing the rifle against the wall, he cupped his hands round his eyes and crushed them against the pane, peering first to the left, then to the right.

Having done the latter, he spied Klinko and his men in the distance, making their way stealthily along the side of the track, the bulls-eye of a dark lantern lighting the way.

His senses were so utterly concentrated on following their progress, being convinced that they were about to set some sort of dreadful death-trap for the trains, that he completely failed to notice the arrival, from the opposite direction, of a familiar face.

"Chessie," purred a soft voice. "It is you, isn't it? Are you alone?"

Henry Chesterfield spun round to see Elizabeth Clarke on the other side of the window making the strange finger-sign. The detective un-bolted the door enthusiastically and let her inside. "He took you on then?" she said. "I thought he would."

Chess was sorely tempted to come straight out and ask the girl about her involvement with Klinko, but he resisted with difficulty.

"Yes," he said. "Piece of cake. Money for old rope."

The girl took off her coat, laid it across a nearby chair, then lay down on a grubby mattress made up of several discarded carriage seats, in the far corner of the spartan room.

Chess remained near the window, staring out into the darkness and trying not to think of the sweet slice of humanity that lay a few feet from him. He was fully aware that if he interfered with the girl that, a few days ago, he had even gone as far as considering marrying, he would lose his life in this back-of-beyond place to the awful rogue that had unexpected-ly come between them.

"Aren't you going to come over here, Chessie?"

The detective ignored her.

"Don't you love me anymore? I did get you the job, like you asked."

Still he ignored her, but with difficulty.

"Chessie, I'm lonely over here."

It was no good. Henry Chesterfield's heart was racing now as he re-called the wonderful times that he'd had with her. He wanted her again, but was torn between lust and self-preservation. He considered for a moment, and decided that it would be most unlikely that Klinko would return just yet, and anyway he reasoned, surely this would be an excel-lent opportunity to quiz Elizabeth about where he was, and what sort of stunt Klinko was planning to pull.

With this thought uppermost in his mind, he groped his way across the dark shed and took the girl in his arms, kissing her without a word. "Ah apassionata," he said softly.

Without even waiting to be asked, she moved back so that she was silhouetted against the moonlight streaming through the window, and began seductively removing her clothes. A deep, monstrous rumbling rose up and subsided once more as a train rushed by outside, oblivious to the sensual display within. When silence reigned once more, Elizabeth was sitting on Chess's lap without a stitch on. The girl gasped with genuine pleasure as Chess kissed her neck and then ran his lips down to her silky-smooth chest, his moustache tickling the soft flesh and making her wiggle sexily...

"Is this Hampshire?" Chess asked when it was all over, and the pair were lying, out of breath, on the mattress, still entwined.

Elizabeth giggled. "No Chessie darling, this is love," she said, pulling herself into a sitting position. "Of course it's Hampshire, Alresford actually. You mean you really don't know?"

Chess shook his head. "No," he said. "They brought me here blind-fold from London. Are they going to blow up the troop trains?"

Elizabeth shrugged. "I don't know," she said, "I've found it best not to ask too many questions, but I've heard something said about the importance of some boxes of watercress, but I'm not sure about-"

The sound of footsteps outside the shed made her break off in horror, and the pair turned their attention to the door. Chess gasped with fear as it opened, and scrabbled in the gloom for his clothes before clambering shakily to his feet, trying to formulate some sort of plausible explanation for his compromising position. As Klinko's menacing egg-head appeared around the woodwork, he knew it was useless and gave up, "I can explain," is all that Chess managed, knowing full well that he couldn't.

His mouth clammed shut as Klinko came towards him, his face as hard as rock. Guessing that the gang-leader probably had a gun, Chess put his hands up in the air in a gesture of surrender. As he did so, his trousers, which he had not had time to secure, slid down to his knees. Simultaneously, Klinko shot his right foot out into a savage kick that slammed into Chess's groin with a sickening force. The young detective arched up in the air and fell screaming in pain to the floor, doubled up. As he writhed there he heard slaps and cries nearby and realised that Elizabeth was taking punishment too.

By now, the other two members of the gang had entered the wooden headquarters and were watching the moonlit proceedings with interest.

"Kill the bastard and be done with it," said one.

Klinko drew himself up to his full height, which was in excess of six feet-four. "No," he said with a cruel smile so wide that it stretched his facial scar until it went white. "We shall have a much more glorious fate for him soon." He looked down at Elizabeth, spat on the floor, then lashed out with his boot. "You, bitch, can kiss goodbye to the land of the livin' too," he bellowed. "I ain't interested in no soiled women. No-one cheats Klinko and gets away with it."

★   ★   ★

Little did Chess know, but help and a pair of friendly faces were, at that very moment, close at hand: Max and Wilbur B. were doing their rounds at Alresford station, the former taking considerable interest in his surroundings, being determined to ferret out anything suspicious that could be associated with his unprovoked attack on the previous evening. Everything looked quite normal as he patrolled the station's goods yard and peered at the large agricultural warehouse that bordered the sidings. Nearby there were several piles of wood awaiting collection, a bundle of newspapers bound for Winchester and several dozen bundles of watercress. Max attempted to move one of these aside to look behind in case anyone was hiding in the shadows beyond, but his nerves got the better of him and he abandoned the idea after struggling to move one of the heavy bundles. Instead, he wandered across to the iron railings and opened the gate onto the platform, just as a troop train came through, southbound on route from Aldershot. The fat man held his breath, convinced that something was about to happen to it as he recalled Holmes's comments, but it soon rattled on out of sight, and Max breathed a sigh of relief.

Satisfied that everything at Alresford station was as it should be, he decided to venture along the side of the track in the direction of Ropley in the hope of stumbling across some clues.

After a walk through a deep chalk cutting, he came out on to somewhat leveller ground, with the lights of the old village of Bishop's Sutton twinkling away through the inky blackness to the south. Here the railway line meandered through cornfields, and Max led Wilbur B. to the fence and shone his storm lantern out across the field towards the watercress beds beyond, recalling how Holmes had mentioned a connection between watercress and the Klinko affair, and wondering if he and

Watson had finished their so-called 'allied business' revolving around the watercress sellers in London.

For a few minutes, he leaned lazily on the fence in thoughtful silence, then, patting the dog who was waiting patiently at his side, he spoke up. "Well," he said out loud. "I don't know about you, Wilb., but I can't see what the flippin' 'eck the connection can be, old fella. I hope your Mr Chess is getting more results than... bloody 'ell!"

Max froze.

He blinked a couple of times to make sure his piggy eyes weren't playing tricks on him, then he peered for a second time along the beam of his lantern.

It was still there.

A body, laying face down in the centre of the nearest watercress bed.

A body that looked very similar in dimensions to that of Henry Chesterfield.

A body that had a head of thick black hair.

"Mr Chess," Max gasped, clambering over the fence, pausing just long enough to secure Wilbur B to a post. "For God's sake no." He hurried across the cornfield and, without a second thought, plunged into the slimy mud of the watercress bed and fought his way towards the figure. It was an agonisingly slow process, and several times he fell headlong into the waters. The lantern, which he had somehow managed to keep dry, still burned, and he shone it towards the form, his eyes peering helplessly at the head that lay face-down before him, certain that the exciting partnership that they had forged was now suddenly at a tragic end. By the time he had reached the body, he was cursing Sherlock Holmes for involving them, and a barrage of unrepeatable language was ringing out over the otherwise silent and deserted landscape.

"Mr Chess," the fat man wailed, his voice breaking into a sob.

It was a further minute – a minute that, to Max, seemed the longest in his entire life – before he managed to reach the form. By now he was soaking wet and covered in smelly, clinging mud, with bits of watercress all over him. However, he thought nothing of his own state as, puffing and panting like a steam engine, he reached down and heaved the lifeless form face-up.

The head was covered in water mould. Water striders and other freshwater insects that had been making themselves at home on the flesh darted away as the beam fell on them. The skin of the face had crinkled in the water, but the deathly expression that returned Max's gaze through unseeing eyes filled Max's heart, not with dread, but with joy. There was no thick moustache and no delicate blue eyes. This wasn't Henry Chesterfield at all, but another dark-haired individual of similar height and build!

After recovering from the shock, Max joyously began searching through the poor fellow's pockets for some means of identification, but there was absolutely nothing. He suddenly realised that he was in full view of the railway line, and that the lantern must be very conspicuous in the middle of the large expanse of flatlands, and to make matters worse, Wilbur B. had taken to baying at the moon that was on the rise in the star-studded sky.

The more Max thought about it, the more he realised that he was in a most compromising position. What reason could he possibly give for being in a watercress bed with a dead body in the middle of the night? Deciding that things could look very black for him indeed, should he be seen, he squelched back towards the line, leaving the body as he'd found it, unhitched Wilbur B., and made off back down the gentle gradient towards Alresford, planning to wire Holmes as soon as possible in the hope that he would come down and shed some light on the curious sequence of events.

It was as he hurried along the trackside, hoping that he wouldn't be spotted in his disgusting condition, that his thoughts returned to his friend, and he began wondering if he had managed to meet Klinko yet. He smiled. At least there wouldn't be any women involved in this case to take his friend's mind off things, he reasoned.

*   *   *

"I don't know how much longer I can bear this, Chessie," sniffed Elizabeth Clarke.

The pair were tied to a support post in the old wooden shed, their hands behind their backs. For almost two days they had been permitted no food and had remained uncomfortably on the floor the whole time, save for brief respites of five minutes each morning and evening for bodily functions.

All the while, Henry Chesterfield had been struggling to free his hands, but all he'd got for his trouble were a couple of deep, red weals on his wrists where the unforgiving rope had severed the skin. He was just as depressed and scared as the girl beside him, but with a concentrated effort, he had made a reasonable job of concealing it, and now, with Klinko and his gang out of the headquarters, he had hatched a plan.

"Elizabeth, let me nuzzle your corset for a few minutes will you? It's important, I've got an idea."

"Don't you ever think of anything else, Chessie," the girl protested. "Can't you put your efforts into getting us out of here?"

"I am," Chess replied. "With respect, whilst your breasts are quite desirable, I don't recall them being quite as pert as your corset would have me believe."

"If my hands were free, I'd smack your face, you-"

"Steady on, I'm just trying to find out what sort of support you're wearing, that's all."

"Whalebone, satisfied?"

"Perfectly, now if you'll excuse me." Henry Chesterfield eased his way around the pillar to the front of the girl and plunged his face into her chest, undoing the buttons on her cotton blouse, one by one, with his teeth, then setting to work on the corset beneath.

"You'd better have a damn good reason for this," Elizabeth blazed as her breasts fell out.

"I have," mumbled Chess, tugging hard at the corset and tearing the fabric with his teeth. A few moments later he had a piece of whalebone in his mouth, which he beat against the wooden post to which the pair were secured. After a considerable effort, the whalebone snapped in two, with both pieces falling to the floor.

"That ought to do it," he said, before proceeding to pick up one of the sections in his mouth. He held it between his teeth, sharp, broken side outwards, and began using it as a saw on Elizabeth's bonds. It was slow, painful work, but he was rewarded as, one by one, the threads that made up the thick rope were cut through until eventually the girl was free.

She got shakily to her feet and rubbed her sore wrists. "Your turn," said Chess, offering up his tied hands towards her.

"I don't know if I can," Elizabeth replied, tugging at the tight knots.

At that moment, the murmur of distant voices filtered through the thin wooden wall. "Bloody Hell," hissed Chess. "Why now? We only needed a couple more minutes." He looked up at the girl who was hovering, unsure of what to do next. "Go, Elizabeth," Chess commanded. "Out the window quickly. Find my friend Maxwell Shore, he's a fat man, probably working somewhere on the line. Make him hotfoot it

130

round here at the double before Klinko knocks the last breath out of me."

Elizabeth didn't need a second telling, and fairly dived through the open window. Chess listened intently as the footsteps receded in the opposite direction to the approaching voices. The door of the shed was thrown open a few moments later, and Henry Chesterfield froze as, first a gun barrel, then Nathaniel Klinko, appeared.

*　　*　　*

Max was waiting patiently with Wilbur B. for the next train to arrive at Itchen Abbas station. Sherlock Holmes had promised that he and Watson would be aboard, and, being the first station down the line from Winchester, all had considered it the ideal meeting place. With the imminent arrival of the eminent detective, Max's spirits were high. He looked at the station clock that showed three forty-five.

"Not long now, Wilb. old fella," he said to the sad-eyed hound that sat patiently at his side, peering gloomily up the track. "Only another quarter of an hour to wait."

The station was deserted that afternoon, save for an old woman with a straw hat who sat knitting on one of the bench seats, and a bowler-hatted businessman at the other end of the platform who had opened his briefcase and was feeding the swifts that flitted around the eaves with little pieces of bread from his uneaten sandwiches.

Max watched him lazily, revelling in the peace and tranquillity that seemed to envelope the country station, certain that his troubles would soon be over. It was as he watched that, in the distance, along the side of the track, he caught sight of a figure rushing headlong towards the station. The fat man squinted against the low, wintery sun and peered down the line. As the figure came closer, he realised that it was a woman, and a most attractive one at that.

She continued to make her way towards the station looking terribly dishevelled and clearly racked with pain and fatigue. Max's first thought was that she'd been accosted, as he noticed the appearance of her blouse, which was half undone. He walked smartly along the station platform towards her, dragging a less-than-keen Wilbur B. along behind. However, before he could reach her, there came a commotion on the road outside, and a battered brougham with blackened windows, drawn by a particularly mangy-looking horse rattled up and pulled to a halt in a cloud of dust. The driver leaped down from his box, rushed onto the platform and went hurrying off towards the girl who he manhandled back to the carriage.

For a moment Max was unsure of what to do and simply watched the action that was unfolding in front of him, too startled to move. It was a sudden flash of recognition as the girl was hauled past him that galvanised him into action. "Elizabeth Clarke!" he exclaimed. "Mr Chess's girlfriend." He had only seen the woman once, and only then for short time, but he was certain that it was her. He ran through the station entrance, meaning to apprehend the black-bearded abductor, but he was too late. All that remained when he got outside was a cloud of dust where the brougham had been. The vehicle itself was hurtling up the road at a considerable lick.

The sound of an approaching train caught Max's attention, and he wandered back in a daze towards the platform. A few moments later Holmes and Watson were beside him.

"It is indeed a pleasure to renew our aquaintance, Mr Shore," said the former. "Pray, give me the description of the person that you have been chasing up the road."

Max stared open-mouthed. "I've heard talk of your abilities, Mr Holmes," he said, "but I never expected you being a mind reader, that's for sure. How did you know I'd been chasing anyone?"

"I am not a mind reader, Mr Shore. It is elementary deduction, but it is easier to know it than to explain it. However, I shall try to furnish you with a few simple facts. I notice that there are beads of perspiration on your brow. As the weather, whilst sunny, is hardly warm at this time of year, I conjectured that you had embarked on some physical exertion. From your appearance, it is evident that you do not make a habit of taking exercise for its own sake. And then there are your shoes. They are covered in dust of a similar sort to that which I perceive, by looking through the station entrance, to be covering the road outside. A man walking at normal pace would not kick up the substance around his feet. A man who was running, most certainly would."

"Brilliant!" said the fat man. "I feel better already with you both here. You are right of course, Mr Holmes. I've just witnessed a young lady being abducted. Ran towards me up the track she did, then a chap came rushing into the station, grabbed her and took her off in an old brougham afore I could get a word in edgeways." Max hesitated.

Sherlock Holmes narrowed his eyes. "The facts," he barked. "The full facts, Mr Shore, if you please."

"I reckon you'll think I'm a fool for sayin' it," Max continued apprehensively, "but I had a feeling that the girl was Elizabeth Clarke, Mr Chess's girlfriend."

"And Nathaniel Klinko's fiancee," Holmes added. "Come, Watson," he said striding purposefully out of the station and proceeding to examine the ground outside. "The game is very much afoot."

Max bustled along, keen to assist in any investigation. He pointed to the approximate spot where the brougham had been standing. "The tracks are here, Mr Holmes," he said pointing into the soft earth. "Perhaps we could follow them."

Sherlock Holmes's expression was pained. "You really are doing remarkably badly all round, Mr Shore," he said. "First you allow yourself to be slugged in the middle of the night, then you let a key figure in the case slip through your fingers, and now you bungle over the tracks."

Max blistered. "What do you mean bungle," he blazed angrily. "They're here, as clear as day, look."

"My dear, Max, the marks that you are alluding to are bicycle tracks. I am familiar with forty-nine different impressions left by tyres. This you will perceive, is a Dunlop, with a patch on the outer cover, and these," he said, pointing to another nearby set, "are Palmers. They always leave longitudinal stripes. All you have managed to do successfully so far is chance upon a body, for which I must congratulate you."

Holmes bent into a half-crouch and scoured the road. After a few moments, he jumped up. "These," he said pointing a long, bony finger to the floor, "are the tracks left by the brougham. See the hoof marks between the two?"

Max nodded sheepishly. "Yes," he said. "Sorry, I was just trying to help."

"And failing most completely," said Holmes hurrying off up the road. "But no matter, we are on the scent now."

Doctor Watson walked up to Max and patted him on the shoulder. "Don't take it to heart," he said in an undertone. "He's always like this."

The pair, with Wilbur B., followed the great detective silently and dutifully for about five minutes. Holmes's eyes had kindled, and a slight flush had sprang to his thin cheeks as he hurried along. His face was fixed with the red indian composure that had made so many regard him as more of a machine than a man.

Max, who was bringing up the rear, puffed and panted, but through it, his senses tingled with excitement at being a party to an investigation by Holmes, the great master, feeling considerably more confident now that he was, at last, nearby.

After walking about two miles, Holmes stopped. "Alresford, I believe," he said, pointing to a cluster of houses before them.

"How the deuce do we find out where the carriage went?" Doctor Watson enquired of his friend. "There must be hundreds of tracks down there, Holmes."

"We use our good friend Mr Shore's observations to bring about our result. You say that you located a body in the watercress beds on the far side of the town, correct?"

Max nodded. "On the line to Ropley," he said between puffs.

"Excellent, then it is in that area that we will look. I should be most surprised if the two events are not connected."

The men walked on in a silence, which was, after five minutes or so, broken by Holmes. "I have decided," he said, "not to preserve my rule, in this case, of keeping the facts of the case under wraps until the outcome, but to relate them to you, Mr Shore, in the faint hope that you may be able to shed some light into a few shady nooks and crannies of the affair that are still troubling me somewhat. But first, tell me, on your second night's duty at Alresford station, was there anything out of place? Anything different from the night before?"

The fat man scratched his rotund head and considered. "Nothing to speak of," he said. "Course, there were different goods in the yard, but—"

"What different goods?" Holmes interrupted.

"Cartons of watercress," Max answered, a little surprised at his companion's interest in the matter. "There's nothing odd about that is there?" he added. "I had a good look around but there was nothing else, save for a few loads of timber."

"Did you move any of the cartons of watercress?"

"Well, yes and no, that is, I started to, I was going to see if anyone was hiding behind the pile. I was a bit edgy at the time, having been clobbered the night before, but I didn't in the end."

"Why?"

"Well, to tell the truth, I started to pull one aside, but they were bloody heavy, and-"

"Weight, Watson. That is the key to the whole affair!"

Doctor Watson looked askance at his friend. "I'm sorry, Holmes," he said. "I confess I don't follow."

"Tut, tut, friend. Shake yourself awake. Watercress is not heavy, is it?"

Watson blistered with annoyance at not seeing the obvious, but no-one was more embarrassed than Max. Holmes rounded on him next: "I am rather surprised that you, Mr Shore, did not draw any conclusions from your find. I would have thought it obvious what the boxes contained."

Max shrugged. "Obvious to you perhaps," he said. "You're forgetting that you haven't given me the low-down on the details of the affair yet."

"I am well aware of that," retorted Holmes, beginning to lose his patience, "but I have explained that Klinko and his men are planning to blow-up the troop trains. Dynamite sticks are heavy. It is an elementary connection to draw."

Suddenly it all became clear, and Max cursed himself for not investigating further the other night. "Are you certain, Mr Holmes," he ventured, "I mean REALLY certain?"

"I would not say it if I were not," came the reply. "It is borne out by the investigations that Watson and I conducted in London on behalf of a pair of watercress seller girls who we first met on an affair that Watson chronicled as The Friesland Case. They visited us recently at 221b to report a spate of complaints from their customers, many of which had fallen ill and blamed their conditions on the cress. When we looked into the matter, we found that many of the bunches being sold were impregnated with cordite, our investigations at Covent Garden market indicated a potentially explosive situation. The London shipment originated here at Alresford. Your comment about the weight of the aforementioned boxes rather confirms it, don't you think?"

"It does look that way," said Max, "but what I don't understand is where the dynamite had gone when the cress reached London, and why it's been put into the boxes at all."

Sherlock Holmes held up his hand to stem Max's flow of dialogue. "One question at a time. Your queries come at me like bullets, but no matter, you shall have your explanations."

"If we cared to look, we would certainly find that a local watercress farmer has been engaged in a lucrative dynamite smuggling deal with some despicable rogue."

"A watercress farmer?" Max said. "Why wouldn't Klinko get the dynamite himself?"

"He is a very cautious and astute man. By distancing himself from such dealings, he can remain one step ahead of me. I would not have drawn any connections had our watercress-sellers in London not chanced to contact me regarding the contamination – a point both the farmer and Klinko didn't bargain for."

"So the farmer hid the dynamite in the cress and simply delivered it to the station in the normal way, by cart?" said Max.

"Exactly," replied Holmes, "Klinko arranged to intercept the watercress cartons at the station as planned, rifling the cress under cover of darkness, removing the dynamite, then letting the contaminated cress go on its way first thing in the morning. But there will be no more such shipments now."

"How can you be certain of that, Holmes?" asked Watson.

"Our friend here said he found a body in the watercress fields. Doubtless that of the farmer involved in the smuggling operation. When the time had come for the pay-off, Klinko promptly drowned the chap to silence him."

"I'm beginning to see why I was slugged the other night," said Max.

Holmes smiled. "Precisely. The last thing Klinko wanted was a security guard hanging around when he and his men went in for the dynamite pick-ups. Frankly you were exceedingly fortunate that you were not killed. Klinko has men in the most unexpected places."

Max swallowed hard, the thought just didn't bear thinking about. He gestured towards the town that stretched out before them. "I suppose Klinko is based somewhere in that lot now," he said haphazardly. "I'm blowed if we're going to be able to find him."

"My dear Max, it really is quite a simple matter. If Klinko wishes to strike the troop trains, then he will need to hole up near the railway line. It is further quite clear that his headquarters must lie somewhere along the line between Ropley and Alresford."

"How the deuce do you work that one out?" enquired Watson.

"Elementary deduction, my dear fellow. The troop trains travel from the Alton end of the Mid-Hants line, through Winchester Junction at the other, down to the port of Southampton. You told me, Mr Shore, that the body you found was in Watercress beds between Ropley and Alresford, which indicates to me that Klinko must be based in a nearby area. Further to this, and bearing in mind that the dynamite had to be concealed in the watercress before the pick-up at Alresford station, it is clear that it would have been dropped off at the closest station down the line - and the one nearest the watercress beds – Ropley."

"So simple when you explain it like that," said Max in admiration, "and you think that Mr Chess is with the gang in this trackside head-quarters?" he continued.

"I sincerely hope so," replied Holmes. "His was a simple task. I should be most surprised if he has not become a valued member of Klinko's team by now."

*   *   *

"A few more hours, Chesterfield, then that's it f'you," Klinko's deep voice boomed out across the wooden shed. "And you an' all," he bellowed, giving Elizabeth a sharp, stinging slap, full across her tear-stained face. The girl bit her lip, but more tears still came. She'd been brought back into the shed after her recapture, putting Chess's spirits at a dreadfully low ebb.

"Did you contact Max?" he enquired in a cautious whisper as the two sat, lashed together, on the floor. She shook her head sadly.

"Couldn't," she sniffed. "They caught me too quick."

Realisation that they were doomed to death struck on Chess's soul like a hammer blow. Elizabeth saw his face drop. "It's the end for us, isn't it?" she said, "and it's all my fault."

Henry Chesterfield said nothing, but the scared look in his delicate blue eyes conveyed more than words ever could. Not only had he condemned both of them to death, but he'd also failed most entirely to carry out the task Holmes had set, and soon hundreds of British troops would be dead. Added to that, he figured that he would now be remembered, not as a great detective in the Holmes mould, but as a dismal failure.

"Keep your traps shut or we'll tape your gobs up," growled one of Klinko's men, lashing out viciously with his boot and catching Chess in the kidneys. He winced with pain. Klinko laughed, a horrible gravelley laugh that struck fear into both of the helpless prisoners.

"Get the fireworks, Clint," he said. "Let's show this Chesterfield fella just what's comin' to 'im."

The mousy-haired assistant went to the back of the shed and fished inside a wooden box, withdrawing a stick of dynamite which he tossed casually across the room to Klinko.

"This is where you get it for what you did," Klinko blazed, thrusting the stick roughly between Chess's legs.

The young detective quivered with fear, and a sweat broke out across his brow as Klinko proceeded to light a match and bring it close to the fuse. Chess found himself shaking so much that the stick that was standing erect wobbled back and forwards as he scrabbled unsuccessfully to get away.

Again Klinko's laugh filled the room. "You won't be ballin' no more women," he said.

Chess closed his eyes and waited.

Nothing happened, and when he re-opened them, Klinko had blown out the match, and he and his fellows had their hands up to their faces suppressing their laughter.

"I'll let you stew a bit longer yet," Klinko said savagely. "You'll go up to heaven with them British troops on the next train through here. Maybe we'll meet up there sometime, you an' me?"

"I doubt it," Muttered Elizabeth under her breath. "I doubt it very much."

*   *   *

Wilbur B., along with Max, Watson and Holmes, hurried tirelessly through the gathering dusk, along the edge of the railway line between Alresford and Ropley. Holmes was entirely transformed from the logician that Max had heard of at Baker Street. He was hot on the scent now, and his nostrils dilated and the sinews stood out like whipcord on his neck as he hurried along, his inscrutable grey eyes darting this way and that.

Through the lips that were drawn into a thin line, there came the occasional hiss of triumph and grunt of disappointment. "We are at close grips," he said suddenly, drawing himself up to his full height. "Mr Shore, I would be most grateful for the use of the scent hound that you are looking after."

"Certainly," said Max, passing Wilbur's lead to the detective. He was about to add that it was rather unlikely that the basset would co-operate, but before he could do so, the dog put its nose to the ground and strained hard at the leash, keen for the off.

"Capital!" said Holmes, "quite another Toby, eh, Watson?"

Max frowned.

"A dog we borrowed for an earlier case," Watson explained.

Wilbur B. scrambled enthusiastically along the deep, chalky railway cutting. "Find your master. Good boy. That's it, where's he gone?" Sherlock Holmes kept the hound encouraged and moving at quite a lick. Even when a stray cat crossed their path, the basset didn't balk, and Max marvelled at the dog's sudden tenacity, which he hadn't seen the like of since the affair with the Jacquelle jewels down in Southampton a long while back, when the dog had been led by a particularly heady perfume.

By now the dusk had advanced to such a point that almost all the colour had drained from the clear skies, and one or two stars had begun twinkling here and there in the heavens. It was as Max gazed upwards at them that Wilbur suddenly stopped. Holmes came to a halt too, and Max, not noticing, cannoned his huge belly into him, almost knocking the detective off his feet. "Sorry," he gasped, using the unexpected break to get his breath back.

The dog seemed unsure of which way to go, and stood panting heavily at the start of a point where two paths met at a junction a few hundred yards past Ropley station. Holmes surveyed the right-hand path with interest, lighting his dark lantern and, by its tiny beam, examining the foliage minutely. "Very recent damage," he said indicating a thin branch that had been snapped off and was hanging by a thread. "The leaves still live. If this had been broken more than a day or so ago, then they would have withered by now."

He turned his attention to the ground in front of the trio. Wilbur B. was sniffing it keenly, but still seemed unsure of what to do. His tail, which had previously been wagging nineteen-to-the-dozen and standing up like a beacon, its white tip waving excitedly, was now tucked down between his legs.

"He seems to have lost the scent," Max said. "What a blasted nuisance, I'd have thought he'd have been able to finish the job after leading us this far."

"There are a good many conflicting smells here," said Holmes. "He's not trained in this work as he should be, and consequently he is finding it rather difficult. Pray, observe." Holmes pointed to three separate sets of footprints in the soft soil. "Now you see why."

Watson, taking great care not to obliterate the tracks, walked a few yards further on and peered around a bend that doubled back on itself towards the curve of the railway line. There, silhouetted against the fast-fading gold of the skyline, was a large wooden shed. As he surveyed it, the door suddenly opened out and five shadowy figures emerged. The doctor gave a start and turned on his heels, hurrying back to the others. "We've got company," he hissed. "There are people coming out of a shed up ahead, five of them."

Holmes pointed his long, spindly index finger to the thick foliage at the side of the path, and the trio fairly dived through, getting cut to ribbons on briars and being stung by nettles as they did so.

Sherlock Holmes placed his hand round Wilbur's jaws and forced the dog's mouth securely closed, both to stem the loud panting, and to ensure that he didn't bark as the party passed by.

Thirty seconds or so later, the figures to which Watson had alluded came into view. Max let out a sudden gasp and sprang forward before anyone could restrain him.

"Mr Chess," he called as he broke cover.

The quintet looked startled and half-turned as Max crashed through the bushes towards them. The welcome party consisted of Klinko and two of his accomplices who were hauling Chess and Elizabeth, still securely tied at the wrists, along the path.

Without a thought for his own safety, Max blundered into attack on Klinko, managing to slug him in the stomach with a flailing right. The man growled in a combination of pain and anger, and was about to retaliate when Holmes and Watson scrambled out of the undergrowth.

A shot rang out.

Max screamed in pain and fell to his knees on the path, clutching at his stomach.

Klinko rushed his prisoners away into the darkness.

"Mr Shore," called doctor Watson. "Are you alright?"

Max couldn't be certain. A sharp pain was searing his stomach, and his hand, which was grabbing hold of it, seemed ominously damp.

"I-I d-don't know," he replied weakly as the medical man knelt down beside him and examined the wound.

"By heaven you've been lucky!" Watson exclaimed a few minutes later. "The bullet's grazed across your stomach. There's going to be a nasty scar, but it's not a matter of life and death."

Satisfied with his colleague's examination, Holmes rounded on the unfortunate fat man. "You are quite the most awful buffoon," he blazed. "Not only have you given away our existence and position to Klinko, but also you've ruined our chances of preventing the attack on the train. Surprise was our most powerful weapon."

Max, who was wincing in pain and feeling rather sorry for himself, hung his head, creating a super-abundance of surplus flesh which formed itself into a double chin. "S-Sorry," he mumbled, "it's just that... Well, when I saw Mr Chess... I-I just wanted to do something, make amends, that's all."

"Your loyalty to your friend is utterly misplaced on this occasion. Your actions have placed him in considerably more danger than ever. Now that Klinko knows about his involvement with outsiders, I should not be surprised to find Mr Chesterfield with a bullet in his back, half way up this path. Can you walk?"

Max nodded dumbly.

"That is something, I suppose," retorted Holmes. "Then we must continue. If we hurry, we may yet still be in time to prevent the troop train being blown, and also to save your colleague."

*   *   *

"In there," said one of Klinko's men, ripping the cupboard and drawer out of a particularly capacious elm, baker's hand-vehicle that was standing, dilapidated and unwanted, at the rear of Ropley station. Chess and Elizabeth were shoved roughly inside, the door slammed shut behind them and the bolt shot.

Elizabeth was whimpering but, on this occasion, Henry Chesterfield was in no mood to console her. He had heard the earlier gunshot and seen Max fall and was now desperately worried that his fat friend could, at that very moment be dying alone on that path. He beat with all his force on the mahogany panels of the covered cart, but to no avail.

Outside on the line, Klinko and his men were busy with several discarded railway sleepers which they were heaving across the track.

"That should do it. Got the dynamite ready?" Nat Klinko spat the words savagely out of the corner of his mouth.

His black-bearded accomplice nodded. "All set, boss," he said in his gravelly voice.

In the distance, the sound of an approaching locomotive broke the silence of the night.

A smile flickered across Klinko's savage face as the train rumbled onwards, oblivious to the obstruction.

Inside the delivery cart, Chess, too, had heard the train as he sat with the girl waiting to learn of his fate.

"If only I'd spoken to your friend when I escaped," the latter wailed.

Chess said nothing. He sat in silence, straining his ears for clues as to what was transpiring outside. All that he could be sure of was that the train was coming to a halt - a terrible, screeching, sudden halt!

Splinters of wood cannoned through the air as the locomotive slammed into the sleepers across the line. The spectacle was watched gleefully by Klinko and his two henchmen who were, by now, well hidden in the trees at the trackside. As the train came to a halt, the driver began clambering down from the footplate. As he did so, Klinko sent a dagger spinning through the air, its blade glinting in the steely moonlight as it travelled, straight and true, to land with a sickening, dull thud in the engine driver's back. He fell, silent and lifeless, to the rails. One of Klinko's men heaved him away after pulling off his cap.

"Everything alright, driver?" called a voice from the rear of the train.

"No problem," Klinko's man called back. "Branch has come down across the line. We'll be on our way in a couple of minutes."

"Do you want some of the troops up to help you move it?"

"Nah, let 'em sleep, conserve their energy, I'll do it."

With that, the guard shut his door and waited for the journey to resume. Klinko, however, had other ideas and, keeping to the shadows, hurried up the side of the train and burst into the guard's van, a leather belt from his trousers gripped so tightly in his hands that his knuckles were white. A few minutes later, another body lay in the foliage at the side of the line, the life strangled from it.

"Get Chesterfield and the girl," Klinko growled. "Chuck 'em in here, an' gag 'em well first, mind."

Clint did as he was bid and, with handkerchiefs tied securely around their mouths, and their hands bound with ropes, the two prisoners were hauled roughly along the trackside and bundled aboard the guard's van.

As they were manhandled past the carriages, Chess caught sight of

Klinko thrusting sticks of dynamite into every available nook and cranny underneath the carriages. "Don't worry," he said quietly as Chess passed him. "I've saved some for you."

Nathaniel Klinko was as good as his word, and once Chess and Elizabeth were aboard, he entered the van with a wooden box full of dynamite sticks. Chess watched helplessly as he set a long fuse and placed the box between his legs.

Up front, Clint, flashing his decaying smile, got the locomotive going and the train began to move forwards once more.

"Have a nice trip," Klinko said to his prisoners, lighting the fuse, then turning and jumping from the train.

It crackled and fizzled away, throwing a garish illumination across the guard's van.

Elizabeth mumbled some indistinct prayer through her gag, while Chess squirmed around trying to snub out the deadly sparkler, his eyes fixed on its relentless progress towards the wooden box between his legs, aware that, once it had blown up the other sticks in the box and put and end to both his and Elizabeth's lives, it would start a chain reaction with the sticks that Klinko had placed under the carriages, and the two hundred or so troops travelling on the train would suffer the same fate.

As the train began to gather speed down the incline towards Alresford, Clint leaped from the footplate, cackling excitedly as the doomed engine lumbered on.

★   ★   ★

"Holmes!" Watson gasped, pointing towards the track, "We've missed it. The troop train, look. There it goes."

The pair, together with Max and Wilbur B, hurried to the trackside. "We must alert the driver to possible danger," called Holmes as the train approached. He pulled out his white handkerchief and began waving it frantically in front of the locomotive.

Still it came on.

"Why the deuce doesn't he stop?" cried Watson.

With the train only yards from Holmes's thin frame, he was forced to leap clear of its path. "There's your answer, Watson," he shouted above the noise as the train steamed past. "There's no driver. I'll wager that Klinko has already done his work. Max, how do we stop the-"

Sherlock Holmes broke off in surprise. Max was not at his side. The corpulent character was hanging from the footplate of the speeding locomotive, his body dragging painfully along the sleepers as he struggled to haul himself up into the cab of the runaway train.

"He's not going to make it," remarked Watson, as one of Max's fat hands lost their grip. Holmes darted along the trackside shouting words of encouragement to Max who, spurred on by the shouts, managed to scramble aboard, wincing with pain from his stomach wound.

For the second time in as many miles, the train ground to a shuddering halt. As it did so, Holmes began battering on the doors of the carriages with his fists. "Get off, quickly. Off. Off. The train is dynamited. Run for your lives!"

Watson took up the initiative and did likewise, and even Wilbur B. seemed to understand the gravity of the situation, and gave out a series of deep, melodious barks.

A few moments later, the track was swarming with activity as sleepy soldiers spewed out of the carriages. Watson watched them, recalling his own military service in the Afghan campaign, but Holmes's attention was elsewhere, and his deep-set, grey eyes were looking over the heads of the army personnel as they scrambled away from the train, to the moonlit fields beyond. There, in the distance, he had made out three figures.

"I am Sherlock Holmes," he bellowed to the nearby soldiers. "Ask no questions now, just do as I say. See that trio over yonder? They must be killed. I will take full responsibility for your actions. Do it. Do it now."

After a few seconds apprehension, the battalion gave chase.

"Three?" said Max struggling down from the footplate and making his way towards Holmes. "But where are Mr Chess and the girl?"

Holmes gestured towards the train. "In there," he said grimly. "Take cover, Mr Shore, you have done more than your fair share to-night. Watson and I will do everything that we can to save your colleague and diffuse the situation."

The Baker Street duo rushed up the side of the train at top speed. "They must be in the guard's van," Holmes called back to Watson, who was having trouble keeping pace with his athletic friend. Sherlock Holmes was a man who seldom took exercise for exercise's sake, looking upon aimless bodily exertion as a waste of energy. However, when there was some professional object to be served, he was absolutely untiring and indefatigable.

They had almost reached the end of the train when the night sky was split by the flash of a huge explosion on the far side of the train. A bright orange fireball rose up and illuminated the track and the fields beyond, highlighting too, the very one-sided battle that was, at that moment, raging in the distance.

As the sound of the explosion died away, the air was filled with gunfire – barks of pistols rang through the trees and tiny flashes of fire, as the weapons spat their deadly cargoes, lit the fields for split seconds, until the cries of three dying men signalled the end, and a deathly silence swept over the scene.

Holmes and Watson exchanged dejected glances. "A few minutes earlier and we'd have been in time," said Holmes.

His grey eyes dimmed for a moment and the veil lifted on his cold and calculating exterior, revealing the great heart as well as the great brain. But then the gaunt features hardened once more, and, with a face as hard as steel, he turned towards Max who was struggling up the line towards him.

"They got Mr Chess," the fat man said in a voice choked with emotion. Tears welled up in his piggy eyes. "I saw the explosion."

The three of them, with Wilbur B., walked helplessly to the end of the train, expecting to see the shattered remains of the guard's van, but it was still intact. Holmes raised an eyebrow as a long, slender leg emerged from the half open door, followed by another thick black hairy one. Seconds later, two familiar faces appeared.

"Mmm gmmfph," said Henry Chesterfield through his gag. Holmes rushed forward, and with the help of Watson, untied Chess and the girl. "That was a close one," said Chess nonchalantly when his gag had been removed.

"Mr Chess... How?" said Max. "How the bloody hell did you do it? I thought you were-"

"So did I," laughed Chess, "It's really all due to Elizabeth here," he said.

"I confess I don't quite follow," said Watson in his inimitable way.

"Oh, it's really quite simple, I whipped off Lizzie's bloomers with my feet, hooked the elastic round the stick of dynamite that had the fuse connected to it, and catapulted the whole shooting-match out through the open door on the far side of the guard's van, con forza."

"Trust you," laughed Max, patting his friend on the shoulder. "No-one else would have had the gall to even consider such a scheme."

Elizabeth blushed a deep crimson.

"You must be cold, my dear," Holmes said, removing his jacket and gallantly putting it around the girl's shoulders.

"It's not that that's cold!" said Chess trying to keep a straight face but failing most completely. "Well, Elizabeth, I don't know why I got you out of the scrape, you'll be the death of me sooner or later, truly you will, if you hadn't tempted me in that shed then we'd—"

"You got me out of it because you love me," Elizabeth interrupted, gazing into the handsome detective's eyes, "and I love you."

"You really have redeemed yourself very well," remarked Holmes, "and saved the train."

But Henry Chesterfield wasn't listening. He had fallen into a most passionate and clinging embrace with Elizabeth. Max groaned loudly, and, together with Holmes and Watson, turned discreetly away.

Only Wilbur B. continued to look at his master, his sad eyes fixed on Chess, and his tail waggling as enthusiastically as the detective's moustache.

"This is a case that I shall certainly chronicle when I have a lull in my medical practice," said Watson. He paused and motioned towards Chess and Elizabeth, who really seemed to have the hots for each other all of a sudden. "However," he continued, "there may be one or two scenes that I shall have to edit out!"

The Signalbox at the Summit

"Whatever possessed me to let you talk me into this?" moaned Max, pulling his coat around him to protect his fat form from the flurries of snow that, whipped up by the icy wind, scurried across the Hawes Junction railway platform. "What do we do now?"

Henry Chesterfield shrugged. "I don't rightly know," he said haphazardly. "I must say, I didn't expect to meet such severe weather up here. Mr and Mrs Clarke didn't say anything about the possibility of it when they invited us up to Carlisle for Christmas. If they had, then I'd have thought twice about dragging all the way up here from London, even though I do admit to missing Elizabeth like mad."

"At least she's put a stop to your amorous encounters," Max said. "Since you've been engaged to her, we've had no such trouble. How far is it to her parent's house from here?"

"Fifty miles or so, at least," came the reply.

"Hmph!" retorted Max, looking back at the locomotive which, up to a few minutes ago, had been issuing forth a thrilling medley of hissing pistons, clanking coupling rods and roaring exhaust as it made its way over the backbone of England and across the lean lands. Now it stood silent on the tracks, a few hundred yards from where Max was standing, little more than a smudge in the mist, completely unable to continue on its journey due to snowdrifts that were blocking the line ahead.

"I suppose I'd better call the Clarke's," Chess said, his eyes traversing the station and coming to rest on the signalbox. The slender telephone wires that emanated from the building had become welded into solid cables of ice that sagged to the ground, dragging down a nearby stout parent pole.

He handed Wilbur B's lead to Max and made off towards the signalbox, whose windows glowed with a comforting golden gaslight. "I hope the damn 'phone works," he called back.

"So do I," muttered Max under his breath, bending down and patting the sad-eyed dog at his side.

"No problem!" said Chess, returning a few minutes later. "A real stroke of luck actually. Mr Clarke apparently knows a chap who lives in a cottage just up the line at a place called Ais Gill. He's some sort of bird photographer by all accounts. Goes by the name of John McCarthy. Mr Clarke's going to give him a ring, chat him up a bit, and persuade him to let us stay at his cottage until the trains can get through to Carlisle. You know, Christmas spirit and all that."

Max nodded. "Well, that's something I suppose," he said. "How do we get to this back-of-beyond place?"

"We walk," came Chess's reply. "I don't think it's all that far by all accounts."

*   *   *

The uncompromising Pennine weather was the small community of Ais Gill's worst enemy. Unbeknown to the trio who trudged wearily towards a cluster of lonely cottages, pockets of snow could often be found in shady places in late June. The small population took most of the vagaries of the weather in their stride, but it was the winters that they really dreaded, when the snows were so heavy and the frosts so severe, that the railway line could be closed for weeks on end, and their exposed homes, could all but disappear under waves of white on the windward side.

The tiny hamlet stood on the lean lands in the distinctive shadow of Wild Boar fell, so named because it was supposedly the place where the last wild boar was killed by one of the Musgrave family. It was a wind-swept and lonely place, over which you could walk all day and never witness another living soul. Here, the summit of the railway was reached, 1,169 feet above sea level, making it the highest main line in England.

It was guarded by a handful of isolated cottages, and it was out of one of these that John McCarthy emerged as the weary travellers arrived. He was a rather weather-worn fellow with light blue eyes and hair like sun-bleached grass. His warmest admirers, if indeed he had any, could hardly claim for him that he was a handsome man. He possessed a high-beaked nose and a prominent chin, and held his head in a birdlike fashion. Birdlike, too, was the pecking motion with which he threw out his words in a high-pitched, sqwalky voice.

"'Bout time too. I was just goin' out to get some shots," he said in a corrosive tone, gesturing in his peculiar birdlike way to the elaborate-looking photographic paraphernalia that he was carrying.

Chess remembered his recent telephone conversation, and recalled that the man was a wildlife photographer, 'birds mainly' he'd been told. Now, standing face-to-face with the fellow, he realised how extraordinarily suited McCarthy was to his work, being almost a bird himself!

"Sorry to have inconvenienced you," Chess said apologetically. "We came as quick as we could. It's rather hard-going back there."

"Quite, quite," came the reply.

Chess peered into the light blue eyes and was met by a sneer. He read a measure of surly ill-will in them, and reasoning that such malevolence could not be directed against a couple of complete strangers, he began to suspect that, for some reason, his father-in-law-to-be was not as popular a man with McCarthy as he'd had him believe on the telephone. Chess decided to clear the air and quiz him on the matter. "I understand that we have a mutual friend," he began. "A Mr Clarke from Carlisle."

"Friend?" exploded McCarthy in a loud sqwalk. "Hardly a friend. He's been tryin' to get me to sell this here cottage for the last six flamin' months. Wants it for a weekend retreat he says. I ain't havin' none of it. I told him to go to hell. Then he phones up out of the blue, askin' me to get you blokes out of a tight spot. Well, normally I'd have told him where to get off, he's such a..." He broke off, sighed, and then continued in a warmer tone. "Oh, hang it all, it's Christmas isn't it. You can't be wandrin' old Wild Boar in weather like this, you'll catch your deaths. You best come along inside."

"Thank you," said Chess, his voice tinged with relief. "That really is most kind. I do have some money with me, and I'd be more than glad to—"

McCarthy held a hand up. "I'll hear none of that," he said as he ushered the tired trio inside. "Perhaps me doin' you folks this little favour'll get Clarke of me back once and for all."

The room that Chess and Max found themselves in was sparsely furnished, yet exhibited a comforting homely ambience, especially noticeable following the harshness of the exterior conditions. A welcoming fire burned in the small, brick grate, and the flickering flames cast strange shadows of birds on the walls. Chess frowned on noticing this, and instinctively looked up to find an array of stuffed birds on twine, affixed to the stout oak ceiling beams. There were six creatures, each turning in the warm convecting air, as if still possessing the gift of flight.

"I'll get you something to eat and drink," McCarthy said. "Best be having something warm inside of you."

"But what about your photography? We certainly wouldn't wish to hold you up," said Chess.

"Tomorrow'll be another day," McCarthy replied, his weather-beaten face cracking into a lop-sided smile. "You make yourselves comfy and take the weight off your feet, you'll be goin' out again soon."

"Out?" Max couldn't help himself. "I -uh- thought you said we could stay here?"

McCarthy sqwalked with laughter. "That you can, that you can, but 'tis a few days from Christmas now, and it's my turn to do the carol singing 'round here tonight. You be any good at singing?"

Chess smiled. "As a matter of fact we are," he said, giving Max a sideways glance and recalling how well he had performed in the Bishop's Castle choir concert during one of their earlier escapades.

"Grand," said McCarthy. "We'll do the rounds later on. Have to be at about elevenish tonight, I'll be out until then."

*　*　*

"This is the Cowley's cottage," McCarthy said as they arrived outside. "Tom's the signalman just up the line, his missus should be in, though. All ready, then?"

Chess and Max nodded, and John McCarthy rapped on the peeling, blue woodwork of the cottage door.

They began...

"Once in Royal David's City, Stood a lowly cattle shed,"

As the hearty harmony was issued forth, Mrs Hilda Cowley opened the door, and, beaming all over her large, round face, proceeded to join in...

"Where a mother laid her baby, in a manger for his bed, Mary was–"

"Help, someone, help, please, there a body."

The singing stopped abruptly in mid-phrase, and the tiny congregation at the cottage door turned to see a young man, who couldn't have been more than twenty years old, running for all he was worth through the snow towards them. As he came on, gasping for breath, Chess cast his eyes over his attire, and, by the boots and back pack, immediately took him to be a walker. "What do you mean, body? Where?" called Chess. The festive atmosphere had dissolved, and suddenly it seemed very cold once more.

"Over there," said the walker. "I've just come down off Wild Boar Fell, past the signalbox." He paused for breath.

150

"And?" prompted Max.

Mrs Cowley's smile had disappeared now.

"That's where it was," the stranger continued, between gasps. "The body. In the signalbox. Slumped backwards over the levers with a dagger in his chest and a look of absolute terror on his face. Like he'd seen a ghost or something."

"God, it's Tom," said Hilda in a somewhat strange tone of voice. Chess shifted his attention to her and looked into her face.

There were no tears. In fact, there was nothing. The woman's face was utterly blank and expressionless.

Chess exchanged glances with Max, then turned to John McCarthy who had regained the surly look which the pair had witnessed when they had first arrived.

Chess sighed heavily before speaking. "In certain spheres, my colleague and I have a reputation for dealing with murder," he said. "We'll visit the signalbox. Mr McCarthy, I should be most grateful if you would call the police, and also take this young fellow's particulars in case we should need to speak to him again." Then, in an undertone, he added, "and take care of Mrs Cowley, will you."

*   *   *

"I just do not believe it!" exclaimed Max as the pair, along with Wilbur B., trudged through the thick snow towards the Ais Gill signalbox. "It's at times like this that I reckon we're bloody magnetic or something."

Chess frowned.

Max continued, drawing breath through his teeth, and then expelling it in a misty cloud that condensed in the cold atmosphere. He shook his round head in disbelief. "It's like death is drawn to us," he finished.

Chess shrugged. "Maybe it's the other way around," he said. "Anyroad, I must confess to being rather surprised at the reactions of McCarthy and Hilda Cowley. I think that we were more shocked at the ghastly news than they were."

Max nodded but said nothing. He had spotted the signalbox standing out like a beacon in the dark, its windows flickering with yellow gaslight. He was about to rush towards the door, when Henry Chesterfield pulled him back.

151

"Wait," he said in a commanding voice. "We must make an investigation of the surroundings first. There could be clues. For once, we're first on the scene. Nothing's been buggered about with yet, let's take advantage of it."

So saying, Chess began scrutinising the ground in the immediate vicinity of the signalbox, while Max stared up at the illuminated windows, his eyes fixed upon the silhouetted form slumped over the levers. He braced himself to face what he felt might be a rather unpleasant ordeal.

"Curious!" exclaimed Chess after a time.

"What is?"

"The fact that there are no rogue footprints in the snow anywhere near the signalbox. Look!" He pointed to a trail that led down from the fell, but stopped ten yards or so short of the signalbox, then headed off in the direction that they had come. "These are the fell-walker's tracks," Chess said. "Clearly the walking boots he was wearing."

"And these?" enquired Max, pointing to an altogether different set that ran right up to the door.

"I daresay they belong to the victim," Chess replied. "We'll know for certain when we examine his shoes in a moment."

"But no other tracks?" Max said, blowing his cheeks out and considering. "How the hell was the murder carried out then? And why?"

"That," Chess replied, "is what I intend to find out."

So saying, he led the way over the snow-covered railway tracks and up the steep, icy steps to the door.

He grasped the handle.

"Stranger still," he remarked.

"Locked?" enquired Max.

"Locked," confirmed Chess.

"What the deuce is going on?" The fat man directed the question at no-one in particular as his piggy-eyes gazed along the railings that bordered a narrow walkway that almost circumnavigated the box. They came to rest on a section that stood out from the rest as being different. Different because the snow had been scraped from it.

"D'you make anything of that, Mr Chess?" Max enquired of his friend, pointing to his find.

Chess shook his head. "Not really," he said. "High winds probably caused the snow to blow off. Any windows open?"

Max walked around the signalbox trying each in turn. "Nope," he said on completing his task.

"That leaves us with no choice then."

Crash!

Chess put his elbow through the bottom left-hand pane of glass in the door, reached through and unsecured it with a key that had been left in the lock on the inside. A few seconds later, both men, together with a rather excited Wilbur B., were inside the signalbox, and while the dog began sniffing around on the floor, Chess and Max proceeded to examine the body.

It lay balanced, its back on the large levers. A dark red stain had gained a fatal prominence around the heart into which had been plunged a rather ornate dagger. Chess's eyes went to the face. It was convulsed in a look of absolute and utter terror. The sightless eyes bulged wide inside their red-rimmed sockets, and the mouth was wide open with the lips drawn back from the teeth in a soundless death scream.

Max shuddered as Chess took the dead man's hand. "Still warm?" he enquired.

Chess nodded and let the hand fall back. "Must have happened tonight."

"Looks like you were right about the tracks, Mr Chess," Max said, gesturing towards the dead man's shoes. "Same sole pattern as the ones leading up to the door."

"This affair really does seem to be rather singular," Chess said, straightening up. "A real-life locked-room mystery in fact. A lonely signalbox, miles from anywhere, secured from the inside, surrounded by virgin snow. If we can solve this one, Max, then I'm damn sure we'll be able to solve anything."

He stooped down once more and began going through the victim's pockets. After a few moments, he drew himself back up to his full height and turned to Max. "One solitary letter," he said, opening out a piece of paper. His eyes widened as he peered at it. "Whew! Mr Cowley here was certainly in a bit of a tight spot. This is a bank statement, and it's redder than a ripe tomato."

"Are you suggesting suicide?" ventured Max.

Chess chuckled. "That would be an ideal explanation in the circumstances, but no. At least I don't think so, for two reasons. First, you can't fake that expression," he nodded towards the body, "and second, look at this." He turned the bank statement so that Max could see it, and stabbed his finger several times at the figures. "Here," he said, "and here and here. Payments made to an insurance company. Large payments too. Surely most odd, especially in view of the existing serious debts." He folded the piece of paper and pocketed it. "Now then, any more clues?"

"Not that I can see," said Max.

Suddenly Wilbur B. yelped making both men start violently. "Wilbur!" shouted Max in annoyance, "you'll be the death of me," he added, putting his hand to his rapidly beating heart.

"What's up, boy?" said Chess, bending down and patting the dog, who was sitting on the signalbox floor offering up one of his stubby front paws. Chess took it in his hand. "Little trick I taught him when he was a pup," he said with a chuckle. "Shake hands, Wilb.," Chess increased his grip. However, as he did so, the dog yelped again, even louder this time, and Chess pulled his hand away in surprise, only to find that it was slightly bloodied.

"He's cut his paw!" exclaimed Max. "Looks like this is the culprit." The fat man bent down and picked up a length of rusty wire. "Damn silly thing to leave lying around."

"He'll be alright," said Chess, fondling the dog's long, velvety ears. "He'll have to be, we've got work to do."

"Work? What work?"

Chess gestured towards the body. "We can't leave it here for everyone to see, can we?" he said. "Better get the poor chap back to his cottage and his wife, it's the least we can do."

"Hadn't we better leave it for the police?"

Chess looked thoughtfully at the scene. He hesitated for a few moments before replying. "No," he said at length. "We'll tell them all they need to know, come on, let's take him home, it's been one hell of a day."

*   *   *

"She's a very brave woman, Mr Chess," said Max in an undertone, as the pair clattered downstairs in the Cowley's cottage, after placing the body in the bedroom where Hilda was fussing over it. "I'd be consumed with grief," he added, "but she's taking it all in her stride."

Chess nodded in agreement. "Perhaps the ghastly truth hasn't sunk in yet," he said, "or maybe it was something she was expecting all along!"

154

They entered the small sitting room where John McCarthy was seated, stony faced, next to a glittering Christmas tree that now seemed suddenly out of place. "When are the police arriving?" Chess enquired.

"Um, well, they're not – at least they might be, I don't know, I–"

"What do you mean, you don't know? You called them like I asked didn't you?"

"They-They we're engaged. I couldn't get through."

"Didn't you try again?"

McCarthy shook his head. "Er, no, I was busy consoling Hilda."

"Where's that fell-walker chap?"

"Ah yes, he's gone on to Kirkby Stephen. Here's his address, like you asked." McCarthy handed over a piece of paper.

"That's something then," replied Chess, snatching it out of McCarthy's hands. "Where's the 'phone?"

The photographer made a pecking motion with his head, towards the tiny hallway.

"Thank you," said Chess, leaving the sitting room and slamming the door behind him. "Bloody fool," he mumbled under his breath as he dialled the number. It rang three times before it was answered by a rather official-sounding gentleman who announced himself as a member of the local police force.

"My partner and I were travelling over Ais Gill by train, and–"

"Alright," the policeman interjected, "what have you had stolen, sir, and quick now, we're busy here."

Chess was somewhat taken aback. "Nothing," he replied. "No, I'm calling to report a body found in the signalbox up here. A Mr Tom Cowley."

For a moment there was no reply, and Chess found himself listening to the crackles of static that seemed to almost be forming into a recognisable percussive rhythm.

"A body you say?" The policeman's voice suddenly came back, sounding rather shocked. "That's different sir. Very different, and I do beg your pardon, your name is?"

"Chesterfield, Henry Chesterfield. When can you get over here?"

"That's exactly what I was asking myself, sir," came the reply. "You're in a darn remote spot up there on the summit, I can tell you, and with all this weather we've been having, Ais Gill's become all but cut-off from the rest of civilisation round here. Frankly, you're jolly lucky that you've managed to find a 'phone that's working. To be honest, sir,

155

it's going to take days, not hours before we can get through. You sound a sensible fellow, if I may say so. Can I rely on you to cope?"

"Of course you may. In fact, my partner, Mr Shore and I, do have some experience in allied matters. Leave it to us."

"Hmm," came the reply. "I don't have much choice, do I? You just make sure you keep me abreast of any developments, and I'll have some men up there just as soon as it's humanly possible."

Henry Chesterfield replaced the receiver slowly and thoughtfully, then returned to the sitting room. John McCarthy eyed him, looking somewhat embarrassed. "Did you reach them?" he enquired.

Chess nodded. "Yes," he said in a proprietorial voice. "As they can't get through, they have authorised Max and I to take charge of the situation."

McCarthy narrowed his eyes slightly and got up from the chair. "Good," he said stiffly. "If I can be any help, like, you've only got to ask." With that, the photographer strode across the room. "See you back at me cottage," he said, taking his leave.

On hearing the click of the door close behind him, Chess and Max began talking in low voices.

"Do you suspect him?" enquired Max.

"I don't know," came Chess's reply. "Frankly, at this stage, I'm more interested in how the murder was carried out. That signalbox was locked from the inside, and there were no footprints anywhere near, save from the ones we've explained away. I just can't see how it could have been done, can you?"

Max shook his rotund head. "Nope," he said. "This one's fair got me baffled, Mr Chess, truly it has."

Just at that moment, there was the unmistakable sound of footsteps on the stairs, and Hilda Cowley entered the sitting room.

Both men turned to face her. "The police will be here just as soon as they can get through the snow," said Chess. "Max and I want to offer our most sincere condolences with regard to your husband's death, and if there's anything at all that we can do, then please—"

"There is nothing," Hilda replied in a short voice. "What's done is done."

Chess nodded gravely. "Quite true," he said. "However, perhaps we can at least find out who was responsible."

Hilda gave a rather strange look and pursed her lips. "Uh, yes, I suppose so," she said unenthusiastically.

Chess continued gently. "Tell me," he said. "Did your husband always lock himself inside his signalbox?"

Hilda nodded. "Quite often," she replied, "especially after dark. I've walked over there many a time when he's been on duty and had to use my spare key to get in."

"I see," said Chess. "Look, I know you can't feel like answering questions at this terrible time, so I'll make this my last one. It may be a little upsetting, but it's important that I have your thoughts on it all the same. Mrs Cowley, I put it to you. Do you think that your husband may have committed suicide?"

"Oh dear," said Hilda, looking genuinely upset for the first time in the whole affair. She lowered her head and stared down at the floor. "Tom'd have no reason to take his own life. He was happy, far as I know," She looked up again and gathered herself. "Our daughter was about to have her first baby. He was looking forward to that."

"Tragic," Chess said, shaking his head. "I wonder, Mrs Cowley, would you mind if my colleague and I made a search of your cottage? We may be able to find some clues that'll help us investigate your husband's death further."

Hilda frowned. "I'd much rather you didn't, I mean surely there can't be anything here."

"Please," Chess spoke in a persuasive tone. "Do let me be the judge of that."

The woman shrugged. "As you wish," she said. "I'll be in the kitchen if you want me. You won't pull the place apart, will you? I couldn't bear that."

"Of course not," Chess replied, "and we'll be as quick as we can." He turned to Max as Hilda left the room. "We'll start in here," he said, "then nip up to the bedrooms above."

Max smiled. "Doesn't look like we're going to get much assistance from your sleuth-hound," he said, prodding Wilbur B., who had settled himself in front of the fire and fallen fast asleep.

Chess smiled, "probably just as well," he said.

Max raised an eyebrow. "Hilda really is either an entirely unfeeling woman, or she knew that her husband was going to meet his end," he said in a hushed tone. "What are we looking for?"

Chess came across to him, and spoke in a similarly low voice. "I want to try to verify the state of the Cowley's financial affairs," he said. "See if there's any material indication of the debts that were shown on that bank statement."

"I see," replied Max. "Well, there certainly doesn't seem to be much of an air of real poverty about this place. It's not particularly grand, but then again, it hardly indicates destitution either."

Chess nodded. "Let's look around," he said.

It was soon clear that, as far as Chess was concerned, the living room provided no clues, and, while Wilbur B. continued to slumber blissfully in front of the fire, the pair trooped up the wooden stairs to the bedrooms above.

"This is all a bit vague isn't it, Mr Chess?" said Max, as they peeped in at the door of one of the rooms to see the body of Tom Cowley laid at rest on the bed, covered by a blanket. "Really, should we be poking our noses in here at all?"

"I promised the police that I'd do all I could," said Chess. "We mustn't leave any stone unturned. Let's look in there." He nodded towards the other bedroom that led off from the tiny landing. On entering it, it became obvious that it was the spare. It was sparsely furnished with an austere pine chest and a simple bed, nothing more.

The plain, whitewashed walls were unrelieved and cobwebs had gathered in the corners.

"This is more the sort of appearance I would have expected the rest of the house to exhibit in view of that bank statement," said Chess.

"Well," sighed Max, "so much for a search. We've learned bugger-all, and probably upset Hilda into the bargain." He sat himself down on the edge of the bed. Suddenly his fat face creased up in a frown.

"What's up?" Chess enquired.

"Feels lumpy, this bed," said Max, getting to his feet once more and scrutinising the mattress.

On the particular corner on which he had sat it seemed to be somewhat raised. The two amateur detectives exchanged glances, then Chess stepped forward and heaved the bedding up.

"Bloody hell!" exclaimed Max, his piggy-eyes widening to almost double their normal size as he peered underneath. "Banknotes," he gasped, "there must be a good few thousand's worth here."

Chess replaced the bedding and stood in rather stunned disbelief. "Looks like the Cowley's are better off than we thought," he said after a time. "Come on, Max, let's get back downstairs, and not a word about our find."

"Was your search fruitful?" enquired Hilda Cowley, coming

through from the kitchen on hearing the men returning to the ground floor.

"Yes," said Chess carefully, "I do believe it was."

★   ★   ★

Next morning, John McCarthy provided a hearty breakfast for his guests, and, come eight-thirty, Chess and Max were tucking into substantial bowls of steaming hot porridge oats, watched attentively by Wilbur B. who was hoping against hope for any left-overs.

Max finished first, pushed his empty dish aside, and sat back in his chair. "No good hanging 'round me, Wilb.," he said, "it's all gone." The dog seemed to understand this and plodded eagerly around to the other side of the table where McCarthy and Chess were seated, still eating.

"Who else lives up here?" enquired the fat man. "I noticed a few other cottages."

"Well, there's Harold Morton, he's a wicker worker – and getting on a bit," replied McCarthy, "and then there's his young wife, Violet."

"Anyone else?" enquired Chess between mouthfuls.

"There is one other chap," continued McCarthy, "a bit of a strange one, he is. Wouldn't be surprised if he had something to do with the murder, either."

Chess raised his eyebrows, and his moustache twitched on his handsome face. "Really?" he said. "Do go on, what's this fellow's name?"

McCarthy's reply came as something of a surprise to both men. "Count Mehemet Azhar," he announced.

"Blimey, he sounds important," said Max. "What in heaven's name's he doing up in this neck of the woods?"

McCarthy looked grave. "No-one's actually asked him directly," he said darkly, "he's sort of, well - sinister."

"I really ought to meet these other residents," Chess said. "Can you possibly arrange something, perhaps a get-together round here? I'll foot the bill for any beverages and so on."

"Don't see why not," replied McCarthy, "though I doubt if they'll all show up."

"They will if you tell them that I want a word with them about the murder," Chess said. "After all, no-one will want the finger of suspicion to fall upon them for being unco-operative, will they?"

"N-No," came McCarthy's rather unsteady reply. "I suppose not,

I'll fix it for tonight then, shall I?"

Henry Chesterfield nodded solemnly.

*   *   *

That evening when darkness had fallen on the smowbound summit, the complete community of Ais Gill were gathered together in John McCarthy's cottage, taking up every available chair in the tiny sitting room. In addition to McCarthy and Hilda Cowley, there were the three new faces for Chess and Max to meet.

The one that proved to be most startling was that of Count Mehemet Azhar, a tall man with statuesque features, a broad brow, well rounded chain and a curiously dusky complexion. Chess's first thought was that the fellow had the distinct appearance of an Egyptian from some ancient dynasty. The angularity of the shoulders and the narrowness of the hips were alone almost enough to identify him as such, but it was the skin that really held Chess's attention: Over the cheekbones and temple it was glazed and shiny, rather like varnished parchment, but from brow to chin it was cross-hatched with a million delicate wrinkles.

Chess exchanged glances with Max who was also taking an interest in the Count. He followed the direction of the fat man's gaze and noticed that it was held in the stare of a pair of vitreous and strange dark eyes which exhibited a misty, shininess. Chess jerked his head away, aware that he'd been staring too long, and, with a slight shudder, decided that there was something distinctly inhuman about this oddly-titled fellow with the sphinx-like face.

"What's your business here?" Chess enquired casually.

A strong emotion seemed to gather in the deep depths of those eyes, and they rose and deepened. "I look into the unknown," came the singular reply.

"Oh," said Chess, rather taken aback. "I-I see. Well that's – that's most interesting, I'm sure."

Max nodded in agreement. For a moment, he was certain that he had sensed the cozy room with its blazing log fire turn a sudden icy cold. In consequence of this, he began to conjecture that the look of terror on Tom Cowley's face, when they had found him dead in that lonely signalbox, could perhaps have been associated with Azhar. Maybe it was due to some occult manifestation, he reasoned, even going so far as to consider that it could even have been a poltergeist thingummyjigs that was responsible for hurling the dagger.

Henry Chesterfield fought to regain his composure and control over the gathering, before turning his attention towards Harold Morton and his attractive wife, Violet, a pretty, dark-haired girl with a sweet innocent face that could only have been half the age of that of her husband's.

Harold Morton spoke first, "Pleased to meet you, Mr uh-"

"Chesterfield, and this is my friend, Max."

Morton nodded. "I hope that your enforced stay up here is a pleasant one," he said. "It's a good spot normally. We rarely have tragedy like this thrust upon us."

Chess nodded thoughtfully at a pair of old brown eyes that looked up at him from beneath shaggy eyebrows, rather like a couple of scouts from beneath a bush. Harold Morton's figure was clearly the framework of a giant, but now his coat hung in a shocking fashion from a pair of broad and bony shoulders. Chess arrested his gaze to the young woman, and a slight smile tugged at the corners of his mouth as he wondered whether she was responsible for her husband's emancipated appearance. Perhaps she was proving too much for the old boy in bed, Chess considered.

Max noticed the all-too-familiar look on his friend's face, and spoke up quickly. "Jolly awful business," he said, "and just a few days away from Christmas too." He began transferring his gaze slowly from Chess to the floor. However, as he did so, he caught sight of Harold Morton's hands. For a few brief moments, his attention was caught by their unusual appearance and he found himself staring fixedly at a pair of knobbly wrists and excessively long, gnarled hands.

Henry Chesterfield made his was across to the fireplace, shoving a slumbering Wilbur B. aside.

"Ahem."

He cleared his throat and watched as all eyes shifted to him. "Thank you all for coming here at short notice," he began, transferring his weight somewhat uneasily from one foot to the other as Azhar gave him one of his dark, sinister looks. "I'm sure that most of you would like to join me in extending our deepest sympathies to Mrs Hilda Cowley for the tragic loss of her husband. I say most of you, because..." He hesitated. "...Because the murderer is in this room amongst you."

Silence fell.

Silence relieved only by the crackling of the log fire and the distant howling of the wind outside on the lonely Wild Boar fell.

Chess continued, his voice commanding and strong now. "I have spoken to the police, and, owing to the fact that the weather has made it impossible for them to get up here, they have asked me to look into the matter. Without going into detail, suffice it to say that Mr Shore and I have considerable experience in the investigative field. I warn you that we shall stop at nothing to uncover the murderer amongst you. I am sure that we can rely on your full co-operation."

Heads nodded.

All except one.

Count Azhar narrowed his eyes. "You are mistaken, gentlemen," he said. "The murderer is not in this room at all."

"What do you mean?" countered Chess. "If you have relevant information, then reveal it, sir. Pray, where, in your opinion, is our murderer?"

Again, Max had the distinct impression that the room's temperature momentarily dropped a few degrees.

"In the nether regions," Azhar answered mysteriously. "In the great beyond."

Chess cast his eyes around the room, expecting to see sniggering faces behind hands, or at least a few eyebrows raised in surprise. Instead he was met by expressions of deadly earnest. The small assemblage seemed to be hanging on to the Count's every word.

"Ghosts?" Chess said. "Are you seriously suggesting that ghosts are responsible?"

"I would rather term them 'restless souls'," came Azhar's reply. "There are many such spirits on the ancient fell."

Chess wanted to laugh out loud, but the serious looks of the locals, and of Max, prevented him from doing so. Instead he found himself asking for more information. "What restless spirits," he said hesitatingly. "What do you mean?"

Azhar looked Chess straight in the eye and began: "Amongst hills between the fine River Eden and the road not far from here, lie the ruins of Pendragon Castle," said he gravely. "It was built by Utherpendragon himself, father of King Arthur. It overlooks Wild Boar Fell."

"And?" said Chess, "what of these so-called spirits?"

"I suggest that you do not take what I say lightly," Azhar replied. "There is a power up here, an awesome power. Tom Cowley crossed it. Now he is dead."

"Please," Chess interjected. "If you have something to say, do come to the point."

The Count's dark, mysterious eyes burrowed into Chess, and he found himself fidgeting. His moustache quivered somewhat as Azhar continued.

"Hugh de Morville's spirit lies there. He was an owner of the castle in a later century. If you know your history, then you will recall that he was involved in the murder of Thomas a Beckett. They have met once again in the great beyond, and there is a terrible battle raging between them that I have come here to witness."

Chess stole a look around the rest of the room to see everyone, including Max, held spellbound and silently staring at this strange Egyptian-looking Count Mehemet Azhar.

"The battle rages on here, on the lonely fells," the sphinx-like fellow went on in a dark voice. "But I have discovered more since I have been here. The spirit world does not dangle in time spans of a few earth years. It is vast. Souls travel back and forth down the centuries. I have felt the presence of older, much more ancient spirits here, more dangerous and more powerful than any I have witnessed before."

"D-Do we know of these?" enquired Max in a somewhat meek voice that made Chess groan.

The count nodded solemnly. "In Arthurian times, the castle of which I speak was in the possession of Sir Bryan de les Illes. However, Sir Lancelot deprived him of it, and gave it to a brave young knight, nicknamed La Cote Male Tayle. Sir Bryan cannot rest. He still seeths with rage. A terrible rage. A rage so powerful that it is wont to rise up out of the spirit world and touch our own."

Azhar turned to Chess. "So you see, sir. The murderer is not necessarily in this room at all."

The statement was put so strongly and categorically that Chess found it almost believable. However, he immediately forced his mind to concentrate on more down-to-earth matters, and was about to address the assemblage when Max suddenly piped up;

"Let Utherpendragon do what he can,"

"Eden will run where Eden ran,"

He spoke the words with in a far away voice, and turned towards Henry Chesterfield, who raised his eyes in desperation.

"Sorry, Mr Chess," Max said, blushing, "it's just something I remembered from the Arthurian legend when I read the books as a lad."

"Well," said Chess. "I'm sure we'd all like to thank Mr Azhar for that fascinating tale. It certainly would be most interesting if one was in the right frame of mind to receive it. I'll – er – bear it in mind in my investigation, which I must warn you all, may well prove to be a complicated and lengthy one."

"Mr Chesterfield," said Azhar. "I can save you much time and trouble if you so wish. You have only to ask one person a simple question about the murder and you will have all the answers that you desire."

Chess frowned. "Who is this all-knowing person?" he enquired, with more than a little scepticism creeping into his voice.

Azhar's answer startled all of those present.

"Tom Cowley," he said levelly.

"But Tom's dead!" exclaimed Chess.

"Precisely."

"Alright, Count Azhar. This has gone far enough. I must ask you to have a little more respect for Hilda sitting here, she–"

"Mrs Cowley, would you like to talk with your husband one last time?"

The widow looked terrified and said nothing.

"Please, I must insist," interrupted Chess.

Azhar glared at him. "Let us vote, I believe that is the democratic way, is it not?"

Chess stared down at the floor, feeling his anger rise. However, suddenly a thought struck him and he realised that here was a chance for him to spot the murderer. These scared people were hanging onto Azhar's every word. If they did believe that the Count could contact the spirit of Tom Cowley, and that the latter would spill the beans about his death, surely, he reasoned, the murderer would not vote in favour of holding a seance, for fear of being found out. A negative answer to Azhar's suggestion would be a clear indication of the guilty party. Chess looked up, rather excitedly. However, he was met by a complete show of hands. Everybody present, including Max, had voted to hold the seance, and the detective's hopes of an early conclusion to the case were dashed.

"Tomorrow night at eight, in my cottage," said the Count. "And come with open minds." He stood up and breezed out.

*   *   *

"Well," said Max in a low voice, as he and Chess sat up in adjacent

164

beds in the tiny spare room of McCarthy's cottage that night. "What do you make of all this spirit lark?"

Chess could hardly contain himself. "Poppycock!" he growled. "Utter preposterous bloody nonsense. A blind by that infernal Count whatisname to throw me off the scent. I noticed you were taken in though, Max. You swallowed it hook, line and sinker."

Max shrugged. "Sorry Mr Chess," he said apologetically. "It's just that the chap put it over so damn convincingly, and to be frank, we've got little else to go on at this stage, surely?"

Chess thought for a few moments. "I suppose you're right to an extent," he said. "We certainly haven't got anything as glamorous as ghosts as our suspects, but there is the matter of the bank statement and those debts, and then finding all that money in the Cowley's. That doesn't add up, does it."

Max agreed, keen to make amends for his earlier behaviour. "Quite true," he said somewhat over-enthusiastically, "and Mrs Cowley said she had a spare key to the signalbox. I suppose she could have got in there that night and done the dirty deed. That would solve the riddle of the door being locked from the inside."

"True," Chess agreed. "She could also just as well have lent the key to someone else – we'll interview her in due course and ask to see it. However, even that doesn't solve the riddle of the untouched snow all around the murder scene."

Max nodded. "Blimey, I forgot about that. Hey, d'you reckon that piece of wire that Wilbur cut his foot on's got anything to do with it, it's over there on the table."

Chess peered through the flickering candlelight at it. "Perhaps," he said, "but I can't figure out any connection at present, and anyway, it still doesn't alter the fact that there were no footprints anywhere near the box. I haven't entirely ruled out suicide," he added. "That would account for everything – the door locked from the inside, and the virgin snow."

"So would the visitation of an angry spirit," Max pointed out, recalling the look of terror on the victim's face.

"Hmmph!" exclaimed Chess, blowing out the candle and settling down in his bed. "Get some sleep, Max, and mind you don't have nightmares!"

*　　*　　*

Externally, Count Mehemet Azhar's cottage was little different from the others. However, the interior decor was decidedly odd, as it featured imaginative pictures of fairies, animals and allegoric figures of all sorts, which rubbed shoulders with strange white statuettes of what Chess took to be mythical monsters.

"Please be seated," said the Count, gesturing to two remaining chairs around a large round table with an odd-looking heraldic emblem in the centre of it. Chess and Max nodded their greeting to the expectant faces of the rest of the locals and took their places.

The light was subdued, yet sufficient to allow everyone to see each other plainly. "Will you be going into a trance?" Chess asked somewhat jovially.

"Not exactly, Mr Chesterfield," came the serious reply. "However, I am always aware of extreme sleepiness." The Count eyed the gathering from his place at the table, onto which he carefully placed his hands, face down. "Evil thoughts are a danger," he said darkly. "There is much that is bad on the astral plane, bad that we must not bring here."

Tension mounted in the room.

"Now we will begin," said the Count, reaching over and extinguishing the lone light on a nearby table and throwing the room into utter blackness.

"For goodness sake," said Chess, "what's the damn point of sitting in darkness?"

Azhar replied in a pained and impatient tone. "The force with which we deal is a vibration of ether, and so also is light. We have the wires of communication all to ourselves now."

"Hmmph!" Chess replied, completely unconvinced.

Max, on the other hand, felt himself being drawn deeply into the exciting atmosphere, and he sat quietly, staring into the darkness. At first it had seemed utterly pitchy, but now his eyes were becoming accustomed to it, and he could just make out the presence of his fellows, albeit very dimly and vaguely.

"Place your hands on the table." Azhar's command seemed to slice through the darkness. "We now sit and expect."

Chess stared out into the blackness, his senses straining. A clock ticked, and far away, the wind moaned on Wild Boar Fell.

While wondering why the hell he was involving himself in this nonsense, he became aware of some strange sensations. There was an icy cold around his feet, and his hands began to tingle slightly. He frowned as he felt a peculiar glow on his palms and a sudden cold wind on his back. It was so convincing that he craned his head around to see if someone had opened the door, but so far as he could tell, it remained firmly closed.

Next to him, Max had become conscious of a heady feeling of expectancy which seemed almost painful.

A rigid, absolute silence fell on the room. Then suddenly a sound came fast out of the darkness...

Chess made a start, and, for no apparent reason, found himself shaking. He checked his behaviour and listened. It was a low, sibilant sound, which, after a few anxious moments, he realised was the quick, thin breathing of the Count. It came quicker and faster, from between clenched teeth, to end in a loud gasp.

Chess felt himself losing his sense of balance and struggled to try to orientate himself in the darkness, convinced that he was swaying most alarmingly from side to side. It was at that moment that he realised it wasn't he who was moving, but the table that he still had his hands resting on. He peered through the darkness at the Count's outline, certain that the strange fellow was manipulating it himself in some way.

No wonder he insisted on turning off the light, Chess said to himself.

Turning his attention back to the table, he thought that he could feel it throbbing. He screwed up his eyes and shook his head violently to clear his brain, then stared again, dimly aware of an easy swooping motion under his fingers.

The detective was about to reach over and fumble for the light to end the charade, when gasps went up from those around the table as a greenish-yellow luminous vapour began rolling, wreathing and undulating over the centre of the table in dim, glimmering folds, turning and swirling like a cloud of smoke.

"Hilda..."

Chess had had enough. "Who said that?" he barked. "Who spoke. McCarthy, was it you?"

"N-No," came the strangled reply. "I t-think it was the Count."

"It wasn't his voice."

"I am using the organs of your medium," came a strange, deep voice. "While I am here, he is happy in another plane of existence. He has taken my place, as I have taken his."

Chess breathed a heavy sigh. "Alright," he said, "tell us who you are and be done with it."

"I am one who has died, as you will die."

Chess was losing his patience fast. "Poppycock!" he growled.

The cloud still swirled faintly over the table, much duller now, but glowing in Azhar's direction.

Max was petrified. "Mr Chess," he hissed, "for pity's sake don't annoy it."

"Ask how it died," sqwalked McCarthy in his bird-like voice, "go on, before it disappears."

Chess spoke lightly and flippantly. "How did you meet your doom," he chuckled.

"I was murdered."

"Where?"

"Close by."

"Have you been dead long?"

"I cannot reckon time. Our conditions are different."

"How were you murdered?" Chess went on, rather beginning to enjoy the game that he believed he was playing, not with the veil of the eternal, but with Count Azhar across the table...

"A dagger through my heart," answered the voice.

"Who did it?"

Suddenly the swirling green fog faded, and the darkness seemed to grow blacker still. "Hilda, my love," said the voice. "Why?"

At this, Chess threw back his chair in disgust, stumbled to his feet and re-lit the gas. "Enough is enough, Azhar," he blazed.

His moustache twitched involuntarily as he looked round the table at the scared, white faces.

Violet suddenly burst into tears. "It's beastly," she sniffed. "Beastly and horrible." Harold Morton took his long, bony hand from the table and put it round his young wife. She nuzzled her head into his shoulder.

"Mrs Cowley," Chess said, turning his attention to the other woman present, who was shivering uncontrollably. "I am so sorry, really I am. Count Azhar should never have done that. It is quite unforgivable."

"I did nothing," came Azhar's reply. "It was the spirit."

*   *   *

"Blimey, Mr Chess, I was terrified back there, I don't mind admitting," said Max when they were alone in the bedroom of McCarthy's cottage later that night. "That light, and those voices!"

"Pshaw!" exclaimed Chess. "Azhar, if indeed that is his real name, is an intelligent man with a very clear and logical brain, I shall concede that much. However, he is also a master of deception, and probably a member of some magic circle or other if the truth was known."

Max shrugged. "It all seemed pretty convincing to me," he said. "The way that voice sounded."

"Have you not heard of ventriloquism, Max?"

"Yes, but-"

"But nothing," said Chess rather heatedly. "For God's sake pull yourself together. I knew it was a mistake to agree to that blasted seance, really you are so gullible sometimes!"

Max sighed. "I suppose you're right," said the fat man, suddenly feeling rather embarrassed. "Sorry."

Chess smiled. "Let's get some sleep, old friend. We're going to have a difficult day tomorrow."

"We're beginning the questioning?"

Chess nodded.

"May I ask who with?"

"Hilda Cowley of course," came Chess's reply.

*   *   *

"Thank you for taking the time to see us once more," Henry Chesterfield said, as he and Max sat down in Hilda Cowley's sitting room. Wilbur B. settled himself across his master's feet, his appealing eyes fixing themselves on the woman who perched herself on the edge of a chair opposite. "What did you want?" she said enquiringly.

"I've got a few more questions for you, Mrs Cowley, it won't take long."

"All right," came the reply, "but I've told you everything."

Chess nodded, "we'll see," he said. "You told me that you had a spare key to the Ais Gill signalbox that you sometimes used when your husband had locked himself in at night."

Hilda stiffened slightly and nodded.

"I'd like to see that key now," Chess said gravely.

"Oh dear, I, well – you know, I don't rightly know where it is, I–"

"I should be most grateful if you would do your utmost to find it. It is of considerable importance in my investigation into your husband's death."

169

The woman stood up looking flushed and flustered. "Certainly, yes, I'll look now, shall I?" she babbled. "It could be upstairs."

Chess nodded solemnly and then, after she'd gone, shot Max a knowing glance. "I'll lay you twenty-to-one she won't find it," he said. "It's quite clear that she's lent it to someone, and that someone must be the murderer. We should soon have this wrapped up now."

Max nodded excitedly. "Don't forget to ask her about that bank statement we found on the body, though, Mr Chess," he said quietly, "and those insurance premiums on her husband's life."

"Never fear, Max, I – shhh!" Chess had heard Hilda coming back down the stairs. She re-entered the sitting room in a dreadful state.

"I hope it's not TOO important, that key," she said. "I can't find it anywhere, it seems to have disappeared."

"You didn't perhaps lend it to anyone, did you?"

"Oh, heavens no. What would I do that for?"

Chess hesitated before replying.

The tension built up.

"That's what I aim to find out."

"But I didn't lend it. It's lost, simple as that. It was-"

"Mrs Cowley, do you recognise this?" Henry Chesterfield pulled the bank statement out of his coat pocket and held it up for Hilda to see.

"Well of course," she said angrily. "Where did you get that? It's private. I know you're conducting an investigation, but you've no right to go prying into our financial affairs, they've got nothing to do with Tom's death." Hilda reached forward and tried to snatch the piece of paper from Chess's grasp, but he pulled it away.

"That's where you may be quite wrong," he said. "It was found on your husband's body. Your financial affairs could have everything to do with your husband's death. From looking at this, it's quite clear that you have fallen deeply into debt, yet on this statement I notice that large payments, financed by your considerable overdraft facility, have been going to the Highland Life Assurance Company. Bearing in mind that I can verify your answer with a simple 'phone call, tell me, is this a policy taken out on your husband's life?"

Hilda Cowley sank back into her chair and closed her eyes. "Yes," she said quietly.

Chess was grave. "Then I put it to you, madam, that you killed Tom Cowley for the insurance money. What have you got to say to that?"

For the first time since the beginning of the investigation, Hilda Cowley broke down in tears. "It's not true," she pleaded. "Tom told me to do it. Said it was a sensible precaution. He was over fifty and he said that he needed to be sure that I was financially alright if anything happened to him."

Chess frowned. "Have you no ready money in the house?" he asked, remembering the banknotes that they had found under the mattress.

Hilda shook her head.

Chess frowned again, more deeply this time. "From what you've just said, it leads me to suspect that your husband was fearing for his life. Was he?"

Hilda shrugged and dabbed at her eyes. "I don't know," she said. "I just did as he said, and now all this has happened. I know people do kill their partners for the insurance money, but truly, Mr Chesterfield, I never did it. You do believe me, don't you."

"At this moment, I do not know what to believe," Chess replied crisply. "Did your husband have any enemies to speak of?"

"Well, sort of, there was one."

"Pray tell me the name, Mrs Cowley, it may save you from the gallows."

Again the woman broke down, rather uncharacteristically Chess thought. "Count Mehemet Azhar," she said between sobs. "That awful man. How could he suggest at that seance that I killed Tom. Horrid, horrid man."

"Please, Mrs Cowley, I must ask you to get quickly to the point. Why was he an enemy of your late husband?"

"Oh dear," Hilda sniffed. "I'd hoped that this was all over and forgotten, but now it looks like it's going to rear its ugly head all over again." She stopped and took a deep breath before continuing. "It was a while back now," she said. "In a public house in Hawes. Tom was drinking in there by all accounts when the Count walked in. Tom'd had a few by that time. He liked his drink he did, and anyway, he started taunting the Count about his odd appearance and his strange ways. I don't know exactly what was said, but it got very heated and they nearly came to blows. The Count stormed out threatening to put some sort of ancient curse on Tom. We didn't take much notice of it at the time, but now – well – I don't know."

*　　*　　*

"I wish this blasted snow would thaw, Mr Chess," said Max, looking out of the sitting room window of John McCarthy's cottage. "This affair's starting to get a bit too complicated if you ask me. I'll be glad when the police can get through and we can be on our way, what say you?"

Henry Chesterfield frowned. "I don't know," he replied. "Half of me wants to be moving on and half wants to stay and solve the riddle of this murder. It's the challenge I suppose. What I am certain of, though, is that I don't want to spend Christmas here with this bunch of hermits."

"Seconded," said Max, "It'd be bleedin' awful, but there's only a few days to go now. I can't say I'm very hopeful. Still, at least this murder business is giving us something positive to do to while away the hours. It'd be damn boring just sitting here doing nothing." The fat man hesitated..."like we're doing now," he added tentatively. "Isn't there someone we could be interviewing? Something to investigate?"

Chess sighed. "You're right, of course," he replied. "I suppose we are wasting precious time." He flipped out his Benson's pocket watch. "Three-thirty," he remarked. "It'll be dark up here in an hour or so this time of year. I vote we snoop around on Wild Boar Fell tonight and see whether we can find any clues."

"It'll be cold as charity up there. Surely we'd have more chance of seeing things in daylight?"

Chess nodded. "Quite probably," he said, "but I'd rather go under-cover of darkness so that no-one sees us doing it. We don't want to arouse suspicion. If we miss the clues first time in the daylight, and someone sees us doing it, you can bet your life that they'll bugger things around so we never find anything. On the other hand, if no-one knows we're poking around up there, and there is something..."

"Whatever you say, Mr Chess. Though I can't for the life of me think what we're looking for."

"An indication of how the murderer managed to get into that signalbox without leaving any tracks," said Chess. "I've got a theory, and I'd like to see if I can find anything to fit it."

Max shrugged. "When do we leave?"

"Midnight," came the reply. "McCarthy should be back from his photographic trip soon. We'll have high tea and supper in the normal way, appear to be tired and turn in early. With any luck we'll be able to grab a bit of shut-eye before we sneak out in the middle of the night." He nodded towards the window. "If the sky stays this clear, then we should have quite excellent visibility. It's more or less a full moon tonight."

*   *   *

When they set out, Chess was bitterly cold but wide awake and much refreshed, unlike his companion. The complete silence on the lonely fell was impressive. There was neither a creak or murmur, it was as if the snow had suppressed all life from the lonely landscape.

Chess fell into a reverent and thoughtful mood as he considered the awesome and powerful forces of nature that were evident on every side, and had, for several days, marooned he and his companion in a white wilderness.

A sense of utter insignificance spread over him as he gazed dreamily across the undulating ground, all silvery with moonlight. Suddenly he caught sight of the distant, yellow glare of a lantern, way out across the fell, advancing slowly towards him, pausing from time to time, then coming jerkily onwards. He tugged at Max's sleeve, and, putting a finger to his lips, pointed out what he had seen.

Max's sleepy nerves were suddenly all on edge as, instinctively, the pair darted behind a gorse bush. The fat man shivered with a combination of the cold and a growing anticipation as, with a thrill of fear, he observed a face which appeared to be floating on air, behind the flare of the lamp.

Chess strained his eyes to see who or what it was, hoping that it would steer a course away from their tell-tale footprints.

They waited.

The figure's body was wrapped in shadow, but the lantern light fell full upon the strange, eager face. There was no mistaking those metallic-looking eyes. "Count Azhar," Chess hissed in his companion's ear. His first impulse on learning this was to come forward and address the man, but as he came closer, there was something so stealthy in his movements and so furtive in his expression, that Chess stayed put.

Gasping breath thrilled the flame of the lamp as Azhar passed by some yards off. Chess and Max crouched silently behind the gorse and watched the fellow keenly, both convinced that his nocturnal errand was of sinister import.

"Grab Wilbur B.," Chess hissed. "Muzzle him before he starts barking and gives us away."

173

Max did as he was bid and clamped his hands round the bewildered basset's jaws, while continuing to watch the progress of the Count over the lower reaches of the fell. His lamp swung in broad arcs in front of the fellow who was peering closely at the ground in front of him as he approached the signalbox. "He seems to be looking for something," Max remarked.

Chess nodded. "Very suspicious if you ask me," he replied in a low voice. "He could well have lost something and be returning to the scene of the crime for it. Murderers do that, don't they? It's how a lot of them are caught."

"I think you could be right, Mr Chess. After all, there's no other earthly reason for him to be up here in the middle of the night, is there?"

The pair watched as the golden glow of Azhar's lantern faded into the distance in the direction of the cottages, before breaking their cover. Wilbur B., pleased to be free again, romped off through the thick snow. Seconds later the still night air was penetrated by a rather surprised 'yelp', as the dog disappeared down a deep hole in a nearby snowdrift.

"Trust him!" groaned Chess, hurrying across to the struggling hound. The two men knelt down, one each side of an almost rectangular hole in the deep snow, which, at this particular place, was about three feet deep. With difficulty, they managed to haul the unharmed dog out.

"What do you make of this, Mr Chess? It looks man-made to me, see those smooth sides."

Chess nodded. "Yes," he agreed. "I'm sure it is, and it's something we'll have to talk to McCarthy about."

"McCarthy?"

"Yes," came Chess's reply. "It's obviously one of his ornithological hides. Imagine the excellent photographic opportunities one could get from sitting in there. Birds would be unaware of your presence and come up close, and it'd be easy to photograph the creatures from their own level. The best shots are always those taken from unusual angles. Yes, Max, building a hide in the snow is a damn good idea. The trouble is, it's also damn dangerous. All manner of animals could fall into it and be unable to get out again."

"I see," said Max bending down to try to imagine the photographic angle that McCarthy was achieving when in his hide. As he did so, he caught sight of a little bag that had been thrust into a nearby gorse bush. He drew himself up to his full height, hurried over and snatched it up. "A clue Mr Chess?" he said, undoing the top which was secured with a length of string, and plunging his podgy hand inside.

174

Chess watched excitedly as his fat friend withdrew a handful of gold rings from the bag. "What the deuce are they doing here?" he gasped.

Max shook his head. "Dunno," he said, "But I'll wager that they're worth a pretty penny. Look at the size of those diamonds. Here you have them." Max handed the find over to Chess, who, after a few moments, replaced the rings in the bag and pocketed it.

"Anything to do with the affair d'you reckon?" Max enquired.

"Not sure," came the reply. "Maybe it's what Azhar was looking for, or perhaps it's something to do with McCarthy. After all, it was found jolly close to his hide."

"Well," said Max, blowing on his hands, which had turned blue with the cold, "at least our little nocturnal ramble hasn't been completely in vain. Can we head back now?"

"Indeed we can," replied Chess, feeling suddenly quite tired. "We'll take a different route down the fell," he said. "The more ground we cover, the more chance we'll have of coming across further clues."

So saying, the two men, together with Wilbur B., made their way down through the lower reaches of the fell towards civilization once more. It was as they came in sight of the cottages that Chess caught a glimpse of something glinting in the moonlight. He pointed it out to Max.

The fat man smiled. "I don't believe it," he said. "Surely we can't be lucky a second time."

As the two men got closer, it became clear that the object to which Chess had alluded was a large sausage-shaped metal cylinder. It lay in a hollow, almost obscured by a thick propensity of foliage and leaves. By the look of the surroundings, until recently, it had been entirely obscured by snow, but the recent winds had caused the drift in which it had lay, to dissipate, and now the object was revealed to the curious couple.

"Merciful heavens!" said Chess, grabbing Wilbur B. and pulling him away. "You know what this is, don't you Max?"

"No I don't."

Chess shivered with fear. "It's some sort of unexploded device – a shell I think," he said apprehensively. "Best keep well away, it could go off."

Max stared in horror, first at the metallic cylinder, then at the cottages beyond. "It's a bit close to them," he said. "Is it likely to be powerful?"

Chess shrugged. "God knows," he said. "We'd better keep this one

175

quiet, we don't want to spread panic among the locals. Frankly, there's nothing that can be done until an expert can get up here and look at it. I'm certainly not going poking around near it, that's for sure."

"Do you think it's another clue?" Max enquired haphazardly.

Henry Chesterfield thrust his cold hands deep into his overcoat pockets and frowned hard. "I wish I knew," he said quietly and thoughtfully. "I really wish I knew."

*　　*　　*

"I'm not looking forward to this," said Max with a shudder, as he and Henry Chesterfield, accompanied by Wilbur B., prepared to pay a visit on Count Mehemet Azhar the next morning. "He gives me the blinkin' creeps!"

Chess smiled. "Don't let him get to you," he replied. "All this ghost business he keeps on about is probably just a blind to throw us off the scent."

Max nodded. "Maybe," he said, "but what of his appearance? He looks the spitting image of those ancient Egyptian types."

"All part of the act no doubt," Chess replied with a dismissive snigger, "probably comes from Manchester or something."

Notwithstanding this, Max was still full of apprehension when, a few minutes later, his companion was knocking on the Count's cottage door.

Azhar answered after a few moments. "Could we come inside?" Chess enquired. "I've got a few things that I'd like to ask you."

Azhar nodded curtly. "As you wish," he said, stepping aside. "But I was under the impression that I had already provided the necessary information for you to solve your murder investigation – I take it that this is what this unexpected visit is all about?"

Chess nodded, recalling, as he did so, the seance in which Azhar had pointed the finger of suspicion at Hilda Cowley.

The trio were led into the small living room and settled themselves around the table - the same table that had appeared to swoop and dive so violently and unexpectedly the other night.

Max had imagined that he would be terrified on re-entering the room, but thankfully, he found that he wasn't. The daylight that streamed in through the window had transformed the room from a haven of horror to a rather homely little abode which, if you discounted the strange white statuettes, had an air of complete normality about it.

"Alright, Mr Azhar," said Chess in a commanding tone, "I'll come straight to the point. What were you looking for on the fell last night?"

Azhar made a slight start, his eyebrows raised and his mouth opened slightly. It was almost imperceptible, but Chess, who was searching the fellow's face, noticed it at once. "Well?" he said, re-inforcing his question.

The Count breathed a heavy sigh and glared at Chess through his vitreous, dark eyes. "It is, of course, none of your business," he said slowly and positively. "However, as you enquire, I was conducting an experiment."

"Go on," said Chess sharply.

"I was making an attempt to contact Tom Cowley's spirit. I have reason to believe that it may not have risen to the astral plane yet."

Henry Chesterfield raised his eyes to the ceiling. "Mr Azhar," he said in a pained voice. "Surely you do not seriously expect me to believe any more of this twaddle, you-"

"We all believe what we want to believe, Mr Chesterfield," the Count interrupted. "That you choose not to accept the fact that there are worlds beyond this one in parallel dimensions, is your own concern."

"Fact that there are worlds beyond this one?" Chess exploded, echoing the Count's words. "Fact my ass! Mr Azhar, you returned to the murder scene last night to retrieve something which you lost when you killed Tom Cowley."

The Count opened his mouth to answer but Chess cut him off. "Well, you can save yourself the trouble. Max found it. Things are looking black against you now. Your ghost clap-trap won't wash with me and it won't wash with the police either."

The Count turned his attention to Max. His face was full of hate and anger now. "If you do not immediately stop meddling into affairs which do not concern you, then I will evoke a curse upon you. A powerful Egyptian curse from which there will be no escape. I suggest that you do not doubt my powers."

The Count's eyes shifted to Wilbur B. who was sitting on the floor, his sad, droopy eyes turned towards Azhar and his tail thumping on the ground. As the animal's eyes met those of Azhar's, the dog suddenly began behaving most strangely. He cowered away from the table and yelped twice, most alarmingly.

"I understand that it would not be the first time that you have evoked your so-called powers on this community," Chess said defiantly.

"We spoke to Hilda Cowley and she told us of your little fracas with her husband in the public house."

Azhar glared at Chess across the table. "I will not be humiliated," he growled, banging his fist on its surface to re-inforce each syllable. "Especially by a mere signalman. Where I come from, such unwarranted behaviour usually results in death."

"And where DO you come from?" asked Chess levelly. Max, having recovered from Azhar's stare, felt a slight smile tug at the corners of his mouth, and he wondered whether the Count would say 'Manchester', as Chess had smugly suggested earlier. But, of course, he didn't...

"I come from the land of the Pharaohs," came the distant-sounding reply.

"You said 'such unwarranted behaviour results in death'," said Chess quoting Azhar's words. "Am I to take that as a confession?"

"You do not hear well, Mr Chesterfield. I said 'usually results in death,' actually. In the particular instance that you mention, it did not, at least not by my hand. However, I was driven to the very precipice of revenge, and I was not sad to see Thomas Cowley meet his doom."

"You are making a very poor defence, Mr Azhar, tell me, what –"

"I shall answer no more of your futile questions. You have become tiresome to the extreme. You must leave now." The Count stood up, and Max, together with a rather agitated Henry Chesterfield, did like-wise. The latter tried to begin again: "I was just going to ask –"

"Enough," bellowed Azhar, losing his patience suddenly. "If you do not have faith in the results brought to you by the spirit world, then try looking to your host, John McCarthy. The man continues to behave in a strange manner. He is involved, mark my words. He is also in love, and that can be a very powerful – powerful enough even to kill for. McCarthy knows Wild Boar Fell, every inch of it, like the back of his hand."

"This is more like it," said Chess warming to the unexpected down-to-earth information. "Are you saying that you suspect him?"

"No," replied the Count. "I trust in the spirit world. They cite Hilda Cowley, as I have already told you. However, Mr Chesterfield, you must follow your own intuition to bring about your result."

"So Hilda Cowley and John McCarthy are lovers?" Chess enquired.

Azhar shook his head. "I did not say that. Once again, Mr Chesterfield, you have not heard well. Good day!"

*　*　*

Instead of returning directly to the warmth of McCarthy's cottage, Chess and Max decided to take a walk with Wilbur B. along the railway line.

"Go on, Wilb.," said Chess, "Off you go, boy."

The dog bounded along, flibbedy-flopping across the tightly-packed icy surface, while the two men picked their way gingerly behind him.

"I dunno what to make of that Count Azhar," said Max. "Did you see what he did to old Wilb. back there?"

Chess nodded. "Yes that was rather spectacular. However, if I was a dog, then I'd probably be petrified of such a wierd individual. What I'm more concerned about is what he intimated about McCarthy."

"Now hang on a minute, Mr Chess," said Max. "We've got to be jolly careful there. We can hardly start accusing our host. We could find ourselves out on our ear. And I, for one, don't relish the thought of sleeping rough up here in this weather."

Chess smiled. "I'm sure that it won't come to that," he said. "It really is disappointing that I couldn't draw the Count further on McCarthy. It was the first time since we've met him that the man behind the mask, so to speak, began to emerge."

"Hmm," replied Max, kicking out at some soft snow along the side of the railway line. "He maintained that you were jumping to conclusions over McCarthy and Hilda Cowley. That only leaves one other."

Chess nodded. "Violet Morton," he said, recalling the young attractive wife of Harold that he'd met a few days earlier. A familiar glint came into his eyes. "Con amore!" he said. "That's one suspect that I will certainly enjoy interviewing!"

Max groaned loudly. "Don't start all that stuff again, Mr Chess," he said in a pained voice. "You know it always gets us into trouble, and besides, you're engaged to Elizabeth Clarke now. Your amorous behaviour really has to stop."

"I suppose you're right," Chess sighed, his face dropping somewhat. "Still," he said, "it'll be nice to talk to a pretty young lady, there's a marked absence of the adorable creatures 'round here."

Max didn't answer and the pair walked on in silence under a pale late-morning sun that made the white landscape glisten with gold.

"Halloa, Mr Chesterfield, halloa!"

Chess squinted and peered into the distance at a figure waving its arms about. He frowned. "Can't make him out," he said. "Can you, Max?"

The fat fellow stared hard. The figure was tall, yet very thin and bony against the snowscape. "I do believe it's Harold Morton," he said after a few moment's scrutiny. "Yes, I'm sure of it."

Max was soon proved right, and five minutes later the three men were held in conversation...

"Well, yes," said Henry Chesterfield, "it really is most kind of you to offer. I'm sure we'd love to come to dinner tonight, what say you, Max?"

The fat man nodded enthusiastically. As his rather large bulk clearly indicated, he had rarely seen it fit to refuse offers of food. "Of course," he said. "Thanks Mr Morton, it'll be a pleasure."

The older man smiled. "That's settled then. I'll have Violet rustle up something for about eight o'clock, that suit you chaps?"

"Perfectly," replied Chess. "We'll see you tonight then."

"Looking forward to it," Harold Morton said, hurrying off in the direction of his cottage.

"Well, that was a stroke of luck," said Chess when he was safely out of earshot. "Exactly the people we want to interview next."

Max frowned. "Maybe they're trying to butter us up a bit?" he said.

"I don't doubt it," came Chess's reply. As he spoke, he fished in his pocket and withdrew a half-sovereign. "I've a feeling that McCarthy may not be best pleased about us talking to Violet, especially if there's any truth in the affair he's supposed to be having with her. He knows we're in an investigative mood, and I'll wager that their liaison is a very closely guarded secret."

Max looked at the coin and laughed. "Surely you're not going to try to bribe him to let us go out to dinner?" he said with a chuckle.

Chess smiled and shook his head. "No," he said, then suddenly flung the coin into the air. "Quick, Max, call! Loser gets to tell McCarthy we're out to the Morton's tonight."

"Heads."

Chess retrieved the coin from the snow. "Bad luck, old friend," he said. "Tails I'm afraid. Break it to him gently. Like you said earlier, we don't want to be sleeping rough up here, do we?"

★ ★ ★

It was just after eight when Chess and Max sat down to dinner in the Morton's cottage. Up until the point of their arrival, the men had endured a rather difficult evening. Max had told John McCarthy that they had intended to dine out, and, as expected, he had protested strongly. However, when Chess had asked him why he was so against the idea, he had shut up like a clam and the dusk had been thick with a sullen and unfriendly atmosphere. The detective was well aware that this was due, in part, to the secret affair that McCarthy was conducting with Violet. However, he sensed by the violence in which the man was opposed to the casual visit, that there was something more to it than that.

"I saw your hide on the fell," Chess had said, trying to make conversation.

"I've built no hide," McCarthy had snapped back. "Where was it?"

"On the lower reaches," Chess had said.

"Never even go there. Always take my photographs further out where the birds are less timid of strangers," and that was that.

Now, Chess and Max were enjoying a meal at the Morton's in a much more convivial atmosphere. "A nice place you have here," said the latter, nodding appreciatively around the small lounge/diner.

A good many houseplants were displayed, many in small wicker pots and baskets. Max remembered that Harold and Violet were interested in craftwork, and, between mouthfuls of roast chicken and vegetables, which were helped down with a most agreeable white wine, he enquired politely about the wickerwork.

"Ah yes, my little business. I do them in all shapes and sizes. Good material is wicker."

Chess felt he ought to draw himself into the conversation, and eyed the room for another suitable talking point. Noticing the abundance of photographic prints featuring birds in flight, he decided to comment on them, touching, entirely by chance, on a rather delicate area: "Really, Mr Morton, these photographs are quite excellent," he began.

Their host for the evening chuckled. "Yes," he replied, "aren't they just. That McCarthy chap that you're staying with is responsible for all these. He's jolly talented. Violet goes out on Wild Boar fell quite regularly with him, helps with all that paraphernalia he uses to get his shots. You're learning rather a lot from him, aren't you dear?"

Violet blushed slightly. "Er – yes," she said awkwardly. "It's very interesting really. Mr McCarthy's very kind. He gives us copies of all his prints. Harold's keen on them."

Both Chess and Max smiled inwardly at the way the young woman had wriggled out of her tight spot. It was quite clear that Harold was utterly oblivious to his wife's affair, and he continued enthusiastically:

"Damn nice fellow, McCarthy," he breezed. "Look at those creatures in the shots, all swooping and darting and soaring."

Chess smiled politely as Morton went on and on... "What a life they must have, eh? Not a care in the world, flying around all day, wonderful life. Smashing little things."

"Aren't they," said Chess, looking at the prints and feeling secretly rather bored as it became evident that he was talking to a wildlife fanatic of the highest order.

"Don't get out and about to see the little devils as much now," he went on. "Bit of back trouble put me in hospital recently, but I'm taking the air a bit more now. It's rare up here, I can tell you."

Violet returned a few moments later with a scrumptious apple tart, into which all tucked enthusiastically, temporarily suspending conversation.

Max, being the first to finish as usual, took up a dialogue once more. "You sew, don't you?" he said nodding towards Violet.

The girl lowered her pretty eyes. "A little," she said rather sheepishly.

"A little?" roared Harold, finishing his tart. "Nonsense, my Violet is far too modest. She is an excellent seamstress. Quite the very best in the whole district actually. Isn't that so, dear?"

"I wouldn't say that really—"

"She works in silk. Costs and arm and a leg, but only the best for her. Go on, dear, show these gentlemen a sample of your work. How about that cushion over there for a kick-off?"

Violet left the table and walked across the room, picking up a most exquisite cushion, which she handed to Chess with a shy smile. It was perfectly made with small, neat stitching and a beautifully embroidered flower motif in the centre.

"Wonderful," Chess said in admiration. "Truly it is. You are both very clever people."

"She makes much bigger items too," Harold said. "Practice makes perfect, that's what we always say about our projects, don't we dear?"

"Uh, yes, yes of course," said Violet.

Evidently one of the other things she had perfected was a knack of appearing to be perpetually embarrassed.

Max found himself wondering if she was desperately shy, and was trying to think of a suitable after-dinner joke to crack in an attempt to bring her out of herself a little, when Harold Morton spoke again. This time his face had lost much of its earlier animation, and his tone was grave.

"Mr Chesterfield," he began. "With regard to the matter of the murder. I think there's something that you should know."

"I see," said Chess. "Pray then, Mr Morton, do please continue."

"Well, it's no secret 'round these parts that Mr and Mrs Cowley were going through a pretty lean financial patch. She'd lost her job, and Tom's railway money wasn't much, and well – um – I, I don't quite know how to put it, but Violet, being the only other woman up here, sort of got friendly with Hilda, didn't you dear?"

Violet nodded dumbly.

"It's just something she told me, got me thinking something was afoot. This was before Tom was killed, you understand."

"Say what you want to say," said Chess.

"Alright, I'll come to it. Hilda Cowley was forever going on to my Violet about insurance payments that she was making on her husband's life. Big payments, too. We reckon that she's responsible. She did it, killed her husband for the payout. I wouldn't have said anything, but then, the other night, what with the outcome of that seance business, well, we thought it best that we spoke up to you, didn't we dear?"

Violet nodded again.

"Thank you," said Chess, "I shall look into it. It does seem most strange, but you understand, I do have my own suspicions."

*   *   *

"Well, we learned bugger-all from the Mortons about the murder," said Max next morning as the two men rose from their beds, "save for the confirmation of the affair. We knew about Hilda and the insurance lark already."

"I learned a great deal actually," said Chess.

"Any theories?"

"Several," came the reply. He lowered his voice. "One is that John McCarthy may perhaps have killed Tom Cowley because he learned about the affair and may have threatened to tell Harold Morton about it."

Max brightened. "I've just had a thought," he said, "maybe the money that we found at the Cowley's was something Tom got from McCarthy as a bribe for keeping quiet about the affair. That fits, Mr Chess, surely it does?"

"Mmm," came the reply. "But it doesn't really shed much light about why Tom was killed, does it? I think we'd better have a talk with our host over breakfast." Chess consulted his Benson's pocket watch. "Come on," he said, "I can smell bacon frying, it's almost half-eight already, best not to keep him waiting, we want him in a good mood."

"Trust you had a good meal at the Morton's last night?" enquired McCarthy stiffly as the pair entered the little dining room.

"Yes," Chess said, sitting down at the table. "But this is an excellent spread too, though," he added, surveying a large plateful of bacon and eggs.

Soon all three men were tucking in.

Chess finished a mouthful and spoke in a casual tone. "You're having an affair with that sweet young thing, Violet, aren't you?" he said.

Crash!

John McCarthy threw his knife and fork down and glared across the table. "Who told you that?" he blazed.

"No-one," said Chess with a shrug. "You forget I'm a detective, I find things out for myself, it's my job."

"Huh!" McCarthy replied, picking up his cutlery once more and continuing with his breakfast.

"You're not denying it then?" Chess ventured.

"I'm saying nothing," McCarthy replied. "You've got no bloody right to be poking your noses in to me business. It's got nowt to do with you."

"It may have if it has a bearing on the murder."

"It ain't."

"Mr McCarthy, with respect, you'll have to let me be the judge of that. I want to ask you some straight questions, and I'd be most grateful for equally straight answers."

"Jesus!" exclaimed McCarthy in annoyance. "I puts you up here free of charge, feeds you both and that dog, then you turn round and do this. Well you can pack your bloody bags and get–"

"Please," Chess interrupted. "I will exercise the utmost discretion, and can assure you that what you tell me will be treated with as much confidentiality as possible. I'm sure you'd rather I discussed the matter with you than with Violet."

John McCarthy sighed. "Alright," he said. "Ask away, and let's be done with it. Go on."

"How did it start? The affair?"

"Harold Morton would often go off to Carlisle to get supplies for their handicraft business, silks and wicker, that sort of thing I think. Well, with Violet on her own and interested in my photography, I sort of

184

– well – you know. I don't need to spell it out for you, do I? Her husband's not as young as he was, is he?"

"Indeed not. How long was he usually away?"

"Couple of days sometimes, he'd return with the stuff in a delivery cart with a driver. Look, Mr Chesterfield, leave Violet out of all this, she's a sweet girl, like you say. She ain't done nothing."

"Maybe not," said Chess. "I was more interested in what it had to do with you. Did Tom Cowley find out about your affair?"

"Not as far as I know. Nobody knows, or if they do, nobody's said."

"I see," said Chess thoughtfully.

"Look, if you want my opinion, it's Violet's husband you ought to be concentrating on. Patronises the poor girl something awful. I can't tolerate him."

"That would be handy for you, wouldn't it?" said Chess. "Harold Morton being the murderer. I'd wager that you'd love to get him out of the way so that you could have Violet to yourself. Frankly, the man's attitude to his wife hardly has much bearing on my enquiries."

"No, but his attitude to Tom Cowley should have."

"What do you mean?"

"Could never put a finger on it, but there's always been a lot of tension between them two. I'll be damned if I know what it was all about. Maybe I'm imagining it. I dunno, best speak to Morton on his own."

"Good idea," said Chess.

"Good opportunity this morning actually. Violet's coming up on the fell along a me, so he'll be on his own then."

*   *   *

An hour later, when John McCarthy and Violet had left for Wild Boar Fell with all manner of photographic odds and ends, Chess and Max, along with Wilbur B., headed for Harold Morton's cottage.

Chess was beginning to look somewhat drained. "This is turning into one of our most complicated and lengthy cases," he said. "I'm really not sure what clue to jump on."

"Let's go through what we've got so far," Max suggested, "one at a time. Perhaps it'll help."

Chess sighed. "Nothing ventured, nothing gained," he said, unclipping Wilb's lead and letting the dog gambol over the snow. "At least the weather's looking up, I shan't be sorry to get out of this place."

185

"Me too," said Max. "Now then, what have we got?" He hesitated. "Let me think. Aha, there's Hilda Cowley's missing spare key, we never did follow that one up, then there's still the possibility of suicide. It's that what's making me think that Hilda's not responsible for her husband's murder. I know about the insurance business and all that, but surely, if she did it, when we mentioned suicide to her as a possibility she wouldn't have poo-pooed it and gone on about how much Tom was looking forward to the birth of their daughter's baby, would she? She'd have snatched on the suicide possibility to get herself off the hook, eh, Mr Chess?"

"I'd have thought so," Chess admitted. "To be honest, I've been suspecting Azhar's involvement somewhere. The way he frightened the living daylights out of everyone at that seance, saying it was Hilda who killed Tom. I'm sure he just did it to throw me off the scent – not that I was actually on much of one at the time."

"And the Count's humiliation in that pub," said Max. "He had a strong motive to do the dirty deed. I reckon he's got the capability to murder - those eyes. And remember that Egyptian curse he was rabbiting on about?" The fat man shuddered. "Doesn't bear thinking about."

"I am more down-to-earth than your good self," said Chess as they walked slowly along the icy lane in the direction of the Morton's cottage. "I was rather wondering whether Tom Cowley may have had some business dealings with his murderer – dealings that may have somehow gone wrong. I'm almost convinced that John McCarthy's had a hand in it all somewhere. That secret affair must be making him very vulnerable to blackmail and suchlike as we discussed earlier. Then there's that hide that Wilb fell down in the snow. McCarthy said he had nothing to do with it. I thought he was lying, but why should he. Unless of course he knew of the existence of that bag of jewellery nearby and guessed that we might have found it. Though God knows where that all figures in this."

"Maybe it's stolen," said Max helpfully.

"I'm sure it is, but where does that get us?"

The fat man shrugged. "Nowhere I suppose," he replied. "Blimey, Mr Chess, all this is giving me a flippin' headache."

"Me too," said Chess. "I feel like I'm trying to fight my way out of a maze, and on top of all this business about the murder, there's that damn shell still in the gorse on the lower reaches of Wild Boar Fell. If it goes off and injures someone I'd never forgive myself for not drawing attention to it, but I don't want to be an alarmist, at least not until I've done everything in my power to uncover the murderer."

"Have you talked with the police again?" Max enquired, "kept them abreast of things like they asked?"

Henry Chesterfield shook his head. "I'm afraid I couldn't," he said, gesturing to the lone telephone wire that, dripping with icicles, snaked along the roadside above their heads. "The weight of all that ice has brought it down somewhere. The line's completely dead. No, Max, we're completely on our own in this. Still," he continued, gesturing this time to the pale blue sky, "looks like the worst of the weather is past. If it holds out, I reckon we could still be at the Clarke's for Christmas Day."

Max crossed his cold fingers. "Let's flippin' hope so," he said.

Henry Chesterfield knocked on Harold Morton's front door, and the pair stood awaiting his reply. After a few minutes, when it had still not come, they ventured around to the rear of the property in search of their lone interviewee. They found him in a large shed in the back garden.

"Mr Morton, can we have a word?"

The man jumped. "Oh, it's you. Of course. Just checking our stock, seeing what I need. Should be able to get through to Carlisle soon. Looks like a thaw's going to be setting in."

"Yes," replied Chess peering into the dark depths of the garden shed and noticing a large quantity of coloured silks draped over some wicker work. "How's business?"

Harold closed the shed door. "Slow for this time of year," came the reply. "Could be better, 'specially if I could have got more of our products into the shops and markets in Settle and Carlisle in time for Christmas. It's a bit of a pain being cut-off up here. Still, mustn't grumble. I've got a lovely wife, and we're getting along famous. That's the main thing."

Chess smiled. Harold seemed such a nice old stick that he decided it would be most unkind to spill the beans about the affair that his wife was, even as they spoke, having with the younger man way up on the fell. "Do you always work alone?" Chess enquired.

Harold nodded. "Just me and my Violet," he said.

"Never thought of forming any business partnership with anyone else 'round here?"

Harold shook his head. "What's the point," he said looking enquiringly at Chess. "It's hard enough making ends meet with just the two of us. Are you suggesting something?"

"Uh- no, of course not," replied Chess.

"You said you wanted to have a word with me about something?"

"It's gone now," said Chess. "Clean forgot what I was going to say, stupid isn't it? Ah well, it's not important. Mustn't keep you. Lovely meal last night, cheerio."

"What do you mean, you forgot what you were going to say, Mr Chess?" said Max. "You're not usually that vague."

"No," replied Chess, as they walked back towards McCarthy's cottage. "I suppose I'm not. I just lost my thread, that's all. When I saw that shed full of stock it just seemed a bit strange, especially when Harold said that business was a bit slow. I can't see the sense in having so much in reserve – and he said he was planning to order more. What do you make of it, Max?"

"Only that it seems as if the weather often traps the inhabitants of Ais Gill up here for ages. Perhaps Mr Morton wanted to make sure that he had enough materials to carry on in case he got snowed in for a long period."

Chess shrugged. "Mmm, I suppose you're right," he said. "Come on, let's get out of this bitter cold and back to McCarthy's cottage. He's out, so we can have a good old chinwag about the case without the risk of being overheard."

*　　*　　*

Chess and Max settled themselves in front of a blazing fire in McCarthy's front room. Max peered pensively at the stuffed birds that twisted round and round on their strings in the warm convecting air, and recalled the first time that he had entered the room. Although it was only a few short days ago, so much seemed to have happened that it felt like an age.

Chess leaned forward, patted Wilbur B. who had settled against the hearth, then warmed his hands in front of the flames. "Well, Max, old friend," he said. "Who do you think our murderer is?"

Max shook his head. "God knows," he said. "There are too many possibilities for me to sift through, Mr Chess. I keep thinking that it has to have been Hilda doing it for the insurance money, but, like I said earlier this morning, even that solution seems to have plenty going against it." He paused, and for a few moments sat in thoughtful silence. "You see," he continued at length, "even if she had the key, I still can't see how she did it. There were no tracks of hers anywhere near the signalbox. The only thing I can think is that she did it before the last fall of snow, what do you reckon, Mr Chess?"

"She can't have done that. The murder took place after we arrived, and there hasn't been a fall of snow since then, so that's scotched that. No, I'm still not happy with Count Azhar's behaviour. He seems a real phoney to me but I can't quite work out what it is about him that makes me suspicious. I'm not sure whether that so-called humiliation in the pub could have been motive enough for him to kill, but then again, we can't rule it out. But whatever, that still doesn't get us any nearer to working out HOW the murder was carried out."

"What about the possibility of some sort of secret tunnel underground leading in from the fell and coming up in the signalbox?" said Max, letting his mind wander. "Maybe the murderer used some sort of clever system of wires that allowed him to lock the door from the outside when the deed was done."

Chess raised his eyes. "I hardly think that it's likely that someone's dug a bloody great tunnel across the fell," he said. "I'm sure it would have been noticed. After all, there would have been tons of earth – even this lot round here wouldn't have swallowed stories of a monster-sized mole!"

Max laughed. "I suppose not," he said. "Thinking back to Azhar though, you don't think that Tom could have been subjected to some sort of poltergeist attack do you?"

This time it was Chess's turn to laugh. "That's even more unlikely than the monster mole," he chuckled. "Still, I think that you may well have something in what you said about wires, not necessarily operated on the door - that'd be too far-fetched - but on one of the windows perhaps."

Suddenly Max became excited. "Bound to be!" he exclaimed. "Remember the murder scene? Wilb cut his foot did'nt he? – and what on?"

"Wire!" said Chess remembering. "You brought it back from the signalbox didn't you?"

Max nodded. "It's upstairs," he said.

Chess turned his attention to the windows of the cottage. "I do believe that these are fairly similar to those on the signalbox. let's try out the theory. Max, nip upstairs and get that bit of wire, and we'll have a shot at opening one of these windows from the outside with it. If we succeed, then at least we'll know if we're on the right track."

A few moments later, Max had returned with the wire and the two men ventured outside. It only took ten minutes for Chess to verify the plausibility of the theory. With some patient bending of the wire, he managed to slide it through a slight gap between the window and the frame surround, and, with a couple of hard upward flicks, lift up the securing catch. "Excellent," he said. "Now let's try and close it in the same way."

That worked too, although this time the wire dropped down inside the cottage. The two men smiled at each other.

"Exactly what must have happened in the signalbox," said Max with a chuckle. "Maybe it wasn't a poltergeist after all."

"No," said Chess. "I think that we should be looking a much more down-to-earth solution."

He paused and looked at Max. "Or maybe that's the wrong way of putting it."

*　　*　　*

The next morning, which dawned bright and clear, saw Chess and Max taking Wilbur B. for a run on Wild Boar Fell. A gradual thaw had set in and now at last, there were considerable patches of verdant green showing through the snowy acres.

"What've you got now, Wilb," cried Max as the basset hound lumbered up to him with a long piece of twig in his slobbery jaws. "Trust you to find a stick amongst all this snow."

Chess was about to bend down and pick it up when a familiar figure came into view. "Good morning Mr Azhar," he said somewhat coldly.

"Hello," came the reply. "I trust that your investigation is progressing well."

"Very well," said Chess, scrutinising the stick that Wilb had found. "I have formulated a theory at last."

"One which harmonizes with the revelations of the spirit world I trust?"

"You're not still on that kick are you?" Chess said rather unkindly. "What's new in the great beyond this morning then?"

The Count's hackles rose. "There really is no need for such intimidation, Mr Chesterfield. In fact, I came over to you to tell you something. Something that re-inforces the fact that you should be looking to the astral plane for your answers."

"What is this 'something' then, Mr Azhar? I am all ears."

"I have, as you know, often had occasion to walk Wild Boar Fell at night. It was during one such ramble a while back, that I witnessed a vast unearthly fire in the sky."

Max was held spellbound.

Chess was his usual sceptical self and remained silent.

The Count continued in a dark, sinister tone. "It was a huge fireball in the air. At first, even I did not believe that it could be anything more than some extraordinary natural phenomenon. However, when I went to investigate the spot on which it landed, there was nothing. It was a fireball from hell, Mr Chesterfield, sent as a warning of the powers that lurk in this lonely and forbidding place."

"Psaw!" exclaimed Chess. "Probably some form of ball-lightning," he said lethargically. "You often get–"

Crack!

In an instant, Chess felt a cold rush of air on his face as a rifle bullet whistled past him. All three men instinctively hit the ground. Chess looked up in the direction of the summit of the fell and was just in time to see a silhouetted figure darting quickly out of sight down the far side. Leaving Azhar to fend for himself, Chess dragged a rather shaken Max to his feet. "Come on," he said urgently, scrambling down the steep slope towards the cottages.

"What's the rush?" said Max, trying gamely to keep up with his much fitter colleague.

"First it'll give us cover from any more shots," Chess called back. "Second, we'll see who's out – that'll tell us whose responsible. The gunman – or woman – won't be able to beat us back to the cottages."

A further couple of minutes of hard running brought them to McCarthy's door. Chess banged on it but there was no reply.

"Has to be him," said Max between puffs.

"Not necessarily," came Chess's reply as he darted off towards the Morton's cottage.

Again there was no-one at home.

Finally he tried the Cowley's with no luck.

"Blast!" he exploded. "Not a bloody soul in sight. That means it could have been any of them. Where the hell are they all?"

"Sunday," Max wheezed. "It's Sunday, Mr Chess. They're probably all making their separate ways to church."

Henry Chesterfield groaned. "So we can't prove categorically who did it," he said angrily. "What a flaming carry-on."

"Do you think someone was trying to kill Azhar – or do you reckon they were gunning for you?" Max enquired.

Chess didn't hesitate. "Me," he said firmly. "I'm sure of it. But not to worry, they missed and they won't get a second chance. I'm certain I know who it was too."

*　　*　　*

"Well, Max, I've managed to get through to the police at last," Chess said next morning before breakfast, "and now the thaw's well and truly set in, both the police and the trains reckon they can get through. I've explained the whole affair to the police and arranged to have them come along at eleven this morning to arrest the murderer."

"You mean you've solved it? You know who did it?"

Chess nodded. "The clues have been there all along. Really, Max, I must have been blind not to have seen it right from the start."

"Who then?"

"Wait and see, old friend. I've asked McCarthy to gather everyone in this cottage at ten-thirty, so you won't have to remain in suspense for long. Why not use the time after breakfast trying to work it out for yourself? As I said, all the clues are there!"

*　　*　　*

"Good morning everyone," said Henry Chesterfield in a commanding voice as he addressed Violet and Henry Morton, Count Mehemet Azhar, Hilda Cowley and John McCarthy in the little cottage sitting room at ten-thirty. "Thank you all for coming here. It is, of course, for the reasons of the murder that I have brought you all together before Mr Shore and I leave. I must confess that the ghastly business did have me rather baffled at first. There have been so many possibilities associated with the case that I have had a tough time sifting the evidence. But that's all over and done with now, and I'm ready to unmask the murderer."

A little gasp went round the room, which then fell as silent as the grave.

Chess, who was standing next to the fireplace with Max, surveyed his audience, all of which were seated. "Amongst the considerable clues, several key things have proved themselves to be relevant. The first of these was a small piece of wire which we found in the signalbox on discovery of the body, and was used by the murderer to secure the window from the outside. It provided a means of access for the culprit, and solved the mystery of the signalbox being locked from the inside."

"Quite ingenious," said Harold Morton.

192

Chess smiled briefly. "Yes," he said. "Wasn't it? Then there was the terror on the victim's face."

At this, Chess turned his attention to Count Azhar. "At first, I reasoned that perhaps there were occult connections. However, it was something that my dog, Wilbur B., found on the fell that made me discount that rather obscure possibility. He found a twig."

Count Azhar laughed nervously, the sound sudden and loud in the quiet room. "Hardly very frightening," he said.

"The terror," Chess went on, ignoring the interjection, "came from the shock of Tom seeing his attacker pull out a dagger and come at him so unexpectedly."

"What's the blasted twig got to do with it?" sqwalked McCarthy, thrusting his head forwards in his characteristic nervous pecking motion.

"Ah yes," said Chess. "I was coming to that. It provided me with the vital clue to the way the deed was done. It was no ordinary twig. It would not have got on to the fell without human intervention. You will recall that I located no footprints anywhere near the signalbox."

The assemblage nodded.

"The stick that Wilbur B. found on Wild Boar fell was wicker – just like the baskets that Harold Morton here makes."

All eyes turned to face the emancipated-looking man. He clasped his long, bony hands together so tightly that the knuckles went white.

"You're not – not suggesting that I had anything to do with this, are you?"

Chess nodded gravely. "Mr Morton," he said solemnly. "You had everything to do with it."

"What do you mean?" Harold protested. "A piece of wicker as evidence? What is all this? What the deuce are you getting at, young man?"

"I have more, much more," Chess said levelly.

Morton refused to give an inch. "Such as?" he said angrily. "Such as?"

"The bird photographs in your cottage for a start," Chess replied. "At first, when you kept on and on about the creatures 'swooping and diving' I took it that you were a wildlife fanatic. Then it came to me. It wasn't of wildlife that you were fond – but flight! Furthermore, the large pile of wicker and silk in your garden shed isn't simply a large stock-holding of raw materials, is it?"

Harold Morton was silent.

Henry Chesterfield turned to John McCarthy. "You recall how I mentioned a deep, rectangular hole in the snow that I took to be one of your hides?"

McCarthy nodded and smiled. "It'd be a bit on the chilly side, that, wouldn't it?"

Chess agreed. "Indeed," he said. "I was wrong there. It was not a hide at all, but a place where a balloon basket came down – a wicker balloon basket with a silk balloon attached to it – all beautifully hand-sewn too!"

All eyes turned towards Violet who blushed. "I-It was a secret," she said quietly. "Harold said we shouldn't tell anyone about it until it was perfected, else we could be made laughing stocks."

Chess was grave. "It is far from being a laughing matter now," he said.

Count Azhar spoke up. "How did you know for certain that they had a balloon. And so what? Surely it's got nothing to do with the murder. I thought that's what we were here to discuss."

"Please," said Chess, holding up his hand. "One question at a time. A few days ago, Max and I saw what we took to be a shell hidden in the gorse on the lower reaches of the fell. In the light of subsequent investigations, it's now clear that it was, in fact, a hydrogen gas cylinder of the type used to inflate the aforementioned balloon – it was this that convinced me of the existence of such a craft. However, it was you, Mr Azhar, who provided me with the final piece of evidence regarding it when you told me of the 'ghostly fireball' which you witnessed one night in the air over Wild Boar Fell a while back. It was indeed a fireball, but with no ghostly connections I'm afraid. It was caused by the hydrogen gas igniting in your first prototype balloon, Mr Morton, is that not so?"

Again the man wouldn't speak.

"Come, come now," Chess coaxed. "I am sure that if I cared to check the hospital records, they would show that you were not admitted for a bad back, as you've had everyone around Ais Gill believe, but for serious burns. What say you to that?"

Harold Morton nodded slowly. "Alright, alright," he said. "Aren't you the clever one? Yes, I admit I've been building a balloon, but, like Violet said, I wanted to keep it quiet. Now the secret's out, it's out. No harm in having a hobby is there?"

"A hobby is one thing. Murder is another," said Chess, flipping out his pocket-watch and checking the time.

It was five to eleven.

The police were due in five minutes.

Violet piped up, looking scared, "it was just a balloon," she said.

"Did you go on any flights?" asked Chess.

The girl giggled rather nervously. "Oh no," she said, shaking her head. "Too scary for me, I don't have much of a head for heights, and besides, Harold only flew it at night."

Chess smiled. "Exactly," he said. "Mr Morton, you killed Tom Cowley. You hovered your balloon over the signalbox, tethered it down to the railing – Max noticed that the snow had been scraped off of a section of it – then climbed in at the open window, thus avoiding leaving any incriminating footprints. Tom Cowley was expecting you, so this method of approach was no surprise to him. In fact, I'll wager that it was not the first time you'd called on him in such an unorthodox fashion to pick up stolen goods. I should have realised right from the outset that there was something amiss - for what other reason would Tom be in his lonely signalbox when the railway line was blocked with snow and there were no trains running?"

The atmosphere in the room had grown tense.

Violet was close to tears.

Harold's brow was deeply furrowed as he sought to find an answer to Chess's allegations. But words just wouldn't come.

He was trapped.

Chess looked out of the cottage window and a slight smile flickered across his face as he heard footsteps. His moustache twitched and he continued in a confident tone. "What Tom didn't expect was for you to produce that dagger and kill him, then climb back into your aerial basket and, using a piece of wire, re-secure the window before flying off. It just leaves it for me to have you arrested for murder."

"You can't – you've got no proof," Morton said in a strangled voice.

"Come in, gentlemen," Chess called loudly. "You're timekeeping is a credit to you. Here is your man, a Mr Harold Morton. Take him away. I'll furnish you with the details later. Oh, and officer, take this. It will be all the proof you need." Chess fished in his pocket and handed over the bag of jewellery.

"What about furnishing US with the details?" said McCarthy as he walked across the room after the police had taken Morton away and put his arm around Violet. The poor girl look fraught and confused, clearly unable to decide just where her loyalties should lie.

Henry Chesterfield breathed a deep sigh. "Alright," he said. "If you insist, but I must be brief, Max and I have a train to catch." He drew a deep breath and began. "Mr McCarthy, you got me thinking along the right lines when you said you'd noticed tension building up between Tom and Harold. We wondered if it was due to some sort of illegal business – after all, this solitary place is ideal for just such a caper. Anyway, this train of thought was re-inforced when I recalled how Max and I had located a huge pile of banknotes in Mrs Cowley's cottage, hidden under the mattress – especially odd in view of their uh, less-than-rosy financial circumstances."

Hilda Cowley gasped. "What money?" she said. "I never knew about this. Are you sure?"

Chess nodded. "Quite sure," he said. "I am sorry, but your late husband was involved in some bad business, probably to try to pay-off debts."

"Oh Lord," groaned Hilda. "We'd have got by, sure we would. Why did he do it?"

Chess shrugged.

"Well, go on," said Count Azhar heartlessly.

"The money was Tom's reward for his part in a series of elaborate railway robberies. Had I been the ideal reasoner, then I should have realised that something was afoot when I first called the police to report the body. I told them that I had been travelling on the Settle to Carlisle railway, over Ais Gill summit, and before I had a chance to mention the murder, I was interrupted by the voice at the other end asking what I'd had stolen. They anticipated my call incorrectly, due, no doubt, to the fact that they'd received many calls on the subject recently from robbed railway passengers in the area, and it had become force of habit."

Max, who had remained silent throughout his friend's masterful summing-up, allowed himself a smile and marvelled at the way Chess has pieced together so many apparently unconnected threads.

"Theft!" Chess went on in a positive tone. "That was the connection. I am sorry to have to say this, Mrs Cowley, but your husband had been stopping night trains up on Ais Gill with the signals, climbing on board and rifling the sleeping passengers' belongings, then storing the booty in the signalbox ready for Harold Morton's ingenious aerial pick-ups."

"And the booty was in that bag that you handed to the policeman just now?" enquired McCarthy.

Chess nodded. "Precisely," he said. "It was a small part of the last haul of jewellery. We found it on the fell near where the balloon had touched down in the snow. Balloon flight is subject to the vagaries of the winds, and it now seems obvious that an unexpected crash-landing was made, during which the bag was accidentally cast out. Knowing the winds up here to be unpredictable, Morton couldn't risk getting out to retrieve it and have the balloon suddenly career off on its own, so he stayed put in the basket which was soon airborne again. It was a bad mistake on his part."

"But why transport the stolen goods by balloon in the first place? It really is a most unorthodox means of travel to say the least," said Count Azhar.

"Speed," Chess replied. "It's as simple as that. Once airborne, Morton could be away over Wild Boar Fell in a matter of minutes in absolute silence. Working undercover of darkness, he could drop off the booty to an accomplice, probably somewhere on the outskirts of Kirkby Stephen. I'll have the police follow that one up."

"I thought my husband had gone to pick-up supplies of wicker and silk for our little business," said Violet getting more and more distressed.

"That's what everyone thought," replied Chess. "Mr McCarthy here told me that Harold would normally return in a delivery cart with a driver – the accomplice. Whilst there may well have been some materials on board the cart, the trip was made mainly to return the balloon to home base. With each successful operation, Tom was paid a share of the money handed over by Morton's accomplice for the stolen property."

This time Violet broke down. "I-I didn't know. Really I didn't," she wailed. "I thought Harold was just testing our balloon in secret, I didn't realise, I–"

"Please," Chess said. "Don't upset yourself so. I did not believe for one moment that you were involved in any way."

"What about that rifle shot on the fell?" Count Azhar said.

"Harold Morton," Chess replied. "The only way he could silence me. He figured I was getting too close to the truth."

"I've got a question," said McCarthy. "Just one last one. Why the murder, Mr Chesterfield. Why was Tom killed, tell me that?"

Chess smiled at Hilda. "Tom Cowley was not a bad man. He was clearly getting apprehensive about the whole business, and suspicion was beginning to fall on him for the thefts. He knew that he was getting in far too deep, and began fearing for his own safety. He even recommended that Hilda should take out some insurance policies on his life which, in the circumstances, turned out to be very sensible. I would wager that, on the fateful night, Tom Cowley told Harold Morton that he was going to the police to clear his name and to hell with the consequences. Morton, on hearing this, had no hesitation in killing him to protect his own skin."

★　★　★

"I had visions of spending Christmas Day on Ais Gill," said Max, as he and Chess, together with Wilbur B., sped towards Carlisle in a first class railway compartment.

Henry Chesterfield lay back in his seat and gazed lazily out of the carriage window at the lean lands speeding by. "So did I," he replied. "You know, Max, I feel a change in myself. I'm actually longing to see Elizabeth Clarke now. A year or so ago, when I first met you, I'd never even have considered a long-lasting relationship with a lady – and now I'm about to plunge myself into marriage."

Max tried to smile, but couldn't.

He recalled their friendship.

The fun.

The half-dozen exciting cases they'd solved together.

A lump stuck in his throat and tears welled up in his piggy-eyes. "I s-suppose that was our last case then," he said biting his lip and looking away.

Henry Chesterfield was about to reply when the compartment door was thrust open and the worried face of a ticket inspector appeared.

"Mr Chesterfield, the detective?" he enquired.

Chess nodded.

"Oh thank gawd! There's been a murder in the next carriage," the railway official blurted. "A young woman. All covered in blood she is."

Henry Chesterfield and Maxwell Shore exchanged glances.

"Isn't this where we came in?" Chess said.